Abstracting Concepts and Methods

LIBRARY AND INFORMATION SCIENCE

CONSULTING EDITOR: *Harold Borko*
GRADUATE SCHOOL OF LIBRARY SCIENCE
UNIVERSITY OF CALIFORNIA, LOS ANGELES

Thomas H. Mott, Jr., Susan Artandi, and Leny Struminger
Introduction to PL/I Programming for Library and Information Science

Karen Sparck Jones and Martin Kay
Linguistics and Information Science

Manfred Kochen (Ed.)
Information for Action: From Knowledge to Wisdom

Harold Borko and Charles L. Bernier
Abstracting Concepts and Methods

In preparation

G. Edward Evans
Management Techniques for Librarians

ABSTRACTING CONCEPTS AND METHODS

Harold Borko

Graduate School of Library and Information Science
University of California
Los Angeles, California

Charles L. Bernier

School of Information and Library Studies
State University of New York
Buffalo, New York

ACADEMIC PRESS   New York   San Francisco   London   1975

A Subsidiary of Harcourt Brace Jovanovich, Publishers

ACADEMIC PRESS, INC.
111 Fifth Avenue, New York, New York 10003

United Kingdom Edition published by
ACADEMIC PRESS, INC. (LONDON) LTD.
24/28 Oval Road, London NW1

Library of Congress Cataloging in Publication Data

Borko, Harold.
    Abstracting concepts and methods.

    (Library and information science)
    Bibliography: p.
    Includes index.
    1.   Abstracting.   I.   Bernier, Charles L., joint
author.   II.   Title.   III.   Series.
Z695.9.B65   029.4   75-13069
ISBN 0–12–118650–4

Contents

Preface

Abstracting Concepts and Methods began as an informal exchange of ideas between the authors on what we should teach and how we should organize our respective abstracting classes. The exchange of syllabi, letters, and phone calls stimulated an intensive examination of the goals and contents of our courses. We also discussed aspects of our curricula with colleagues and examined the literature for relevant material. Gradually, we arrived at a common set of objectives, which we have now synthesized and embodied in this volume.

Our primary goal is to make abstracting and indexing relevant, important, and interesting features of library education. Some librarians abstract; many participate in the acquisition and use of many abstracting publications and computer-based abstracting services. These publications and services are in many disciplines and subject areas. Students of library science need to understand the why, where, and use, as well as the how, of abstracting. Graduate library school study of abstracting should be more than a how-to-do-it course. It should include general material on the characteristics and types of abstracts, the historical development of abstracting publications, the abstract-publishing industry (especially in the United States), and the need for standards in the preparation and evaluation of the product. These topics we call *concepts*.

Librarians do, however, need more than an understanding and appreciation of abstracting services. They not only evaluate and purchase abstracting publications but also frequently are called upon to prepare abstracts for their organizations, patrons, and clients, and to search in abstracting publications and their indexes. They need to know how to abstract, so the text includes a *methods* section containing instructions for writing various types of abstracts, and for editing and preparing abstracting publications. These detailed instructions are supplemented by examples and exercises in the appendix. There is a brief discussion of indexing of abstract publications.

Research on automation has been treated extensively in this work, for we believe that the topic deserves greater emphasis than it has received in the past. Computer use is becoming increasingly important in all aspects of librarianship. Much research effort has been expended on the preparation and evaluation of computer-prepared abstracts and extracts. Students, librarians, and abstractors will benefit from knowing about this research and understanding how computer programs were researched to analyze text, select key sentences, and prepare extracts and abstracts. The benefits of this research are discussed.

Abstracting is a key segment of the information industry. Opportunities are available for both full-time professionals and part-time paid or volunteer workers. Many librarians find such activities pleasant and rewarding, for they know they are contributing to the more effective use of stored information. One chapter is devoted to career opportunities for abstractors.

It is our plan that *Abstracting Concepts and Methods* provide a basis for a well-balanced course of instruction, and our hope that our colleagues will find it a useful vehicle for teaching and stimulating interest in abstracting services and learning to abstract for personal as well as professional use.

I | NATURE OF ABSTRACTS

1 | Characteristics and Types of Abstracts

In our complex world, there is an obvious need to improve communication, perhaps most of all in the transfer of scientific and technical information. Progress and economic and cultural achievements are largely dependent upon research. To foster such progress, all nations spend a significant percentage of their Gross National Products to support research and development (R&D). The United States alone spends more than $27 billion per year on R&D (SATCOM, 1969, p. 1). The product of research is information, and this information must be made available rapidly, effectively, and efficiently.

The abstracting and indexing (A&I) organizations are important links in the chain of communication between the originator of information and the ultimate consumer. These organizations are called *secondary services* to distinguish them from the *primary services* which publish the original research reports and journal articles. The A&I services have grown tremendously over the past century; they have increased their coverage of the literature and developed new products. They now constitute a multimillion-dollar segment of the knowledge industry. In the United States, secondary services include private profit-making organizations, such as the Institute for Scientific Information; nonprofit scientific and professional organizations, such as the Chemical Abstracts Service of the American Chemical Society, the American Institute of Physics, and the American Psychological Association; and various governmental organizations, such as the National Library of Medicine and the National Technical Information Service. There are comparable secondary services in most of the larger, more developed nations of the world. In the United States, many abstracting organizations have formed the National Federation of Abstracting and Indexing Services (NFAIS).

Generally speaking, information publication can be divided into *discipline-oriented services* and *product-* or *mission-oriented services* (NFAIS, 1973). The mission-oriented services seek

> to provide comprehensive coverage of a given field of knowledge by capturing the literature at the time of its primary publication; adequately abstracting and indexing it; making the information available as quickly, broadly, and conveniently as possible; and storing it for later use. There are a limited number of comprehensive discipline-oriented services as these are directly related to the basic division of knowledge into classes (e.g., chemistry, biology, physics, mathematics, engineering, geology, and psychology).
>
> [The mission-oriented services are aimed at] an identified user group that has a specified area of interest usually defined in terms of a task rather than a traditional discipline. For example, the *Abstract Bulletin* of the American Petroleum Institute draws on the literature of chemistry, mathematics, physics, and other fields of science and engineering to service the oil industry. [NFAIS, 1973, pp. 3–4]

An understanding of the distinction between discipline- and mission-oriented services is useful, because it will help one decide where to look for the information desired.

1.1   THE ABSTRACT AND ITS USE

An abstract has been defined as an abbreviated, accurate representation of a document without added interpretation or criticism and without distinction as to who wrote the abstract (Weil, 1970, p. 352). The phrase "without distinction as to who wrote the abstract" has been added to the definition to eliminate the differentiation between an abstract and a synopsis. (The term *synopsis* was formerly used to denote a resumé prepared by the author of a work.) As Weil points out, this distinction is no longer valid; if the statement is an abbreviated, accurate representation of a document, it is an abstract regardless of by whom it was written.

The definition is part of the official *American National Standard In-*

stitute (ANSI) *Standard for Writing Abstracts.* However, no definition is able to capture the nuances of the term or to provide more than an indication of the importance of the concept. To understand better the broad meaning of the term, students find it necessary to consider the various purposes that abstracts serve and the relation between abstracts and other document surrogates.

An abstract condenses the primary scientific literature to one-tenth to one-twentieth the number of words; for instance, a 2000-word article is typically condensed to about 100–200 words. It is this noncritical reduction in size that is the essence of the abstract, but other types of condensation are possible and prevalent. Terms referring to other document surrogates are as follows: *abridgment, annotation, aphorism, axiom, brief, code, command, compendium, conclusion, databook, epitome, excerpt, extract, maxim, precept, précis, resumé, review, selection, summary, summation, synopsis, and terse conclusion.* There are both obvious and subtle differences in the meanings of these terms. Each type of surrogate was designed for a specific purpose, but all facilitate communication and the transfer of knowledge. Some of the differences can be clarified by defining a few of the more common terms used for document surrogates. An *annotation* is a note added to a title or other bibliographic element of a document by way of comment or explanation. An *extract* is composed of one or more portions of a document that have been selected verbatim to represent the whole. A *summary* is a restatement within a document (usually at the end) of the document's salient findings and conclusions; it is intended to complete the orientation of a reader who has studied the preceding text (Weil, 1970, p. 352).

Without surrogates, such as abstracts, search through the accumulated literature would be impossible. The recognition of the necessity for surrogates has led to the growth and proliferation of abstract journals, which now number in the thousands. Some surrogates make reference to the primary literature less necessary. All facilitate the use of the literature. Some of the more significant purposes and uses of abstracts are discussed next.

1.1.1   Abstracts Promote Current Awareness

Every educated person has the ethical responsibility for keeping up with the literature in his field. Sensitivity to this responsibility has led D. O. Myatt and T. E. Upham to write, "In most technical fields today, the thoughtful scientist views his obligation to remain well informed with a sense of acute personal distress" (1961, p. 18). For the same reason, Vannevar Bush wrote, "The investigator is staggered by the findings and conclusions of thousands of other workers—conclusions which he cannot find time to grasp, much less remember, as they appear" (1945, p. 101).* Most of the previously mentioned surrogates help the scientist to keep up. If we cannot read all the words we believe we should read, then we must read fewer words, and these fewer words can be selected and organized much better than present procedures allow. Surrogates repackage data into a more condensed form and thus foster keeping up, but better surrogates and more of the present kinds are urgently needed. There is some evidence that abstracts are being used less for current awareness than they were formerly. The reasons given are the delay in the appearance of the published abstracts and their great number. Specialization has been the traditional means of meeting the increasing bulk of literature, but now the literature is so voluminous that overspecialization is a growing problem (Bar-Hillel, 1957).

It is difficult to gauge accurately the impact of the size of the technical literature upon one's ability to keep up, but some figures are available. The biomedical press, for example, has been estimated to publish 2 million papers each year (McCandless, Skweir, and Gordon, 1964, p. 147). These papers can be read at the rate of two per hour—assuming that the reader is attentive, can read approximately 70 languages, and has the documents at hand. If journal reading is limited to 1 hour per day and continued 365 days per year, then it will take more than 27.4 centuries to read the output of 1 year of the world's biomedical press. Chemists are more fortunate; it would take them about 5.7 centuries to read the annual output of their literature at the same rate. Even in a specialized field, such as cardiovascular pathology, there are estimated to be 10,000 papers a year. These would take 13.7 years to read at the same rate. In the Department of Defense, there were estimated to be 1 million reports per year legally required to meet contract specifications. If each report is one-quarter of an inch thick, then the annual output of reports for this one department would occupy a shelf about 4 miles long. In practically all fields, researchers are finding it difficult or impossible to keep up (Bernier, 1970). As a result, they turn to surrogates, principally abstracts, which may average one-tenth the length of the original documents. Current awareness requires surrogates.

1.1.2   Abstracts Save Reading Time

At best, abstracts can save about nine-tenths of the time needed to read the original documents. Alternatively, they can broaden the scope of reading by a factor of 10. Or the reader can strike a balance between reading time saved and scope of reading broadened. Even more important than reading time saved is the improved assimilation and integration of what is read. New reading tends to crowd out earlier items that are important and should be remembered. After the hundredth document is read, the first one may be forgotten. For abstracts, forgetting may occur only about one-tenth as rapidly as for original documents. This does not mean that the original document can be abandoned. Nearly all the words in the original document are necessary to serve the purpose for which the document was written—namely, to describe one research project and to function as a paradigm for duplication of the author's original work. For this purpose, most primary documents are peerless; they constitute an archive and must be preserved. However, for the purpose of putting the data, findings, and conclusions to prompt use, original documents tend to flood the reader with unnecessary words and numbers. For putting words to work, condensations may be better vehicles than originals (Bernier, 1968, 1970).

1.1.3   Abstracts Facilitate Selection

Titles, as subject paraphrases, are too frequently uninformative—especially with regard to the specific details that are vital to the selection of articles to be read. Titles also tend to be very general because of the necessity for brevity; they often suggest possibilities far beyond what the author actually reports. Thus, titles may be poor guides to the selection of readings (Maloney, 1974). In a few cases, titles may be made deliberately obscure to intrigue the reader into reading the document, and some titles—especially those of patents—may even be made misleading to thwart disclosure. Thus, carefully written abstracts are usually far superior to titles and to index entries for use when selecting documents to be read.

1.1.4   Abstracts Help Overcome the Language Barrier

There are about 70 languages in which reports of engineering and science appear, but the average scientist/engineer is reputed to read only one or two languages. This mismatch can be rectified by providing abstracts in one of the more common languages. Or, if the searcher is fortunate, the abstract will be in his own language. If he is not quite so fortunate, he would still need only two languages, his native tongue and that of the abstract journal. In many cases, abstracts function as surrogates for the original, foreign-language documents, and in others they lead, more reliably than index entries or titles alone, to a translation or to a decision that a translation should be obtained (Maloney, 1974, p. 370).

1.1.5   Abstracts Facilitate Literature Searches

Searches (so-called *retrospective searches*) are aided by the availability of abstracts, for without abstracts, comprehensive search of the literature would now be impossible. There are estimated to be 60,000 to 100,000 serials carrying reports of research and development in engineering, medicine, and science.* It is actually impossible for one individual to assemble and search this mass of literature. The literature of unpublished reports is even larger than the published literature. For example, for the United States military alone, there have been estimated to be 250,000 contracts in effect each year. It is a legal requirement that each contract generate four reports per year, giving a total of 1 million reports. Although few interim reports carry engineering and scientific data, final reports do, and these constitute an important part of the literature. Financial, industrial, business, and research organizations also produce interim and annual reports, as do nonmilitary governmental agencies. The fact that nearly all these reports are unpublished and many are classified (i.e., confidential, secret, or top secret) or proprietary (e.g., industrial secret) has no relation to the value of the content, but it makes obtaining these documents more difficult. In addition, about half the unclassified, nonproprietary technical reports containing publishable data are published within 2–3 years of their appearance as reports (Gray and Rosenborg, 1957, p. 18). Without indexed abstracts, searches of the open and classified literatures would be impossible. Data would be irretrievably lost.

1.1.6   Abstracts Improve Indexing Efficiency

Abstracts can be indexed much more rapidly than can original documents, because there are fewer words to be read and the indexable material is more visible. The rate of indexing can be improved by a factor of 2 to 4. The time and cost involved in preparing the index is reduced with little or no loss in quality.

* Shilling, C. W. Biological Sciences Communication Project, Washington, D.C. The estimate, made in 1964, is based upon serials in the life sciences plus those estimated in other sciences and technology.

1.1.7   Abstracts Aid in the Preparation of Reviews

Abstracts are of special help in the preparation of bibliographies and reviews. Difficulties arising from the large number of documents, the many languages in which they are written, and the lack of ready access to some documents, are all alleviated by the use of abstracts. Abstracts are convenient units by which to organize the writing of reviews and the compiling of bibliographies. Data can be extracted from abstracts for use in reviews more efficiently than from the original articles. Related abstracts can conveniently be assembled for preparing simple or annotated bibliographies.

Abstracts and their indexes can help users to integrate a field of study. Cross-references guide users to specific, earlier abstracts that are related—as a part of a series of articles; by subject; by author; and by reference in the document abstracted. The skimming of indexes gives a rapid and very valuable overview of a subject field, and aids the integration and use of information.

With the usefulness of indexed abstracts so well established, it seems unlikely that they will ever be supplanted. However, they may be supplemented—and there is a trend in this direction—by other surrogates that are much more condensed, such as terse literatures (Bernier, 1970). These developments will be discussed in Section 1.4.2. But first it is important to examine the characteristics and various types of abstracts.

1.2   CHARACTERISTICS OF THE ABSTRACT

An abstract is a well-defined type of literature with definite attributes and a unique style. Abstracting is not a "natural" form of writing; it requires training. The abstract must be brief and accurate, and it must be presented in a format designed to facilitate the skimming of a large number of abstracts in a search for relevant material.

1.2.1   Brevity

One principal virtue of abstracts is that they are shorter than the documents from which they are derived. Brevity makes it worthwhile to use abstracts as surrogates. All natural languages, such as English, are full of redundancy, much of which can be eliminated during abstracting of the original document. Abstract users read abstracts knowing that they must be alert to every word, and they must, in places, read in reasonable surmises. Brevity saves not only the reader's time but also space, thus lowering the cost of the abstract. Although redundancy is pruned in the writing of abstracts, it often serves a useful purpose in other writing, especially in belles lettres. Repetition emphasizes, teaches, sells, persuades, and embellishes, but is dispensable in abstracts.

Actually, redundancy of the kind in the list of redundant expressions (See Appendix, Section I) is not the major source of verbosity in documents. Rather, it is the history or background given to bring the reader up to the point of understanding the work reported that adds the excess wordage. History and background are eliminated from abstracts, because the abstract is written for users of a certain level of education and experience. Descriptions of well-known techniques, equipment, processes, conclusions, premises, axioms, and results—common knowledge, what one educated or trained in the fields is expected to know—are commonly omitted from abstracts. Thus, abstracts become purveyors of the new, carrying newly coined terms and phrases, novel theories and hypotheses, and results and conclusions never before published.

With the removal of the forms of redundancy mentioned, abstracts become almost as brief as they can be made. Further efforts toward brevity are made in handling new data, findings, and results. Only processed data are included, since raw data are so numerous. Samples and examples of data, rather than all, are brought over into the abstract. Salient data are extracted rather than all data. Reasoning, logical arguments, mathematical derivations, proof, and the like are often omitted, as are details of standard equipment, usual procedures, and normal or expected processes. The name is substituted for these details whenever practicable. Brevity without loss of novelty is sought.

Abbreviations and symbols are commonly used in abstracts to save space without seriously interfering with rapid comprehension. Standard lists of abbreviations are supplied to abstract users, abstractors, abstract editors, and indexers. The use of standards imposes an obligation to be consistent. This obligation is costly in terms of time, for abstractors, editors, and indexers must continually refer to the list, at least until it is memorized. Such lists also tend to make policies rigid and changes difficult. Symbols (e.g., those for the chemical elements or for vacuum tubes) are widely used and acceptable to people trained in a field. A standard nomenclature should be adopted in cases where there are several in use. For example, the names of bacteria differ in different countries. Adoption of a single standard avoids misunderstandings and helps users of abstracts to avoid having to translate from one standard to another. Ad hoc abbreviations may be used by abstractors for long words repeated several times in an abstract. Such abbreviations are given in parentheses after the first occurrence of the name in full and are there-after used consistently throughout the abstract. Roman numerals, as ad hoc abbreviations, are commonly printed in boldface type to distinguish them from symbols, such as those for iodine and vanadium.

When all the techniques for brevity are understood and used, there is little need to specify the length of the abstract—not absolute, maximum, or mean length. The more intelligent way to avoid unnecessary length is to specify rules and principles for abstracting and let length take care of itself. Average length of an abstract can be misleading because actual lengths can vary so enormously. It is said that many a man has drowned while wading a river that averaged only 2 feet deep. The answer to the question, How long should an abstract be? is paralleled by the answer to another question: How long should a piece of string be? The answer is this: just long enough to wrap up the package. Predetermined lengths are as absurd for abstracts as for string. Good abstracts have varied from one word to 10,000 words or more. An example of a one-word abstract is the abstract of a study on the spelling of the name of the inventor of the perforated-plate funnel widely used by organic chemists. The article was entitled, "Büchner or Buchner?" The abstract was one word, "Büchner." This abstract is informative, terse, and complete. Details of the study can safely be left in the original article. An example of a necessarily long abstract is that of a monograph written about 1500 or so new chemical compounds developed as insecticides and tried on dozens of kinds of insects. Names of all the compounds and insects had to be abstracted to avoid loss of what was new.

1.2.2   Accuracy

Publication of an abstract journal is a continual, uphill fight against error. It has been said that if an error—no matter how improbable—can be made, somebody, someday, will make it. Since errors are inherent in all human activity, their prevention needs to be conscious and planned.

Errors in the Citation

Some subject-expert abstractors, engineers, and scientists tend to be impatient with meticulous format and accuracy of bibliographic cita-tions. It is necessary to convince them of the importance of correct, standard forms. The usefulness of abstracts is impaired if original docu-ments cannot be found or if they can be found only with difficulty. Accuracy of citation is essential; small errors, such as the transposing of digits in a journal volume number, make finding the original document difficult. Standard names of journals may appear to be unimportant, since many variant abbreviations are intelligible without necessitating the reader's consulting of a standard list. However, in an abstract journal, consistency of citation and abbreviation saves time and space. Such consistency is especially important in avoiding scattering of related entries in a citation index.

Errors can be minimized by increasing the awareness of the abstractor to the types of mistakes he tends to make and to the serious consequences of these inaccuracies. Tactful reminders and feedback help to reduce the error rate. However, to err is human, and so some errors will occur. All abstracts must be checked in manuscript form and again in galleys and page proof. The checking of reference citations can be done by nontechnical personnel who can be trained to detect and correct inaccuracies in the reference portion of the abstract. Multiple checking can reduce the percentage of error to any specified minimum, but this is expensive, and a realistic minimum must be set.

Errors in the Body of the Abstract

Errors of content are much more numerous and usually more serious than errors in the reference portion. Almost anything can occur. The abstractor may translate *kaninchen* into *dog*, while thinking of *canine* instead of *rabbit*. *Polyneuritis* may be abstracted as *polynephritis*. Omissions are the most serious kind of error, for the user cannot be expected to detect what isn't there. Content errors can be reduced in number by instructing and training the abstractor. Feedback is essential, as is editorial alertness. Editors of abstracts seem to develop a sixth sense as to when some content of importance is missing. They look for, and expect to see, certain categories of information, such as methods and equipment used, data collected, and conclusions.

Errors in copying mathematical data and proper names are especially common, and these items should always be checked against the original document. Abbreviations are frequently made incorrectly, or the abstractor may fail to abbreviate. Correcting and adding abbreviations and symbols is the most common change made in the editing of abstracts.

Reducing the number of errors to the barest minimum is a necessary, although expensive, goal of the abstracting service. Users soon come to rate abstracting services in part, by their freedom from error. Maintaining accuracy is costly, but it pays off in increased use, respect, and confidence.

E. J Crane, the editor of *Chemical Abstracts*, summed up the need for accuracy in the following verse, which has appeared in the Chemical Abstracts Service house organ, *The Little CA* (No. 91, 1958, p. 28):

To authors it's fairer
The rarer an error.

1.2.3   Clarity

It is not enough for an abstract to be brief and accurate; it must be clearly written, in a style that is easily read. For these purposes, it is best to write in complete sentences and, so far as possible, to use the author's own words. Use of the abstractor's words in place of those of the author may often obscure or subtly change an author's meaning, and thus should be avoided. However, abstractors always paraphrase the author's work; otherwise they would be extracting rather than abstracting. Ashworth (1973) says that paraphrasing enhances the literary quality of the abstract.

In these preliminary considerations, it is sufficient to stress that the abstract must be brief, accurate, and clearly written. Methods of achieving these desirable characteristics are discussed in Chapter 4.

1.3   TYPES OF ABSTRACTS

An abstract is an abbreviated, accurate representation of a document. Note that this definition does not specify the writer, the purpose, or the form of the abstract. This is done deliberately, for abstracts can be written by different people, for different purposes, and in different styles.

1.3.1   By Whom Written

Abstracts have been prepared by the authors of the original articles, by subject specialists, and by professional abstractors; and there have even been attempts to produce computer-prepared abstracts. Chapter 8 has a discussion of these attempts.

Author-prepared abstracts, although prompt, and prepared by those best versed in the specific subject, vary greatly in quality. Abstracting takes training and experience, both of which authors usually lack. There are rules for abstracting; authors generally do not know them. Authors have been known to omit data and results in the process of abstracting less significant aspects of their papers. An author trained and experienced is the best abstractor, but training all authors to become proficient abstractors would seem to be an impossible task; at any rate, no one has attempted it. Many journals do require authors to prepare abstracts and to submit these with the original manuscript. These abstracts may be used by secondary publications either intact or in a modified form. Subject-expert abstractors of large services are given the option of using author-prepared abstracts if they are satisfactory. Since author-preparation of abstracts is a common requirement, author-prepared abstracts are frequently found in primary publications accompanying original articles.

Subject-expert abstractors are often the choice of professional abstract journals. Those who are trained in abstracting and are also expert in a field write the best abstracts; their abstracts are accurate, comprehensive, lucid, and terse. It is easier to train subject specialists in abstracting techniques than to train abstractors to become experts on a subject. Subject specialists who abstract on a part-time basis have less difficulty keeping up in their fields than do professional abstractors who are abstracting full-time. Prestigious abstracting journals have little difficulty recruiting excellent subject-expert abstractors who work for an honorarium or without pay, because they are contributing to their profession in a way that benefits themselves as well as their colleagues.

Professional abstractors abstract for a living. Such abstractors are employed to handle work, often in other languages, where difficulty is experienced in finding volunteer abstractors. Their work usually is prompt and competent, if within their area of expertise; outside this area, the quality may suffer. Abstracting done by professional abstractors is expensive, but, except for author-prepared abstracts, it is the best way of ensuring that the work will get done on time.

1.3.2   By Purpose

Abstracts serve different purposes, and if the function is known in advance, the abstract can be prepared to serve best the purpose for which it is intended. Abstracts may be informative, indicative, critical, or special purpose.

An *informative abstract* is intended to provide readers with quantitative and qualitative information in the parent document. Informative abstracts often save the user the necessity of consulting the original work. Numerical data usually included are ranges, maxima, minima, formulas, means, medians, modes, reliability measures, and so on. Parts of tables are often abstracted as are findings, results, new methods, novel equipment, and conclusions. Informative abstracts are especially desirable for reports describing experimental work and for documents devoted to a single theme. The method of condensing information is part of the art of abstracting and is covered in Chapter 4. An example of an informative abstract is shown in Figure 1.1. See Figure 1.2 for an indicative abstract of the same material.

The Science Information Exchange as a source of information. Monroe E. Freeman. *Special Libraries* **59**, 86–90 (1968). — More than 100,000 one-page abstracts of ongoing research (that not yet completed or published) are received and updated annually by the Smithsonian Science Information Exchange (SSIE)—formerly the Science Information Exchange (SIE). The abstracts, which cover life, physical, social, and engineering sciences, have a classified, subject index. Index data are stored in a computer file in code, and abstract data in a hardcopy file in full text which is later microfilmed. Project records (abstracts) are registered, analyzed, indexed, and stored for about $10 each. Input or inventory cost is about 56% of the budget. Requests by mail or telephone include those for a subject, name, or list of names related to projects and pending proposals. SSIE answers about 55,000 questions a year and retrieves and dispatches nearly 800,000 documents annually. Compilations of data, computer lists, tabulations, and catalogs are also examples of output. Simple name requests cost about $1.70 each; complicated subject requests about $45. Complex data compilations range upward from $100 or more to catalogs up to $40,000. Product output accounted for 35% of the budget. Demand for SSIE products and services has increased by 10–20% each year.

Figure 1.1 *Informative abstract.* [*Abstracted by permission of the* Special Libraries Association *from the source indicated.*]

The Science Information Exchange as a source of information. Monroe E. Freeman. *Special Libraries* **59**, 86–90 (1968). — One-page records of research not yet completed or published are received by the Smithsonian Science Information Exchange (SSIE)—formerly the Science Information Exchange (SIE). These records, updated annually, are of indexed abstracts of ongoing research in life, physical, social, and engineering sciences. The subject index to the records is classified and computerized. The records are stored as hard copy that is later microfilmed. Questions, received by mail or telephone, may be formulated for computer search. Requests include those for a name or list of names related to projects or pending proposals. Subject searches are also an important service. Other services include compilations of data, lists, tabulations, and catalogs. Copies of records are a common output in response to specific request or as a result of a search. Cost of operation of SSIE was borne, in part, by sale of products and services. Processing costs, as well as input or inventory cost, are given as are costs of products and services, and the relation of these costs to the budget of SSIE. Demand for products and services of SSIE has increased substantially every year.

Figure 1.2 *Indicative abstract.* [*Abstracted by permission of the* Special Libraries Association *from the source indicated.*]

Another kind of abstract is the *descriptive, or indicative abstract*. This form indicates or describes what will be found if the original document is consulted, but it does not contain much data and often cannot be used in place of the original. It is not uncommon for indicative abstracts to be as long as informative ones. One reason for this is that indicative abstracts are frequently used for describing discursive or lengthy texts, such as broad overviews. Such multitopic texts may permit the preparation of only this type of abstract—an indicative or descriptive guide to what the document is about.

A third kind of abstract is the *critical abstract* or *review* (Figure 1.3), in which the abstractor also functions as an evaluator. For indicative and informative abstracts, the abstractor normally functions as an objective reporter; his opinions are carefully excluded. For the critical, or evaluative, abstract, the abstractor deliberately injects his opinions and analysis. The value of critical abstracts is highly dependent upon the subject competence of the abstractor—much more so than for the other types of abstracts. Because it is easy for the abstractor, without benefit of laboratory work or library research, to be mistaken in his judgment, extra care must be exercised in preparing critical abstracts. Abstracting services do not permit critical abstracts because the author cannot be allowed space or time for reply to the criticism. Examples of critical abstracts are found in *Applied Mechanics Reviews* (Figure 1.3), *Referativnyi Zhurnal Mekhanika,* and Herner's modular-type abstracts (Figure 1.4).

Modular abstracts have been proposed and tried (Lancaster and Herner, 1964, p. 404), but they are rare. Since the abstractor must read the original article before abstracting, it was reasoned that he could prepare a *set of abstracts,* rather than one, in but little additional time. These modular abstracts could then be used by a variety of secondary services, which would select those modules appropriate for their readers. The modules to be prepared would include annotations, informative abstracts, indicative abstracts, and critical abstracts. The concept is logical. Reliable critical abstracts proved difficult to prepare.

Abstracts are written to comply with objectives of the service that publishes them. This compliance may result in *slanted* or, less pejoratively,

---

Theory for the ablaton of fiberglass-reinforced phenolic resin.
R. E. Rosensweig and N. Beecher. *American Institute of Aeronautics and Astronautics Journal* 1, 1802–9 (1963). — The theory of ablation of carbon-contaminated glass, extended from the char-layer theory, gives 38% underprediction of results of experiment. A thorough error analysis was not included. Spalding and Scala have treated similar problems.

Figure 1.3 Critical abstract.

Ablation of fiberglass-reinforced phenolic resin. R. E. Rosensweig and N. Beecher. *American Institute of Aeronautics and Astronautics Journal* 1, 1802–9 (1963). —

Annotation:

A model is developed for charring and melting a composite material with glassy ablation combined with char-layer–molten-glass reactions.

Indicative:

Variables in ablation of a fiberglass–phenolic-resin composite include glass ablation and plastic pyrolysis, flow of melt, mass loss, reaction-heat absorption, mass injection, and coupling between pressure and chemical reaction. Mathematical development and approximations are discussed. Parametric examinations are made.

Informative:

Melting and pyrolysis and other chemical reactions are considered in this theory of ablation of phenolic-resin–fiberglass composite. In this theory, reaction occurs in a surface film in which carbon from pyrolysis of the resin reacts with the glass. For IRBM reentry, there is little temperature drop in the reaction zone, usually less than 1% and 6% maximum. Depth of the reaction zone was one-thousandth that of the thermal thickness. The unreacting runoff in the melt was 40–80% and was a function of the possible reaction-enthalpy level. More than 99% of the material reaching the reaction zone was affected. At 1400–2000°C the reaction assumed was: $SiO_2 + 3 C = SiC + 2 CO$. Up to a 25% increase in the ablation rate appeared only at lower reaction rates. Changing reaction enthalpy three times changed the reaction rate less than 10%. The value calculated according to this theory for peak reentry ablation rate was 38% below the experimental value.

Critical:

This theory of ablation of carbon-contaminated glass extends the work of Bethe and Adams (Cr. Avco-Everett Research Laboratory, Research Report No. 38, Nov. 1958) on glasses. Experimental ablation was 38% greater than that calculated by this theory. Thorough error analysis was not included. Spalding (Aero Quarterly 237–74 (Aug. 1961)) and Scala (General Electric Co. MSVD, report R59SD401 (July 1959); ARS Journal 917–24) have treated similar problems.

Figure 1.4 Modular abstract. [*Paraphrased from Lancaster and Herner, 1964, p. 404.*]

special purpose abstracts. Clearly defined objectives of the abstracting organization allow for acceptable abstracts that are considerably shorter than if the objectives were not defined. For example, a chemical abstracting service may abstract the parts of a biochemical work on biology indicatively and the parts on chemistry informatively. This is entirely proper and results in abstracts suitable for chemists. A biological abstracting service, on the other hand, may abstract the chemical parts indicatively and the biological parts informatively. Thus two abstracts of a document prepared for two different services might be quite different; yet each serves its organization admirably. Examples of abstracts prepared from different points of view and according to different objectives are shown in Figures 1.5, 1.6, and 1.7.

1.3.3   By Form

Abstracts written in a highly regularized form—ruly abstracts, if you will—have been tried primarily for facilitating computer search through the abstracts themselves. Such abstracts have been called *telegraphic,* because they sound something like a telegram. Although one purpose was brevity, the main objective was to prepare the abstract for computerized searching while still maintaining human intelligibility. Since computers were—and still are—not very adaptable to the vagaries and subtleties of natural language, the language of the abstract had to be standardized

---

Blood levels of acetaldehyde and methanol during chronic alcohol ingestion and withdrawal. Edward Majchrowicz and Jack H. Mendelson. *Recent Advances in Studies on Alcoholism; Interdisciplinary Symposium 1970* (published in 1971), 200–16 (English). Edited by Nancy K. Mello. GPO: Washington, D.C. — Acetaldehyde does not play a significant role in developing tolerance to, or dependence on, alcohol. In alcoholic subjects during a 10–15 day period of alcohol intake, blood acetaldehyde ranged from 0.11 to 0.15 and 0.04 to 0.08 mg/100 ml when blood alcohol levels ranged from 1 to 400 mg/100 ml after drinking 100-proof bourbon or 50% alcohol, respectively. The higher levels of blood acetaldehyde in the bourbon drinkers come, in part, from the bourbon. During increasing and decreasing phases of blood alcohol, acetaldehyde remained relatively constant. No dose or dose-time relations were found between alcohol and acetaldehyde levels in blood. Blood methanol increased progressively from 0.2 to 2.7 mg/100 ml from the first to the eleventh day of drinking, during which time blood alcohol concentrations ranged from 150 to 450 mg/100 ml. Alcohol was eliminated from blood at the rate of 27.2 ± 3 mg/100ml/hr within 14–18 hr after cessation of drinking. Blood methanol decreased at the rate of 0.29 ± 0.04 mg/100 ml/hr only after blood alcohol levels decreased to 70–20 mg/100 ml. Methanol disappearance lagged the linear disappearance of alcohol by about 6–8 hr. Methanol probably accumulates in the blood as a result of competitive inhibition of alcohol dehydrogenase by alcohol. Endogenously formed methanol or its metabolites may or may not contribute to the severity of intoxication and to the alcohol-withdrawal syndromes.

Figure 1.5 Special-purpose abstract—medicine.

and written in rigid form. Telegraphic abstracts were produced for a time for the American Society for Metals. After tests showed some difficulty in their use, they were replaced with standard abstracts.

The great versatility and subtlety of English and of other natural languages make them especially suitable for describing the outputs of research and development, which are naturally unpredictable. Ability and license of authors to invent and use new terms and to give new meanings and shades of meaning to old terms are the forte of natural language. Artificial languages, codes and classifications must struggle to keep up with what is novel, and invariably lose; they are always out of date. A further disadvantage is that most users find codes, artificial languages, and classifications irritating barriers to communication, and usually resist using them. There is usually so little useful literature in artificial languages that people are discouraged from learning them. The telegraphic abstract was, in effect, a self-indexing abstract produced by humans so

---

Blood levels of acetaldehyde and methyl alcohol during chronic ethyl alcohol ingestion and withdrawal. Edward Majchrowicz and Jack H. Mendelson. *Recent Advances in Studies on Alcoholism; Interdisciplinary Symposium 1970* (published in 1971), 200–16 (English). Edited by Nancy K. Mello. GPO: Washington, D.C. – Blood levels of ethyl alcohol, methyl alcohol, and acetaldehyde were followed in alcoholics for a 10–15 day period of ethyl alcohol intake. Bourbon (100-proof) gave acetaldehyde levels in the blood of 0.11 to 0.15 mg/100 ml; grain alcohol gave 0.04 to 0.08 mg/100 ml. The higher levels of blood acetaldehyde in the bourbon drinkers came from, in part, the bourbon. Blood acetaldehyde was about constant during ascending and descending phases of blood ethyl alcohol levels. There was no dose or dose-time relationships between blood acetaldehyde levels and blood ethyl alcohol levels in any phase of this study. Blood methyl alcohol levels increased progressively from 0.2 mg/100 ml to 2.7 mg/100 ml from the first to the eleventh day of drinking, at which time blood ethyl alcohol concentrations ranged between 150 and 450 mg/ml. Blood ethyl alcohol was eliminated at the rate of 27.2 ± 3 mg/100 ml/hr within 14–18 hr after cessation of drinking. Blood methyl alcohol levels lagged the linear disappearance of ethyl alcohol by approximately 6–8 hr, and decreased at the rate of 0.29 ± 0.04 mg/100 ml/hr only after blood ethyl alcohol levels decreased to 70–20 mg/100 ml. Methyl alcohol may accumulate in the blood from competitive inhibition of alcohol dehydrogenase by ethyl alcohol.

Figure 1.6 Special-purpose abstract—biology.

Blood levels of acetaldehyde and methanol during chronic ethanol ingestion and withdrawal. Edward Majchrowicz and Jack H. Mendelson. *Recent Advances in Studies on Alcoholism; Interdisciplinary Symposium 1970* (published in 1971), 200–16 (English). Edited by Nancy K. Mello. GPO: Washington, D.C. — *Acetaldehyde* [75-07-0] in blood of alcoholics was 0.11–0.15 mg/100 ml after drinking 100-proof bourbon, and 0.04–0.08 mg/ml after drinking 50% grain EtOH [64-17-5] when EtOH in blood was 1–400 mg/100 ml. Blood acetaldehyde was about constant during change in blood EtOH. MeOH [67-56-1] in blood increased progressively from 0.2 to 2.7 mg/100 ml from the first to the eleventh day of drinking, when EtOH in blood was 150–450 mg/100 ml. EtOH was eliminated from blood at 27.2 ± 3 mg/100 ml/hr in 14–18 hr after cessation of drinking. MeOH disappearance lagged the linear disappearance of EtOH by about 6–8 hr, and decreased at 0.29 ± 0.04 mg/100 ml/hr only after EtOH decreased to 70–20 mg/100 ml. MeOH may accumulate in the blood from competitive inhibition of alcohol dehydrogenase by EtOH.

Figure 1.7 Special-purpose abstract—chemistry.

that computers could search the abstract as if it were an index. Thus the difficulties that indexers and index users experience with classifications, and so on, necessarily fell upon the telegraphic abstract, and it failed.

Another special form of abstract is the *statistical* or *tabular* abstract. This is used for certain specialized subjects, such as thermophysical properties, where the emphasis is exclusively on the data. The abstract is a summary of the data presented in tabular form. An example is shown in Figure 1.8.

No. 105. Specified Reportable Diseases—Cases Reported: 1945 to 1967.
Prior to 1960, excludes Alaska and Hawaii, except for tuberculosis. Figures should be interpreted with caution. Although reporting of some of these diseases is incomplete, the figures are of value in indicating trends of disease incidence. See *Historical Statistics, Colonial Times to 1957*, series B 275–281, for rates of selected diseases.

Disease	1945	1950	1955	1960	1964	1965
Amebiasis	3,412	4,568	3,348	3,424	3,304	2,768
Aseptic meningitis	(NA)	(NA)	(NA)	1,593	2,177	2,329
Botulism	(NA)	20	16	12	23	19

[Numbers are in thousands of cases.]

Figure 1.8 Statistical abstract. [*Extracted from* Statistical Abstract of the United States (*Washington, D.C.: G.P.O.*), 1969, p. 77.]

1.4   OTHER SURROGATES

Abstracts are the most popular of surrogates, and abstracting publications have a long, honorable, and useful history. Although abstracts have many advantages, they also have limitations. Abstracts are expensive; their preparation requires skill, knowledge, and time, all of which add to their cost. In addition, the primary literature has now grown so large that even the abstracts are too voluminous to read. Newer and more compact forms of surrogation are called for. To solve the cost problem and to reduce the level of skill required of the average abstractor, it has been suggested that *extracting* be used instead of abstracting. Copyright considerations enter the decision to extract. To increase compactness, new forms of surrogation, called *terse literatures,* have been proposed (Bernier, 1970, p. 316). These are discussed in Section 1.4.2.

1.4.1   Extracts

Of all the other forms of surrogation, extracting is most often promoted as the rival of abstracting. *Extracting* means the selection of verbatim sentences, data, tables, equations, and the like, from the original documents. The major skill needed for the preparation of extracts is the ability to recognize and select the key sentences embodying the important information contained in the parent article. This is a lesser degree of skill than that required of the abstractor, who must also be able to paraphrase the significant concepts. Extracting can be done in less time and at less cost than abstracting; however, copyright permissions may be involved. The extract is not so condensed as the abstract and generally contains between one-fifth and one-third the words of the original. However, this degree of condensation is certainly worthwhile. An example of a document extract is given in Figure 1.9.

1.4.2   Terse Literatures

Terse literatures are condensations of the original document; many varieties are possible.

Terse conclusions (Bernier, 1970, p. 316) closely resemble aphorisms. They condense a document to about one-hundredth the number of words. Hippocrates is credited with two volumes of aphorisms, of which this is an example: "That which is used, develops; that which is not used, wastes away." Terse conclusions can also include quantitative actuarial data: "For males in the U.S. between 15 and 69 years of age, those who

Blood levels of acetaldehyde and methanol during chronic ethanol ingestion and withdrawal. Edward Majchrowicz and Jack H. Mendelson. *Recent Advances in Studies on Alcoholism; Interdisciplinary Symposium 1970* (published in 1971), 200–16 (English). Edited by Nancy K. Mello. GPO: Washington, D.C. — Out of some 15–20 possible candidates we were able to confirm only the presence of acetaldehyde. We detected the occurrence of previously unreported methanol accumulation during ethanol ingestion. Paradoxically, although both congeners were found in the blood and in alcoholic beverages, the actual amounts found in the body fluids were formed physiologically. The subjects ranged in age from 26 to 49 years and reported a history of alcoholism of 12–36 years' duration. When blood ethanol levels ranged between 1 and 400 mg/100 ml following consumption of bourbon, blood acetaldehyde levels averaged .11 to .15 mg/100 ml. During grain ethanol consumption, blood acetaldehyde values were approximately one-half this value for similar blood ethanol ranges. The difference between the blood acetaldehyde levels of the bourbon group and the grain ethanol group could be explained by the presence of acetaldehyde and other congeners in bourbon. No descending dose or dose-time relationship was found between blood ethanol and blood acetaldehyde values immediately following cessation of drinking. As drinking continued, blood methanol levels ranged between 1.1 and 2.7 mg/100 ml when the mean blood ethanol concentrations were between 157 and 435 mg/100 ml. When blood ethanol levels decreased to approximately 70–20 mg/100 ml, methanol levels began to decline (Phase IV). Thus, blood methanol disappearance lagged behind the linear disappearance of ethanol by approximately 6–8 hr and complete clearance of blood methanol accumulation and elimination in grain alcohol drinkers was similar to that of bourbon drinkers. The mean clearance rate of methanol was 0.29 ± 0.04 mg/100 ml/hr. The major finding of this study is that acetaldehyde does not play a significant role in the process of tolerance or physical dependence associated with chronic ingestion of alcohol. However, since grain alcohol contained no detectable amounts of methanol, virtually all methanol found in blood of both groups of drinkers was derived from endogenous sources. Since both methanol and ethanol were metabolized by the same enzyme system and since ethanol competitively inhibits the oxidation of methanol, it is likely that methanol accumulates in the blood because of competitive inhibition of the enzyme that metabolizes both alcohols.

Figure 1.9 Extract.

are 30% over the average weight have an excess mortality of 42% over standard experience."* Saving of reading time, and/or allowing expansion of reading into related areas of interest, are the obvious advantages of terse conclusions. Also, it has been discovered that the reading of

---

* The statement quoted was kindly supplied by telephone from the Metropolitan Life Insurance Company's New York office.

a collection of categorized and indexed terse conclusions often results in the better integration of a small subject area so that appropriate decisions can be made. Decisions, or appropriate actions can include further reading, planning, using new insights, using discoveries, making recommendations, and so on.

Terse explanations describe briefly how things function (e.g., the operation of lasers, drugs, carburetors, pulsars). Terse explanations need to be brief, categorized, and indexed. Study of related explanations in a category (or related by cross-references) should be useful in presenting analogies for teaching and learning.

Terse intentions describe plans, future research, and projections. Research plans are filed and made available by the Smithsonian Science Information Exchange (SSIE) (Freeman, 1968, p. 86) and by the Division of Research Grants of the National Institutes of Health (*Research Grants Index*, 1969, p. vii). Terse intentions of these plans could be prepared, categorized, and indexed to provide researchers with information of ongoing research and development. Such knowledge could prevent the unintentional duplication of work, increase creativity, and avoid infringement.

Terse organizations of data can come from datum signatures (data, usually numerical, plus complete labels) to be used in handbooks and datum-card or computer files. Compendia (databooks, factbooks, and handbooks) have not kept pace with the outpouring of processed data in the primary literature. Related data are scattered throughout published and unpublished literatures in space and time. Finding, extracting, organizing, evaluating, and disseminating these scattered data should be the function of organizations devoted to saving time of engineers, researchers, and scholars (Bernier, 1972, p. 152).

Terse admonitions are terse conclusions expressed as a warning. For example, they are particularly suitable for use in Poison-Control Centers. For such uses, currency, cogency, and terseness are major virtues. With the increasing complexity of civilization, there has come an increased need for more cautions.

Terse advocacy is the positive expression, in some cases, of terse admonitions. Out of development, research, and scholarship should come recommendations—advocacy. If advocacy does not eventually result, then the effort and resources invested in the study have been lost. Recommendations for action can be expressed tersely. Advertising and suggestions can be terse expressions and so fall into this category. Commands and orders are normally terse—and cogent.

Ultraterse literatures are condensations to one-thousandth or less of the original number of words. This degree of condensation is only possible when dealing with a collection of related documents. An example of an ultraterse conclusion derived from about 60 documents in the fields of nutrition, heart disease, and atherosclerosis is this: "Atherosclerosis and coronary thrombosis are probably manifestations of chromium-deficiency disease that is aggravated or provoked by sugars and possibly mediated by too much insulin in the blood" (Bernier, 1971). This ultraterse conclusion (which is also an ultraterse explanation and implies an ultraterse admonition) represents a condensation to about one four-thousandth. Creation of ultraterse literatures normally precedes research and these ultraterse literatures may form the basis of testable hypotheses. The investigator searches the literature and comes up with an ultraterse conclusion that is then converted into an ultraterse intention. For example, a search of the literature on smoking and health could create the ultraterse conclusion, "Smoking cigarettes is dangerous to your health," or the ultraterse admonition, "Don't smoke cigarettes," or the ultraterse advocacy, "Stop smoking cigarettes," or the ultraterse intention, "I will stop smoking cigarettes." The investigator usually does not write terse statements as a result of his literature search, but these are the things that he remembers because he cannot remember everything that he has read. The condensed versions that he carries in his mind may resemble and be expressed as ultraterse literatures.

2 | Historical Review of Abstracting Services

The modern scientist is not the first to experience difficulty in keeping up with the literature in his field. The disparity between the amount of available relevant literature and the time available for reading is not a twentieth-century phenomenon; it has been a problem almost from the very beginning of records. People, generally in a hurry, do not have the time—or do not take the time—to read all pertinent material. Reading always has been done selectively; indeed this is as it should be. That is the point of the abstract—an attempt to get at the essence of the information with none of the historical background, supporting statements, or embellishments.

A colleague, Robert Collison, when explaining the concept of an abstract to his students, used the following analogy. He suggested that they think of a lemon that has been squeezed dry. The juice is the abstract, and the pulp is the elaborative and illustrative matter that gives the fruit its form, aroma, and body. Busy executives and men of responsibility expedite their decisions by employing someone to squeeze the juice out of incoming reports, so that they need attend to only essential information.

2.1   THE BEGINNINGS

The history of abstracting goes back to ancient times when writing was still being done on clay tablets. Francis J. Witty, who has made a thorough investigation of the history of indexing and abstracting, states that a device similar in function to an abstract was first used "on some of the clay envelopes enclosing Mesopotamian cuneiform documents of the early second millennium B.C. The idea of the envelope of course, was to preserve the document from tampering; but to avoid having to break the solid cover, the document would either be written in full on the outside with the necessary signature seals, or it would be abstracted on the envelope accompanied likewise by the seals" (Witty, 1973, p. 193).

Witty also points out that, even in the days of the great Alexandrian library, scholars found it difficult to study large numbers of papyrus rolls; and so, many of the larger works, particularly histories, were abstracted. Even the plays of the great dramatists of the time were abstracted, for it was felt that it would be useful to provide an abstract of the plot (called hypothesis in Greek) along with a list of characters. Witty's article contains a translated abstract of the play *Agamemnon* by Aeschylus; the abstract is reproduced here in its entirety.

> Agamemnon upon departing for Troy had promised Clytemnestra that, if he sacked Troy, he would signal by beacon on the same day. Consequently Clytemnestra set a hired watch to look out for the beacon. Now when he saw it, he reported; she then sent for the assembly of the elders—of whom the chorus is composed—to make an inquiry concerning the beacon. When they hear, some sing a song of triumph. Shortly afterwards Talthybios (herald) makes an appearance and describes in detail the events of the voyage. Then Agamemnon comes on a chariot followed by another chariot in which are the booty and Cassandra. While he then goes forth to enter the house with Clytemnestra, Cassandra, before entering the palace, prophesies about her own and Agamemnon's death and the matricide of Orestes; then rushing in like one ready to die she casts down her insignia. This part of the play is admirable because it arouses fear and proper pity. Characteristically Aeschylus has Agamemnon slain off-stage; says nothing about the death of Cassandra until he displays her corpse. He has Aegisthus and Clytemnestra each rely on personal arguments for the murder: hers is the slaying of Iphigenia; his, the misfortunes of his father at the hands of Atreus. The play was staged during the archonship of Philocles in the second year of the eightieth Olympiad (459/8 B.C.). Aeschylus won first prize with the *Agamemnon, Libation bearers, Eumenides,* and his satyr play, the *Proteus.* Xenocles Aphidnaios led the chorus. [Witty, 1973, p. 195; Murray, 1957, p. 205]

Note that this is more than just a summary of the plot. It is a critical abstract, as indicated by the sentence, "This part of the play is admirable because it arouses fear and proper pity." It also includes a historical note as to when the play was staged and the fact that it was a prizewinning play.

This remarkable document provides evidence not only that the abstract was in use centuries before the Common Era, but that it was a well-developed literary form. Many plays, of both the Greeks and the Romans, were preceded by such summaries, many of which were written in verse.

The purposes of these ancient abstracts (and this remains the purpose of abstracts today) were to provide concise information about the original document and to facilitate the search for, and recall of, specific information. It was also the custom to abstract deeds of sale, contracts, and other like documents.

In the Middle Ages, when monks transcribed manuscripts, they would frequently make marginalia that summarized the page's contents.

It was not only the scholar who used abstracts. Statesmen, then as now, placed great reliance on the use of abstracts. Many kings of old did not know how to read. They were men of action and had little patience for the reports of their officials. Ambassadors were the eyes and ears of their ruler, and they prepared reports of what was happening in other lands. These documents were often long, for the ambassadors were commonly rated on the length of their reports. Even at that time, it was easier to count pages than to evaluate the ideas contained therein. The ambassadors wrote of many things; gossip, social events, trade alliances, political happenings, and so on. These reports would first be read by a royal secretary, who would then condense them for the king to read, or perhaps a vocal report would be made. This too was an abstract, for abstracts can be spoken.

Rulers also had to keep informed about local events. Even in modern times, the president of the United States receives a daily summary of the news. So also in ancient times the events of the day were abstracted and recorded on the court "calendar." Some of these old calendars are still in existence.

The papal court, with headquarters at the Vatican, was particularly powerful; by the year 1000, papal envoys were in most of the capitals of the world, and all were sending voluminous reports to the Vatican. The reports were written in Latin, which was the international language, and even the script was international and was called the *chancery hand* (perhaps the ancient equivalent of the Spencerian script). During this time, the process of abstracting was universally understood and used. Pierce II, a fourteenth-century pope, liked books, and when he read one, he wrote an abstract and sent copies to his friends. He probably didn't really write the abstract; like all busy executives, it is more likely that he dictated the abstract to his secretary.

By the time of the Elizabethans, scientists made frequent use of abstracts. When the scientist finished a project, he sent a complete report of the study to one or two friends, and to the others he sent a short account—an abstract. These people, in turn, may have sent abstracts to their friends, for their purpose was to disseminate the knowledge of the results as widely as possible. The abstract served as a private communication system, from an ambassador to his king, and from one scientist to another.

The use of abstracts eventually changed from a means of private communication to a system of public information dissemination. The single most important event that led to this change was the formation of the French Academy of Sciences by Cardinal Richelieu in the seventeenth century. This was not the first academy, for in Italy many academies already existed, but they were informal groups of intellectuals who met in cafés. In contrast, the French Academy was a formally organized body of elected members who would meet, discuss matters of common interest, and share the results of their studies. The first abstract periodical for public dissemination, Le Journal des Sçavans, was published in Paris on January 5, 1665. It was a weekly journal, initially edited by Denis de Sallo (1626–69) and later by Abbé Gaulois.* The introduction to the first issue stated that the intent of the journal was to inform the reader of what was new and significant. The journal was to catalog and comment on books printed; to speak of the philosophy and the works of those who died; to report briefly on significant happenings in the fields of physics, chemistry, other sciences, and the arts; and to report on the principal decisions of the ecclesiastical tribunals and the happenings at the academies. Nothing of importance that took place was to be unnoticed by the journal.

These were the stated goals, and the journal was very successful. The first weekly issues contained about seven pages each. During the short time that de Sallo was editor, he succeeded in making enemies of almost everyone. The abstracts that he published were critical—abstracts of books exceedingly so. Even the decrees of the Pope were abstracted and criticized, as were the proclamations of the king of France and the works of just about everyone of importance in the intellectual life of France.

After three months, de Sallo was removed from his post as editor, but the journal continued. It had proven its importance and survived the change of editors. The new editor was the Abbé Gaulois. He was less

* For this and other information on the chronology of abstracting, the authors are indebted to Robert Collison, both for discussions and for the chronology he edited entitled The Annals of Abstracting 1665–1970 (Collison, 1971).

critical, but he was also lazy, and he would occasionally skip an issue. He, too, was eventually replaced, and although editors came and went, the journal continued and is still in existence as *Journal des Savants*. Now, it is a "learned journal," a journal for the publication of primary literature, and not an abstract journal.

The *Journal des Sçavans* inspired many similar publications. In 1684, the philosopher Pierre Bayle (1647–1706) issued the *Nouvelles de la République des Lettres* (Amsterdam, 1684–1718). In 1687, Bayle's friend the Protestant historian and jurist, Henri Basnage, Sir de Beauval (1656–1710), published the *Histoire des Ouvrages des Savans* (Rotterdam, 1687–1706, 1708–09).

Each of these early works was the result of the dedicated efforts of one man, and the publication generally ceased when this prime mover lost interest or died. When there was no organization sponsoring the publication, there was no continuity. The *Journal des Sçavans* lasted because it was a publication of the French Academy; the other two publications were without such sponsorship, and they had relatively short lives.

2.2   **THE EIGHTEENTH CENTURY**

Early in the eighteenth century the first of the German abstract journals made their appearance. Some of the more important publications follow:

1703   *Monatsextracte* (Leipzig).

1712   *Deutsche Acta Eruditorum; oder, Geschichte der Gelehrten, Welche den Gegenwärtigen Zustand der Literatur in Europa Begreiffen* (1712–39) Leipzig, Johann Friedrich Gleditsch (1653–1716).

1749   *Zuverlässige Nachrichten von dem Gegenwärtigen Zustande, der Veränderung und dem Wachsthum der Wissenschaften* (Leipzig, 1749–57); supersedes *Deutsche Acta Eruditorum* (1712–39) (Collison, 1971, p. 1).

1778   *Chemisches Journal für die Freunde der Naturlehre* (Lemgo, 1778–81).

1784   *Chemische Annalen für die Freunde der Naturlehre, Arzneygelahrtheit, Haushaltungskunst, und Manufacturen* (Helmstadt and Leipzig, 1784–1803), supplemented by *Beyträge zu den Chemischen Annalen* (1785–99), and *Neues Chymisches Archiv* (1784–91) (Collison, 1971, p. 2).

In England, the first abstract journals were published in the middle of the century. The following two publications were started by publishers as profit-making enterprises, and they did make a profit.

1747   *Universal Magazine of Knowledge and Pleasure* (London, 1747–1815).
1749   Monthly Review (London, 1749–1844) (Collison, 1971, p. 1).

However, not all were successful.

1782   *Abstract and Brief Chronicle of the Time* (London, December 2 and 7).

New abstract journals continued to be published in French:

1756   *Journal Encyclopédique ou Universel* (Liège, 1756–93) and *Année Littéraire* (1754–90).
1772   Société des Gens de Lettres de France published *Esprit des Journaux Français et Étrangers* (Liège, 1772–1815; 1817–18), with the title of the *Nouvelle Esprit des Journaux* for 1803–04 (Collison, 1971, p. 2).
1789   *Annales de Chimie* (Paris, 1789–92; 1798–1815).
1797   Académie des Inscriptions et Belles-lettres, Paris, published *Journal des Savants* (1797; 1816 to date), superseding the *Journal des Sçavans* (1665–1792) (Collison, 1971, p. 3).

The abstract publication efforts of the eighteenth century conclude, appropriately enough, with the resurrection of the new *Journal des Savants* out of the ashes of the old *Journal des Sçavans*.

These early publication efforts need to be understood in the context of the history of Europe during the eighteenth century. During this period, Europe was divided into small duchies or provinces. These territories were often ruled by despots and their courts. Transportation and communication were inadequate, and the people felt isolated. The courts, particularly, needed to know what was going on in other places. They needed intellectual stimulation, and this was provided by the scholarly abstract journal of the period. De Sallo's work for the *Journal des Sçavans* became the model and was copied by many courts in different cities. The abstract journal became a link between the educated people throughout Europe.

2.3   THE NINETEENTH CENTURY

Whereas the eighteenth century was characterized by scientific publications that were general or universal in coverage, the nineteenth century should be considered the start of the specialized publications. Actually the division is not an abrupt one, for Crell started his chemical abstracts journal in 1784 and the French *Annales de Chimie* appeared in 1789. These were the beginnings of the trend toward specialization.

Many new abstract journals made their appearance in this century. An abridged list will provide some indication of the nature of these developments:

1807   *Neues Jahrbuch für Mineralogie, Geologie, und Paläontologie*
           (Stuttgart, 1830–1949) first entitled *Taschenbuch für die
           Gesammte Mineralogie, mit Hinsicht auf die Neuesten Ent-
           deckungen.*

1816   *Annales de Chimie et de Physique* (1816–1913) superseded
           Annales de Chimie (1789–92; 1798–1815).

1822   *Law Journal Reports* (London, 1822–49).

1830   Berlin Academy published *Pharmaceutisches Central-Blatt*
           (Leipzig and Berlin, 1830–49).

1837   *American Medical Intelligence: A Concentrated Record of
           Medical Science and Literature* (Philadelphia, 1837–42).
           *The Jurist: Weekly Periodical Containing Reports in All
           the Courts* (London, 1837–66).

1842   *Nouvelles Annales de Mathématiques; Journal des Candidats
           aux Écoles Polytechnique et Normale* (abstracts in 1842 and
           1843).

1843   *Medical News and Library* (1843–79) superseded the *American Medical Intelligencer* (1837–42).
           Law Times Reports (London, 1843–1947).

1845   *Half-Yearly Abstract of the Medical Sciences: Being a Digest
           of British and Continental Medicine and of the Progress of
           Medicine and the Collateral Sciences* (London, 1845–73)—
           American edition (Philadelphia, 1845–73).
           Die Fortschritte der Physik (Berlin; Brunswick, 1845–1918)
           published by the Deutsche Physikalische Gesellschaft (Collison, 1971, p. 3).

1851   *New York Times Index.*

1853   The British *Annual Abstract of Statistics* (1840–53).

1856   *Chemisches Central-Blatt* (1856–1906) superseded *Chemisch-Pharmaceutisches Central-Blatt* (1850–55).
        The Geological Society, London, issued *Abstracts of the Proceedings* (1856–1952).
1868   The *Jabrbuch über die Fortschritte der Mathematik* (Berlin, 1868–1944).
1871   Abstracts in the *Journal of the Chemical Society,* London (Collison, 1971, p. 4).
1877   *Beiblätter zu den Annalen der Physik* (Halle; Leipzig, 1877–1919).
        Nippon Kagaku Soran (Chemical Abstracts of Japan).
1878   *Statistical Abstract of the United States.*
1884   The *Engineering Index* published by the Association of Engineering Societies.
        Times Law Reports (London, 1884–1952).
1888   The Linnean Society of New York published *Abstracts* (1888–1932).
1889   The Association of Life Insurance Medical Directors, New York, published *Abstracts of Proceedings* (1889–1940).
1891   The *Architectural Review* (Boston, 1891–1910; 1912–21) (abstracts included).
1893   *Reports in All the Courts* (London, 1893–95).
1894   *L'Année Psychologique* published by the Laboratoire de Psychologie Physiologique de la Sorbonne (Collison, 1971, p. 5).

2.4   THE CURRENT SCENE

In the twentieth century, the trend toward an increase in the number and in the specialization of services offered by abstracting and indexing services has continued. There are now about a thousand abstracting and indexing publications in existence throughout the world. The International Federation for Documentation (FID) and the United States' National Federation of Abstracting and Indexing Services (NFAIS) have, in 1972, undertaken to prepare a *World Inventory of Abstracting and Indexing Services.* "The primary objective of the project is to compile a computer data base of information on abstracting and indexing services covering all subjects regardless of the medium of the service" (FID News Bulletin, 1974). As of the end of 1973, over 1000 questionnaires have been returned and keypunched for input to the data base. It is expected that a printed directory will be available in 1975. The data base will be updated regularly and supplements will be published as needed.

The abstracting organizations will prepare and publish an estimated 1.79 million abstracts in 1975. The cost is tremendous. The approximately 30 member organizations of NFAIS alone have published over 1.5 million abstracts in 1972 (NFAIS, 1973). Because of the number and diversity of A&I (abstracting and indexing) services, their control and use have become a problem of concern. Several new trends and developments have now become evident (Bernier, 1970).

2.4.1   Automation and New Services

In order to provide a more comprehensive service and to make search and its recording more convenient, many of the larger A&I services are using the computer for input of human indexing, storage, publication, and searching. The Chemical Abstracts Service, the American Institute of Physics, BioSciences Information Service, Engineering Index, Inc., Medical Documentation Service, and the American Psychological Association are just a few of the larger American A&I services that have prepared computer data bases and use computer typesetting or print-out for their publications.

With automation it becomes possible to do more than publish a journal. Such additional services include searches, selective dissemination of information (SDI) services, preparation of special bibliographies, reports of research and development in progress, and the like.

2.4.2   Cooperation and Standardization

The growth and proliferation of A&I services suggest the possibility for cooperative efforts and the sharing of the work load on both the national and international level. The various A&I services have conducted studies on the extent of overlapping coverage and its desirability (Wood, Flanagan, and Kennedy, 1972, 1973). The services are also concerned with overlapping readership, and the use being made of the abstracts. The object being to improve service through interservice cooperation without increasing costs.

Cooperation implies standardization. In the United States, the responsible organization for developing standards for abstracting is the American National Standards Institute, Z-39 Committee. At an international level, the corresponding body is the International Standards Organization (ISO), and in this particular field the work is closely

related to the International Council of Scientific Unions Abstracting
Board (ICSU AB) (Bernier, 1974). Some of the standards of prime
concern are the following:

1. coding journal titles;
2. abbreviating journal titles;
3. listing abbreviations in English and other languages;
4. writing abstracts;
5. preparing indexes;
6. formatting bibliographic references;
7. formatting records for the exchange of bibliographic references on
   magnetic tape.

The topics of cooperation and standardization will be discussed in
more detail in subsequent chapters.

2.4.3   User Access via Computer Networks

Now that some collections of indexed bibliographic citations (data
bases) have been stored on computer tape and are available at libraries
and other information centers, users are able to search these data bases
instead of, or in addition to, the printed abstracts. Not all libraries have
these data bases, but through a computer network and terminal, users
at various locations are able to share resources. Such services are technically feasible and some already exist, particularly for government-subsi-
dized medical-literature services. Many problems of an economic nature
need to be solved before commercially produced bibliographic data bases
can be made generally available, but in spite of the problems, one can
safely predict that computer networks will increasingly guide users to
abstracts and bibliographic information.

The need for abstracting and other surrogation and indexing services
is increasing along with the growth of scientific literature. The abstracting and indexing services are striving to meet this need and to provide
expanded and diversified services. The current scene is a dynamic one.

3 | Criteria, Instructions, and Standards

In Chapters 1 and 2 we discussed the general characteristics and the history of the abstract. Here, we will discuss the criteria used to judge the adequacy of an abstract.

Abstracting services have prepared instruction manuals to help their abstractors learn to meet the special needs of their readers. These requirements differ from service to service; yet a basic similarity remains, for the abstract is a well-defined literary form. The common elements need to be identified and the unique aspects related to the special functions. Also, in the interest of furthering national and international cooperation, existing standards for the preparation of abstracts need to be examined and compared. Together, the procedures, criteria, instructions, and standards should identify the common and unique elements of abstracts and aid in their preparation.

3.1   CRITERIA FOR ACCEPTABLE ABSTRACTS

Although abstracts and other forms of terse writing have existed for years, there have been few attempts to study this form of literature in a controlled, scientific manner. In 1962, Borko and Chatman surveyed the instructions for abstractors used by 130 scientific publications. The purpose of the study was "to specify a set of criteria by which the adequacy of an abstract could be judged" (Borko and Chatman, 1963, p. 156). It is interesting to note that the investigators' intention was not so much to improve the writing of abstracts but to establish criteria for judging the adequacy of computer-generated abstracts. In 1962 it was already possible to instruct a computer to extract certain sentences from an article. Criteria were needed to evaluate how good these machine-produced extracts were and to develop new programs for making them better. Although work in automated abstracting has continued (see Chapter 8), a more important effect of the study was the improvement of instructions to abstractors and the formation of a basis for preparing standards for writing abstracts.

The researchers concluded that an adequate abstract of a research article must cover purpose, method, results, conclusions, and specialized content.

> *Purpose:* A statement of the goals, objectives, and aims of the research or reasons why the article was written. This statement should be included in both the informative and indicative abstracts.
> *Method:* A statement about the experimental techniques used or the means by which the previously stated purpose was to be achieved. If the techniques are original or unusual, or if the abstract is informative, more detail should be included.
> *Results:* A statement of the findings. The informative abstract tends to be more quantitative than the descriptive abstract.
> *Conclusions:* A statement dealing with the interpretations or significance of the results.
> *Specialized content:* Certain subject-matter fields require that the abstract contain specialized information. Medical journals, for example, require that the abstract contain details of diagnosis and treatment, drug dosages, etc., where applicable. In writing or evaluating abstracts in these fields, the specialized requirements must be considered. [Borko and Chatman, 1963, p. 157]

The above criteria hold for both informative and indicative abstracts, but more detailed quantitative and qualitative data are included in the former. There is also a significant difference in writing style between the two types of abstracts.

> Style-wise in the informative abstract, the abstractor identifies with, and writes from, the point of view of the experimenter; that is to say, he uses an active verb form in the same tense, often the past tense, as in the original

article. In contrast, the descriptive abstract is most often written in the passive voice and in the present tense. [Borko and Chatman, 1963, p. 157]

The following outline sums up the differences between the informative and the indicative abstract:

Informative	Indicative
Active voice	Passive voice
Past tense	Present tense
Discusses the research	Discusses the article that discusses the research

Borko and Chatman's study was a good start. The investigators were able to propose criteria for acceptable abstracts. However, only the *instructions* were examined—not how they were used by the various publications. Borko and Chatman recognized that the next step would be to examine published abstracts to determine whether they were consistent with the criteria. This work, although proposed, was never carried out. Thus criteria are based upon what people say a good abstract should contain and not on what publishers actually accept as a good abstract.

3.2   INSTRUCTIONS TO ABSTRACTORS

All the major abstracting and indexing services, and many of the minor ones, have published manuals of instructions for preparing abstracts to meet the specific needs of their clientele. Although these manuals will not be reproduced here, we will discuss three of them: *Directions for Abstractors*, published by the Chemical Abstracts Service; *Policies and Procedures* by the American Bibliographical Center, which publishes *Historical Abstracts;* and *Guidelines for Reviewers*, prepared by *Applied Mechanics Reviews*. These examples provide different orientations to the writing of abstracts, and thus further illustrate the nature and the art of abstracting.

3.2.1   Directions for Abstractors (Chemical Abstracts Service)

The goal of Chemical Abstracts Service (CAS) is to present timely, accurate abstracts of all published, new chemical and chemical engineering information and to bring it, along with pertinent peripheral material, to the attention of interested scientists by use of all the advanced information processing and dissemination techniques now available [CAS, 1971, Introduction].

To help achieve this goal, CAS has published the *Directions for Abstractors*. "In general, *Chemical Abstracts* (*CA*) contains informative abstracts. Their primary purpose is to give the reader accurately and quickly enough information on the chemical content to the document abstracted to allow him to determine whether he wants to consult the original publication" (CAS, 1971, 1–1). *CA* uses indicative abstracts for chemical reviews, and for historical, educational, and biographical articles.

Significant elements to be included in a *CA* abstract are as follows:

1. purpose and scope of work;
2. new compounds, materials, reactions, and techniques;
3. new applications;
4. results and conclusions.

Directions for Abstractors devotes much space to detailing the style to be used in *CA*. Style includes specific advice on sentence length; punctuation and capitalization rules; the use of superscripts and subscripts, italics, foreign expressions, abbreviations, and so on. These instructions are important in improving clarity and in avoiding editorial corrections.

In addition to general abstracting instructions, the manual provides special instructions for abstracting organic chemistry, biochemistry, and patents. Some particularly important elements in chemical abstracts have to do with writing chemical formulas and structures, chemical symbols, and indications of single and multiple bonds.

Another important section in the *Directions for Abstractors* is the list of abbreviations and symbols used in *CA*. Both general and specialized abbreviations are included in the manual. The manual also includes a useful index—a feature not normally found in abstractor-instruction manuals.

3.2.2   Policies and Procedures (Amercan Bibliographical Center– Clio Press)

The American Bibliographical Center (ABC) publishes abstracts in the field of history and related disciplines. Abstracting instructions in the handbook *Policies and Procedures* (ABC, n.d.) are brief. Reliance is placed on examples and on a relatively few instructions. It is pointed out that abstracts serve the historian and reference librarian in several vital ways.

First, they provide the researcher access to a comprehensive selection of periodical literature in the field. Second, they assist the researcher in deciding whether the contents of the articles abstracted should be read in full. Third, they provide summaries of ideas, concepts, and interpretations so that it is frequently unnecessary to read articles in full. Fourth, they provide a timely reference service for updating course materials and planning curricula in the field. Fifth, they provide the specialist a means of surveying literature in his field and of keeping abreast of developments in other fields of interest and specialization. [ABC., n.d., p. 1. Reprinted by permission of ABC–Clio, Inc.]

These abstracts are either informative or indicative.

The informative abstract is used to abstract scholarly articles based on research or broad interpretations of historical developments. Indicative abstracts merely clarify the title of an article or expand its meaning or intent. Frequently, a single sentence will complete an indicative abstract. [ABC, n.d., p. 1. Reprinted by permission of ABC–Clio, Inc.]

ABC abstracts are not evaluative. *Policies and Procedures* specifies that the content of the abstract should include the following:

1. theme or topic;
2. thesis or conclusion;
3. period or periods of primary significance;
4. names of individuals;
5. geographical locations.

The style guide recommends that verbs in the active voice be used whenever possible, and that unfamiliar terms, acronyms, and abbreviations or symbols be avoided or defined when they first appear. No rules for transliteration, spelling, or punctuation are given. The examples at the end of the booklet and the brief instructions reproduced in Figure 3.1 are intended to provide the abstractor with sufficient guidance. Instructions need not be lengthy to be useful.

3.2.3   Guidelines for Reviewers (*Applied Mechanics Reviews*)

It is the policy of *Applied Mechanics Reviews* (*AMR*) to provide an assessment of the world literature in applied mechanics by means of critical reviews. The reviews are "critical" in the sense that they are selective in the choice of primary source material to be listed, and also in the sense that they include critical, constructive, and evaluative comments in addition to the factual summaries. "Regardless of the source of an item selected for review, the function of the reviewer is to evaluate

ABC - CLIO

ABSTRACTING INSTRUCTIONS

1. Abstract designation
   code ——————————————→ | H | | Office |

2. author and
   institutional affiliation ——————→ | Richard, Guy   (U. of Caen). |

3. article title —————————————→ | DU MOULIN BANAL AU TISSAGE MECANIQUE. LA NOBLESSE DANS L'INDUSTRIE TEXTILE EN HAUTE-NORMANDIE DANS LA PREMIERE MOITIE DU XIXe SIECLE |

4. English title
   translation ——————————————→ | [From the communal mill to mechanical weaving. The nobility in the textile industry of Haute-Normandie in the first half of the 19th century]. |

5. journal, year, volume,
   number, page numbers ——————→ | Revue d'Histoire Economique et Sociale [France]   1968   46   (3)   305-338. |

6. abstract —————————————————→ A statistical analysis of aristocratic ventures in cotton textile production between 1800 and 1850 in an area bounded by the Epte, Risle, Avre, and Andelle Valleys. The aristocratic industrialists were, with few exceptions, members of well-established noble families rather than bourgeoisie who acquired noble status through financial success. Their textile plants were mostly converted water-driven flour mills or forges located along river banks to which they held proprietary title. The growth of such "feudal" enterprises reached its peak during the Orleanist Monarchy (1830-48), only to fall off rapidly with the introduction of steam-driven machinery. Based on documents

7. documentation —————————————→ in the Archives Nationales (series F 14), departmental archives (series S), published official statistics, and secondary works; 3 maps, 6 tables, 2 graphs, 23 notes. Article to be continued. J. R. Vignery

8. abstracter ———————————————→ | ca. 1800-50 | Office |

9. chronology —————————————————→ | Office |

EXPLANATION OF ABSTRACT

1. *Abstract designation code.* The letters A, H, T, TA, HA, TH, THA appear next to the article in the table of contents in the journal(s) sent to you for abstracting. Type the appropriate letter in the box (see page 7 of POLICIES & PROCEDURES for codes).

2. *Author(s) and institutional affiliation(s).* Cite the last name of the author first. Type in the institutional affiliation for each author.

3. *Article title.* Type in all capital letters the title and subtitle of the article exactly as they appear on the first page of the article.

4. *English translation of title.* Type the English translation of article titles published in foreign languages. Enclose the translation in brackets, use upper and lower case.

5. *Journal, year, volume, number, and page numbers.* Underline the name of the journal and cite it exactly as it appears on the cover. Include the year of publication, volume number, fascicle or issue number, the inclusive page numbers in that order — all in Arabic numerals, and the country of publication (except U.S. journals) e.g., Journal of Polynesian Society [New Zealand].

6. *Abstract.* An abstract is an abbreviated, accurate representation of an article without added interpretation or criticism. The abstract is normally 100-150 words in length. Consider the following points

for inclusion: The main theme or topic. The author's thesis or con-clusion. The period or periods of primary significance to the article. The individuals (personal names) of major significance to the article. (Cite full names in the abstract so they can be indexed accurately). The geographical locations of relevance to the article. Avoid using un-familiar terms, acronyms, abbreviations, or symbols; if they are essen-tial, define them the first time they occur in the abstract.

7. *Documentation used in article.* Cite the number of documentary footnotes, when they are consecutively numbered, and the number of maps, tables, appendixes and illustrations. In the documentation show the kind of materials used, e.g., primary and secondary sources, newspapers, government documents, or whether the arti-cle was based primarily on a single source. Give the type of docu-mentation at the end of the abstract in the following order: Based on primary and secondary sources; illus., maps, tables, notes, biblio. Use "biblio." only if there is a bibliography other than the foot-notes.

8. *Abstracter's name.* Type your name at the end of each abstract.

9. *Chronology.* Please include period covered (chronology) at the bottom of the abstract.

Figure 3.1 ABC–Clio abstracting instructions. [Reprinted from ABC–Clio, Policies and Procedures, by permission of ABC–Clio, Inc. © 1973 by American Bibliographical Center–Clio Press.]

its worth to the potential reader and to provide an appraisal of its relationship to the other literature if it is deemed worthy of reviewing (*AMR*, n.d., p. 1).

The instructions maintain that a good review should be as self-contained as possible. It should be informative rather than indicative. The reader should be able to follow the review without having access to the original paper.

Guidelines for Reviewers states that the following elements should be included in the critical review:

1. problem statement including assumptions, treatment, or method;
2. reference to previous research;
3. originality;
4. significant results and conclusions;
5. clarity and readability;
6. reader-appeal group—research scientists, design engineers, graduate students, and so on.

The suggested contents stress the need for evaluative statements. For the evaluations to be useful, the reviewer must be a person of standing in the field. Reviewers are carefully screened, and are invited at the recommendation of other reviewers. The editor recognizes that there may be differences of opinion concerning the reviews and any complaints or comments by the author are referred to the reviewer. Changes or additions are published as "letters to the editor."

No specific guidelines are given on the style of the review. Perhaps this is because a far greater latitude is given to the writers of critical reviews than to other abstractors.

An abbreviated version of the *AMR Guidelines for Reviewers* is reproduced in Figure 3.2.

3.3   STANDARDS

The value of having standards has long been recognized by many services. Yet the standardization of procedures for the transfer of information within nations, and especially across national boundaries, is difficult to achieve. The problems involved in standardization are many and complex. To say that people and organizations are basically uncooperative and do not want to change present practices for the common good is unfair; to accept at face value the facetious remark that all organizations should standardize by adopting "my" particular method is foolish. The

APPLIED MECHANICS Reviews

See full GUIDELINES for
more complete information

ABBREVIATED GUIDELINES FOR REVIEWERS

The following items are abstracted from the AMR GUIDELINES FOR REVIEWERS. If further explanation is desirable, the original guidelines should be consulted.

Timeliness: Publications should be reviewed and returned within 4 weeks if at all possible.

Criticality: Constructive comments; no derogatory or petty statements. Be objective. Pointing out deficiencies acceptable, if substantiated.

Critical Review Elements:

   Problem Statement (overview of publication)
   Nature of Treatment
   Reference to Previous Research
   Originality
   Results and Conclusions
   Clarity and Readability
   Reader Appeal Group

Length: Commensurate with publication length and importance.

Subject Classification: Main heading and cross-reference number(s) entered on the EVALUATION REVIEW form; use only nonintersecting cross references. For main headings and code numbers, see backside of this sheet.

Typing: Double spaced on both front and back of the form. Additional plain sheets permissible for continuation.

Reviewer's Identity: Typed beneath the review on the form with country identification (use official United Nations country designations).

Reviewer's Change of Address and Title: Use proper space on form.

Title Translation Change: Corrections to be made on form.

Mathematics: Minimize use of math formulas. If formulas must be used, type on single level. Explain all symbols which are not obvious. Diagrams and tabulations are taboo.

Abbreviations, Acronyms: Spell out.

Units: SI preferred, if publication uses British units, then dual system encouraged.

Referencing: Include in text and only if complete (author's name, journal title, volume, year, issue number, and pages). Do not cite references based on memory.

Proofing Text: Watch for typing errors and missing symbols.

Matching of review and review form: When several reviews are prepared concurrently, guard against mixing reviews and improper titles.

Transfer Assignment: Ask colleague for consent; cross out original reviewer's name; transfer material to colleague; send COMMUNICATION CARD to AMR.

Nonreview: Return all material with COMMUNICATION CARD in envelope.

Reviewer Privileges: If review prepared, retain reviewed material.

Editorial Prerogative: AMR Editors may edit reviews.

AMR LIST OF MAIN HEADINGS   *(over)*

***Figure* 3.2** Applied Mechanics Reviews: Abbreviated Guidelines for Reviewers. [*Reprinted from separate by permission of* Applied Mechanics Reviews.]

people and services involved in abstracting are neither naive nor selfish; the majority are willing to change if the change will give better service at reasonable cost. And there is the problem; it is very difficult to guarantee this.

Each abstracting service has developed a set of procedures for providing abstracts of its specialized material to its own clientele in a useful and economical fashion. The editors know this to be so, for people are buying and using the service. The users have become acquainted with a given format for listing titles, authors, content elements, and the like, and have learned to use the service efficiently. Why change just for the sake of uniformity? Why change when any change will be costly, disruptive, and possibly not so good as the present system? Can a single standard serve equally well for both discipline- and mission-oriented secondary services, and for subject matter as diverse as science, technology, humanities, and the arts? Can a standard be devised that is sufficiently prescriptive, yet flexible enough to allow for individual differences? And, even if such a standard could be produced, what advantage would there be over present ways of writing abstracts? These are difficult and important questions that need to be answered before standardization can be achieved.

Let us first attempt to answer the question, Why change? If it were indeed true that existing abstracting and indexing (A&I) services could, in the future, provide the same level of service that they now provide at approximately the same price, there would be no advantage to changing current procedures. However, there are a number of reasons why it is believed *not* to be true. The volume of literature that needs to be abstracted by any given A&I service is constantly increasing so that the cost and number of abstracts are ever increasing. The users of A&I services are becoming more sophisticated and more demanding of quality. In many services, users insist on coverage of relevant foreign publications. The users also want to be informed of relevant publications in related and peripheral fields, for it is in the area of overlap between traditional disciplines that science grows most rapidly. Users also want a more rapid service, and if it proves to be time-saving, one that makes use of the latest data-processing technology such as on-line interactive retrieval systems. The desired services may be very expensive, in fact, prohibitively so for all but the most affluent organizations. If one accepts the foregoing arguments, then it follows that if the A&I services continue their present mode of operation, services will deteriorate and/or costs will increase.

Is standardization a solution? The answer is *partially,* for standardization provides a means for combining and sharing the abstracts of various services. At the very least, standardization should provide a common format that will make it easier for people to use diverse services when searching for information. At an intermediate level of cooperation, standardization may make it possible for a single abstract of a multi-disciplinary article to be used by more than one abstracting service. This type of cooperation should cut costs and provide broader coverage. An even greater advantage would occur if, because of standardization, the products of a number of different abstracting services were combined into a single, computer-readable data base for research and retrieval.

As a result of this and similar analyses of the A&I service industry, some have concluded that standardization *now* is both necessary and feasible. This is not to say that standardization is simple or that all problems have been solved. What is being said by its proponents is that standardization would cause fewer problems and have a greater long-term advantage than would the proliferation of nonstandard individual A&I services. A major problem to be solved is caused by difference of viewpoints in abstracting. For example, for the chemist the chemical part of a biochemical article should be abstracted informatively and the biological part indicatively. For the biologist, the biological part should be abstracted informatively and the chemical part indicatively. If both parts are abstracted informatively, the abstract may be longer and more difficult to prepare, because the chemist who abstracts the work will also have to know biology, and the biologist who abstracts the work will also have to know chemistry. Those abstracts shared in interdisciplinary fields will have to be different from other abstracts in order to serve best the interests of those in all the disciplines involved. For abstracts strictly within a discipline, such as chemistry, there is no problem because other services in the same language may not wish to compete, and abstracting services in other languages may have exchange privileges. That is to say, the services in a given discipline will exchange abstracts among themselves; for example, *Chemical Abstracts* and *Chemisches Zentralblatt* (or its successor). This type of exchange within disciplines has been in existence for years. Exchange of abstracts between services of *different* disciplines has been of low volume because the disciplines developed as unrelated to each other and suffer from the problem of viewpoint. Some editors, as a result, and in order to make their abstract journals of the greatest service to their own clientele, may use abstract journals of other disciplines only as their guides to the original documents. Then they abstract the originals from the viewpoint of their discipline. Copying abstracts from other services has been handled by agreements for copying.

3.3.1   ASTIA Guidelines, 1962

In the United States, a significant step toward the standardization of abstracting was taken by the Armed Services Technical Information

Agency (ASTIA) with the publication of the *ASTIA Guidelines for Cataloging and Abstracting, 1962.* The publication describes the procedures used by ASTIA in providing guidance to the scientific and technical report literature prepared by and for the Department of Defense (DoD). It was part of their effort "to encourage standardization of bibliographic techniques for technical reports, thereby: (1) increasing the effectiveness of the technical report; (2) avoiding unnecessary duplication and reducing the cost of the bibliographic effort; and (3) accelerating the dissemination process" (from the letter of transmittal (of standards for technical reports to those who produce reports, e.g., government laboratories and contractors of the DoD) signed by Paul Klinefelter, then Acting Deputy for Science and Technology).

ASTIA had a computer for document-security control and for printing of the *Technical Abstract Bulletin (TAB).* The *ASTIA Guidelines* covered various elements in descriptive cataloging, subject categorization (by means of descriptors and identifiers), and abstracting. Because of the nature of the agency, and the fact that the DoD was able to exercise some control over the reports submitted by its contractors, these guidelines became a standard for a significant part of the scientific, engineering, and scholarly community producing technical reports.

3.3.2   DDC Standards, 1968

In the course of time, ASTIA was renamed the Defense Documentation Center (DDC), and transferred to the Defense Supply Agency. The volume of government reports increased as did the emphasis on using computers for information processing. The need for standards became greater, and a more-complete set of abstracting guidelines was issued (DDC, 1968). The introduction to this document explains that "with the interchange of information being planned for complex communication networks, all contributors to this interchange should abide by standard rules so that all readers may understand and rely on what is written" (DDC, 1968).

There were a few more teeth in these standards than in the previous set, for in the meantime the Department of Defense had issued a requirement (DoD Instruction 3200.8, "Standards for Documentation of Technical Reports under the DoD Scientific and Technical Program") that every technical report generated for the DoD must incorporate DD Form 1473 ("Document Control Data—R&D"), which required an abstract. (This form is reproduced in Figure 3.3) DoD Instruction 3200.8 has been superseded by MIL-STD-847A and DD Form 1473 is now a part of this military standard, p. 15 (DoD, 1973).

SECURITY CLASSIFICATION OF THIS PAGE (When Data Entered)

REPORT DOCUMENTATION PAGE		READ INSTRUCTIONS BEFORE COMPLETING FORM
1. REPORT NUMBER	2. GOVT ACCESSION NO.	3. RECIPIENT'S CATALOG NUMBER
4. TITLE (and Subtitle)		5. TYPE OF REPORT & PERIOD COVERED
		6. PERFORMING ORG. REPORT NUMBER
7. AUTHOR(s)		8. CONTRACT OR GRANT NUMBER(s)
9. PERFORMING ORGANIZATION NAME AND ADDRESS		10. PROGRAM ELEMENT, PROJECT, TASK AREA & WORK UNIT NUMBERS
11. CONTROLLING OFFICE NAME AND ADDRESS		12. REPORT DATE
		13. NUMBER OF PAGES
14. MONITORING AGENCY NAME & ADDRESS(if different from Controlling Office)		15. SECURITY CLASS. (of this report)
		15a. DECLASSIFICATION/DOWNGRADING SCHEDULE
16. DISTRIBUTION STATEMENT (of this Report)		
17. DISTRIBUTION STATEMENT (of the abstract entered in Block 20, if different from Report)		
18. SUPPLEMENTARY NOTES		
19. KEY WORDS (Continue on reverse side if necessary and identify by block number)		
20. ABSTRACT (Continue on reverse side if necessary and identify by block number)		

DD FORM 1 JAN 73 1473   EDITION OF 1 NOV 65 IS OBSOLETE

SECURITY CLASSIFICATION OF THIS PAGE (When Data Entered)

Figure 3.3 DD Form 1473. [Reprinted from report documentation page 15 of MIL-STD-847A (DoD, 1973) by permission of the Defense Documentation Center.]

The 1968 guidelines contain instructions for preparing abstracts, as well as an appendix that specifies the symbols to be used in the abstracts, annotations, and title—symbols that allow for machine processing of the data. A second appendix contains sample abstracts.

An outline of the DDC rules for preparing abstracts is reproduced in Figure 3.4.

3.3.3   ANSI Standards, 1970

Both the ASTIA and the DDC guidelines applied only to abstracts of technical reports produced for the Department of Defense. The non-defense community, the main contributors of journal articles, were unaffected by these standards, but they were certainly not unaffected by the problem. The need for standards for writing abstracts was recognized by the U.S.A. Standards Institute, now called the American National Standards Institute (ANSI). The task of drafting such standards was assigned to Sectional Committee Z-39, Subcommittee 6, which is sponsored by the Council of National Library Associations and deals with standardization in the fields of library work and documentation.

Formulating the standards was difficult, complex, and time-consuming.

DDC Rules for Preparing Abstracts
Outline

In brief:
1. Always an informative abstract if possible
2. 200–250 words
3. Same technical terminology as in report
4. Contents
    a. Objectives or purpose of investigation
    b. Methods of investigation
    c. Results of investigation
    d. Validity of results
    e. Conclusions
    f. Applications
5. Numerals for numbers when possible
6. Phrases for clauses, words for phrases when possible
7. No unconventional or rare symbols or characters (see Appendix I, Verbalization Chart)
8. No uncommon abbreviations
9. No equations, footnotes, preliminaries
10. No descriptive cataloging data
11. Security Classification
12. Dissemination controls, if any
13. Review it.

Figure 3.4 DDC rules for preparing abstracts. [Reprinted from DDC, 1968, by permission of the Defense ocumentation Center.]

The aim was to draft a substantive and more useful standard, which would qualitatively improve the writing of abstracts and not just legitimize existing practice; satisfy the requirements of diverse disciplines and missions; and be acceptable to journal editors and the vast majority of the scientific and technical community. The difficulty of the task is indicated by the fact that two committees failed to formulate acceptable standards. However, the task was accomplished by a third Subcommittee 6, appointed in January 1969, under the chairmanship of Ben Weil of Exxon Research. Four drafts were prepared for review, comment, and revision. The fifth and final draft (Weil, 1970) was submitted to, and accepted by, ANSI.

The ANSI standard defines an abstract, types of abstracts, and related terms designating terse writings. It identifies the content elements as follows: purpose, methods, results, conclusions, collateral, and other information. The standard does not prescribe the order in which these elements are to be arranged. It states that

> Most documents describing experimental work can be analyzed according to these elements, but their optimum sequence may depend on the audience for which the abstract is primarily intended. Readers interested in applying new knowledge may gain information more quickly from a findings-oriented arrangement in which most important results and conclusions are placed first, followed by supporting details, other findings, and methodology. [Weil, 1970, p. 353]

Under "Style," the abstractor is admonished to "begin the abstract with a topic sentence that is a central statement of the document's major thesis, but avoid repeating the words of the document's title if that is nearby" (Weil, 1970, p. 354).

The ANSI standard provides recommended guidance on the content and style of abstracts acceptable for publication in learned journals throughout the United States. (Adherence to standards is voluntary and can not be enforced.) However, as was pointed out earlier in this chapter, the common procedures should be supplemented by the separate style manuals of the specialized A&I organizations and publications.

3.3.4   International Standards

The same problems that beset the A&I services in the United States have been felt within other countries and internationally. If anything, it is even more difficult to achieve agreement on international standards than on national standards, and the guidance provided is usually less prescriptive and more general.

The international counterpart of the American National Standards Institute is the International Standards Organization (ISO). *Abstracts and Synopses* ISO/R214, an ISO recommendation concerning abstracts and synopses, was first published in November 1961. It distinguishes between an abstract and a synopsis: A synopsis is prepared by the author of the original article or with his agreement, and it is published simultaneously with the article. This distinction, although it may have originally been valid, no longer holds. The term *abstract* has become preferred, connoting both author- and editor-prepared abstracts, and also referring to summaries that accompany the article and those that are published separately.

The ISO guide is very short; it states that the abstract should be brief, objective, and "should respect the general form and balance of the original" (ISO, 1961, p. 3). It makes no style recommendations.

UNESCO has published a *Guide for the Preparation of Author's Abstracts for Publication* (UNESCO, 1968). The preamble states that it is important for every article published in a scientific journal to have an author-prepared abstract (The term *synopsis* was deliberately avoided.). Concerning the content of the abstract, it is requested that the abstract be brief, and that it should contain a "summary of the contents and conclusions of the paper and should refer to any new information which it contains" (UNESCO, 1968, p. 5). Directives on the style of presentation are equally general, but the guide does suggest that the abstract be written in complete sentences, that it not exceed 200 to 250 words, and that it be written in at least one of the more widely used languages regardless of the language of the original paper.

With the advent of computerization and international abstracting services, the need for more standardization and more specific instructions for preparing abstracts is becoming evident. A first step for such a service is the compilation of a world inventory of abstracting and indexing services. This was started in mid-1971 (Keenan and Elliott, 1973). The work is jointly funded by the U.S. National Science Foundation and UNESCO, and is being carried out by the National Federation of Abstracting and Indexing Services (NFAIS) and the International Federation for Documentation (FID).

The purpose of this joint venture is to provide a machine-readable inventory of information on abstracting and indexing services that would be capable of being indexed and searched by subject, country, language, and other characteristics. It is expected that the file will contain about 6000 entries. But the inventory of A&I services is only one step in a planned development of a world science information system known as UNISIST (1971). UNISIST, which is sponsored by UNESCO, has as one of its goals the sharing of scientific and technical information among the nations of the world. The data, including bibliographic descriptions and abstracts, will have to be prepared in machine-readable form in a well-defined file structure. Standardization is the key to the success of UNISIST and of similar projects.

II | ABSTRACTING PROCEDURES

4 | Contents and Format

Abstracts have three major parts: the reference, the body, and the signature. The _reference_ portion directs readers to the original document. The _body_ contains data from the original document and/or indicates or describes the content of the original. The *signature* identifies the abstractor. The normal order of these parts is as given: reference, body, and signature. However, in some publications, the abstract body may precede the reference.

4.1   REFERENCE SECTION

Precise guidance from the abstract to the original document from which the abstract is derived is essential; therefore the reference must be complete and accurate. Even informative abstracts do not always function as complete surrogates for originals. For example, originals must be consulted for tables of data, diagrams, and details of procedure. When the abstract is descriptive or indicative, the original document usually must be consulted; such abstracts serve mainly as guides to the original. Inaccurate guidance to the original burdens the user of abstracts with extra work and may cause him to give up the search for the original document.

Through the years, content and format (structure and punctuation) of references have evolved. An unambiguous reference with a minimum number of keystrokes (characters plus spaces) has been the objective, for ambiguity makes the reference costly to publish and to use. Placing the reference at the head of the abstract provides users with important clues that help them to decide whether or not to read further.

The reference section of the abstract consists of many parts, as the example from the ERIC (Educational Resources Information Center) abstracts, Figure 4.1, indicates. All the parts should be included if they help the reader to ascertain the relevance of the document and if desired, to locate and obtain the original document. Readability and intelligibility may be improved if more than one font of type is used in the publication.

The more significant parts of the reference portion of the abstract, which will be discussed in detail, are as follows:

1. document identification number;
2. author(s);
3. title;
4. author's affiliation;
5. sponsoring agency and agency report number;
6. contract or grant number;
7. source and date of publication;
8. original language and/or source of translation;
9. descriptive notes;
10. alternative sources for obtaining the document;
11. price of original document.

It should again be pointed out that the ERIC format for writing abstracts is an *example*. It is a good example, but it is only one of a number of possible formats that could be used in preparing abstracts. Other A&I services may prefer variant styles, especially in regard to the reference citation. Obviously the style of the service takes precedence over any rules presented in this section. Nevertheless, it is worth learning these rules, if only as a basis for later modification.

4.1.1   Document Identification Number

The identification number is an accession number that is sequentially assigned to documents as they are processed. The number serves uniquely to identify the particular abstract and document within the abstract service. A special identification-number index is often provided by the publication. In Figure 4.1 the document identification number is the ERIC Accession Number ED 013 371. Although other numbers can be assigned, such as Clearinghouse accession number AA 000 223, only one number can serve as the identification number for the particular abstracting service; in this case, it is the ERIC Accession Number.

The Legislative Authority Code is unique to the ERIC service and is not normally included in abstracts.

4.1.2   Author(s)

There are differences of opinion as to whether the author's name should precede or follow the title, and there are advantages and disadvantages to each position. Prominence is given to the author's name if it is placed first. Some reasons for emphasizing the author are as follows: (1) it provides a means for rapidly identifying the article; (2) it caters to the preferences that certain readers may have developed either in favor of or against the writings of particular authors; (3) it provides a means of selecting all works by the same author while skimming an issue of abstracts. The main disadvantage of placing the names of authors first is that the title of the article provides better guidance for nearly all readers and therefore should receive emphasis. When the title is placed first, the user is able immediately to focus on this item and, by reading only the title, quickly reject most abstracts that are not of interest.

The ERIC abstracts have made a rather ingenious compromise. The author's name is placed first but in a lightface italic type, whereas the title is printed in boldface capitals so that it stands out at the head of the abstract. At this point it should be noted that an all-capital-letter style in titles in some fields, such as chemistry, leads to lowered intelligibility and to circumlocutions.

There are many variations in the listing of author names in abstracts. Several points to consider follow.

Single Authors: Full or Abbreviated Name

The preferred rule is to print the name of the author verbatim as found in the original document rather than to use the family name and initials; for example, *Norberg, Kenneth David,* not *Norberg, K. D.* Note that in the ERIC example in Figure 4.1 only the middle initial is used. This was the way the name was given in the original article, and adding *David* would have taken too much time. Giving author names in full saves look-

SAMPLE ENTRY

Left-side labels:

ERIC Accession Number—identification number sequentially assigned to documents as they are processed.

Author(s).

Title.

Organization where document originated.

Date published.

Contract or Grant Number—contract numbers have OEC prefixes; grant numbers have OEG prefixes.

Alternate source for obtaining documents.

EDRS Price—price through ERIC Document Reproduction Service. "MF" means microfiche; "HC" means hard copy. When listed "not available from EDRS" other sources are cited above.

Center entry:

ED 013 371   64   AA 000 223

Norberg, Kenneth D.

Iconic Signs and Symbols in Audiovisual Communication, an Analytical Survey of Selected Writings and Research Findings, Final Report.

Sacramento State Coll., Calif.
Spons Agency—USOE Bur of Research
Report No.—NDEA-VIIB-449
Pub Date—15 Apr 66
Contract—OEC-4-16-023
Note —Speech given before the 22nd National Conference on Higher Education, Chicago, Ill., 7 Mar 66.
Available from—Indiana University Press, 10th and Morton St., Bloomington, Indiana 47401 ($2.95)
EDRS Price—MF-$0.75 HC-$5.24 129p.
Descriptors—*Bibliographies, *Communication (thought transfer), *Perception, *Pictorial Stimuli, *Symbolic Language, Instructional Technology, Visual Stimuli.
Identifiers—Stanford Binet Test, Wechsler Intelligence Scale; Lisp 1.5; Cupertino Union School District.

The field of analogic, or iconic, signs was explored to (1) develop an annotated bibliography and (2) prepare an analysis of the subject area. The scope of the study was limited to only those components of messages, instructional materials, and communicative stimuli that can be described properly as iconic. The author based the study on a definition of an iconic sign as one that looks like the thing it represents. The bibliography was intended to be representative and reasonably comprehensive and to give emphasis to current research. The analysis explored the nature of iconic signs as reflected in the literaure and research.

(AL)

Figure 4.1 A sample ERIC abstract.

Right-side labels:

Legislative Authority Code for identifying the legislation which supported the research activity (when applicable). *

Clearinghouse accession number.

Sponsoring Agency—agency responsible for initiating, funding, and managing the research project.

Report Number and/or Bureau Number—assigned by originator.

Descriptive Note.

Descriptors—subject terms which characterize substantive contents. Only the major terms, preceded by an asterisk, are printed in the subject index.

Identifiers—additional identifying terms not found in the **Thesaurus of ERIC Descriptors.**

Informative Abstract.

Abstractor's initials.

Figure 4.1 (Continued)

* **The key to these codes is as follows:**

Code	Description
08	Adult and Vocational Education, Public Law 88–210
16	Captioned Films for the Deaf, Public Law 85–905
24	Cooperative Research, Public Law 89–10, Title IV
32	Disadvantaged Students Program, Public Law 89–10, Title I
40	Handicapped Children and Youth, Public Law 88–164
48	Language Development, Public Law 85–864, Title VI

Code	Description
52	Library Research and Development, Public Law 89–320, Title II, Part B
56	New Educational Media, Public Law 85–864, Title VII, Part A
64	New Education Media, Public Law 85–864, Title VII, Part B
72	Research in Foreign Countries, Public Law 83–480
80	State Educational Agencies Experimental Activities, Public Law 89–10, Title V, Section 505
88	Supplementary Centers and Services, Public Law 88–10, Title III
95	Other Office of Education Programs

ing up a full name later should identical initials be discovered in index editing and use. Preventing the grouping of articles written by different authors under the same author entry is an important function of editors of author indexes. Confusion about author names wastes time of index users. If author names (initials or given names and surnames) in an index are identical, then the address or the name of the organization for which the author works can be used to differentiate. Differentiating among identical author names is unnecessary in the abstracts themselves; context provides differentiation.

Multiple Authors

Again there are many variations. All author names can be given or only a limited number can be listed. Some abstracting services give all names, no matter how many there are; other services may specify use of the name of the first author and the substitution of *et al.* for the names of the others. Still other publications set a maximum number of author names to be given—for example, 3, 5, or 15 names. Author names may be printed verbatim, or the given names of authors may be cut to initials or other abbreviations.

The name of the first author may be printed inverted, with the last name first, followed by the first name and middle name. This is done to save rekeyboarding in making up the author-index entry from the abstract by means of a computer. Some services also invert the second and following author names, as in, *Brown, Robert William and Smith, Carol Ann*, rather than *Brown, Robert William and Carol Ann Smith*. The last name is listed first for alphabetizing and cataloging, not of the abstract, but of the index entries or catalog entries (e.g., cards) derived from the abstract by typist or computer. There seems to be no justification for reversing the normal order of author names for manual indexes. If the author index is prepared from assignment cards rather than from the abstracts, there is no reason for inversion of any author names.

Changing of the order of the author's names in a particular reference (e.g., listing them alphabetically) is unacceptable because correct sequence aids identification of original paper and citation counting is made easier. When preparing the abstract, the authors must be listed in the same order as in the original document.

Non-English Names

Names of authors from other countries may contain special letters, such as letters with umlauts. If these special characters are unavailable through the printer, then other letters need to be substituted for the unavailable ones; for example, *ue* may be used in place of *ü*. Family names of Chinese customarily come first, but it may be the practice in abstracts published in occidental countries to place the family name last. Inversion of other than Chinese names is unnecessary and generally not done because there is no reason in abstracts to bring the family name to the fore. Those of Spanish descent may use names of both mother and father. The French may use *M.* for *Monsieur* as well as for a given name, such as *Marcel*. Author names in languages not using the Latin alphabet require transliteration. A Russian–English table for transliteration is given in Figure 4.2. The Hepburn system for transliteration of Japanese may be used (CA, 1960, p. 14).

Other Problems Regarding Author Names

For an anonymous work the term *Anon.* can be used. Titles, such as *Doctor* or *Professor*, are omitted. The abbreviations *Mrs.*, *Mme.*, and *Ms.*

RUSSIAN — ENGLISH

Printed Capital	Printed Small	Written Capital	Written Small	English Equivalents	Printed Capital	Printed Small	Written Capital	Written Small	English Equivalents	Printed Capital	Printed Small	Written Capital	Written Small	English Equivalents
А	а	*Аа*		a	К	к	*Кк*		k	Х	х	*Хх*		kh
Б	б	*Бб*		b	Л	л	*Лл*		l	Ц	ц	*Цц*		ts
В	в	*Вв*		v	М	м	*Мм*		m	Ч	ч	*Чч*		ch
Г	г	*Гг*		g	Н	н	*Нн*		n	Ш	ш	*Шш*		sh
Д	д	*Дд*		d	О	о	*Оо*		o	Щ	щ	*Щщ*		shch
Е	е	*Ее*		e	П	п	*Пп*		p	Ъ	ъ	*ъ*		ʼ (not indicated at end of word)
Ё	ё	*Ёё*		e	Р	р	*Рр*		r	Ы	ы	*ы*		y
Ж	ж	*Жж*		zh	С	с	*Сс*		s	Ь	ь	*ь*		ʼ (not indicated at end of word)
З	з	*Зз*		z	Т	т	*Тт*		t	Э	э	*Ээ*		e
И	и	*Ии*		i	У	у	*Уу*		u	Ю	ю	*Юю*		yu
Й	й	*Йй*		i	Ф	ф	*Фф*		f	Я	я	*Яя*		ya

Figure 4.2 Russian—English table of transliteration. [Reprinted from CAS, 1971, pp. 5–13, by permission of Chemical Abstracts Service.]

are used if the husband's name is used in the reference. For committees, the name of the chairman can be given, followed by *et al.*

Over the years, a large number of rules related to author names have been formulated. Organizational policies have emerged of necessity. For details of these policies and rules, it is recommended that the abstractor contact the abstracting service of interest and consult its printed author indexes.

4.1.3   Titles

Users tend to rely on the title of the work to provide the first guide to the subject content; thus it is logical to print the title so that it is easily identifiable. Good titles are paraphrases of general subjects of works. In the ERIC example (Figure 4.1), the title is in boldface type and in capital letters. In some services, it is the policy to capitalize only the first letter of the first word of titles and subtitles, and to capitalize proper names, and acronyms and initialisms. All other words in titles then start with a lowercase letter. Most titles used in medical, scientific, and technical literature provide accurate guidance to the general subject matter of the article. They are sometimes reproduced verbatim. To save expense in printing and time of reading, they can safely be edited to remove uninformative prefatory words, such as, *On, An introduction to,* and *A study of.*

Although titles do not normally cause any difficulties in preparing an abstract, there are occasional problems.

Ambiguous Titles

It the title is uninformative or unclear, several things can be done. Commonly, words are added to make the title less ambiguous. These added words are placed within brackets. Another way is to place a supplementary title, informative and clear, in brackets following the title of the document. Only rarely is one title substituted for another by the abstractor or by the editor of abstracts. Examples of amended titles follow:

Process Control [for Petroleum Cracking]
[Manufacture of] Hydrazine [by Process XYZ]

If it is the policy of the abstracting publication not to edit the author's title, then ambiguities in the title will need to be corrected in the body of the abstract.

Title incompleteness can occur if the article being abstracted is part of a series, and the title of each article is incomplete in itself. For example,

High Strength Steels for Aerospace Applications should be changed to read *Manufacture of New Steels, Part XIX: High Strength Steels for Aerospace Applications.*

Foreign-Language Titles

For abstracts of non–English–language publications, some abstracting services reproduce both the original foreign-language title and the English translation. The translated title generally precedes the original (for the convenience of users who read only the language of the abstract). Abstracting services that want to save money, space, and readers' time may omit the title in the language of the original.

For language of a non-Latin alphabet, such as Cyrillic, some abstracting services use transliterated titles. (See Figure 4.2.) However, it is difficult to understand the justification for this procedure or the value of the transliterated title.

4.1.4   Author Affiliation

The expressed affiliation of the author helps the reader to identify and evaluate the author, and it also gives the place where the document originated (see Figure 4.1). Sometimes the address of the author may be given in parentheses following the name. Addresses are useful in writing for offprints, but become obsolete.

In the case of multiple authors working for different organizations, policies differ on whether to list the affiliation of only the first author or to list them all. The ideal solution, used by some services, lists all affiliations in the order in which the authors are listed; for example, *Harold Borko and Seymour Chatman. System Development Corp., Santa Monica, Calif.; Univ. of Calif., Berkeley.* Note that the specific location as well as the name of the organization is given, for many companies have more than one office, even in the same state.

4.1.5   Sponsoring Agency and Report Number

The sponsoring agency is responsible for initiating, funding, and supervising the research project on which the report or article is based. The sponsoring agency assigns its own number to the report (see Figure 4.1) unless it is the policy of the agency to encourage publication in the open literature. In this case, it is usually requested that source of the support be acknowledged in the article.

4.1.6   Contract or Grant Number

If the work reported in the article has been performed under a U.S. government contract or grant, this number should be included in the abstract. The same contract may generate many reports; having the contract or grant number enables one to locate all reports prepared under a particular grant or contract.

4.1.7   Source and Date of Publication

This section of the abstract heading is especially important and must be accurate and complete. The purpose is to enable the reader to locate the original document, and to do so by use of the fewest number of keystrokes. The points to be observed are many.

Journal Abbreviations

Many abstracting services use standard abbreviations or codes for names of journals and reporting agencies. Standard lists of abbreviations impose a burden on abstractors and on abstract editors as well as on abstract users, for it takes time to look up forgotten abbreviations in a list. However, the alternative of spelling out the complete title takes more space and keystrokes, which add to the expense of publication. Suggestive abbreviations, such as *J.* for *Journal* and *Soc.* for *Society* do not need to be looked up.

Series, Volume, Issue, Date, and Pages

After the journal name some services place numbers important in locating the work. The *series number,* if there is one, may be placed in brackets immediately after the journal name. For example, in the journal citation "*Ann. chim.* (Paris) [13], 4, 491–506 (1959)" the "[13]" is the series number and means that this is the thirteenth series of volumes of *Ann. chim.* French journals tend to have more series than do journals of other countries.

After the series number comes a comma and then the *volume number* (often in boldface). The volume number may be or may not be redundant with the year; some journals have several volumes per year whereas others may have one volume for more than one year. Bound volumes of journals are commonly shelved according to volume number, which is a very convenient locator. If the journal has no volume number, the *year* is substituted; for example, "*J. Chem. Soc.* **1960**, 476–82."

The *issue number,* if it is used, may follow a colon after the volume number (or year). Another form for writing the issue number is to omit the colon and to use, for instance, "No. 3" instead, as in the following example:

> *Datamation* 14:3, 40–3 (1968)
> or
> *Datamation,* Vol. 14, No. 3, 40–3 (March 1968)

Issue numbers can be omitted if pagination is consecutive for the entire volume. Some abstracting services always use issue numbers to avoid having to decide whether or not the pagination is consecutive. However, issue numbers add redundancy to the reference. This redundancy can save users time in locating the correct pages when there are errors in page numbers of the reference—but it is better to make sure the reference numbers are correct before publication. After the comma following the issue number comes the page number(s). Inclusive pagination is used to give the reader the exact length of the work. Giving only the first page saves keystrokes. For inclusive pagination, digits can often be dropped to save keystrokes without impairing intelligibility. For example, 223–229 can safely be shortened to 223–9. The digit 1, however, when occurring in the teens and hundreds, is not dropped; for example, 18–19; 118–119. Inclusive pages "eighteen to nineteen" or "eighteen through nineteen" would, if shortened to 18–9, be incorrectly read as "eighteen to (or through) nine." The following list illustrates correct usage.

11-17
111-117
21-7
221-37
305-8
2196-202
206.5-6.7
[CA, 1960, p. 18]

For articles that meander among the advertising or other interspersed material, commas can be used to indicate the intervening material. For example, *17–19, 21–7, 53–6, 113–116.*

After the page number(s) may come the year in parentheses. If parentheses are used, no comma ahead of them and following the pagination is necessary because the first parenthesis constitutes an adequate break. Users like to know the date of publication to see how current the work is and to help adjust coverage (time span) of search. If parentheses are not used, a comma should follow the last page number before the year. Included in the parentheses may be the name of the month or date of issue; this information is generally redundant with the issue number, so is often omitted.

4.1.8   Original Language and/or Source of Translation

If the article for which the abstract is being prepared is in a foreign language, this should be stated. For example, the words "(in Russian)" might appear after the title.

If the article originally appeared in a foreign language and was then published in translation, the name and date of the translation journal should be given:

> English translation in *Engineering and Cybernetics* (USA) 4:1, 37–41 (1972).

Indicating the language of the original article may save the reader from turning to (and searching for) an original in a language (s)he does not read, especially when translation would be unavailable, too costly, or too slow. Some services give the name of the language in which the work is printed only if it differs from the language in which the journal name is printed. Other services assume that all works are in English unless otherwise specified, which seems to be the more practical approach. For example, using the first approach, one would expect that all articles in *Helvetica Chimica Acta* would be in Latin, which is not the case. In case the language of the article differs from that of the journal, the name of the language can follow the year and be placed in parentheses; for example, *J. Phys. Soc. Japan* 14, 128–142 (1959) (in French). Some Japanese journals, published in English, may have occasional articles in languages other than Japanese or English.

4.1.9   Descriptive Note

The note simply provides the reader with additional information about the original document and thus helps him to determine the usefulness and relevance of the content (see Figure 4.1). For example, the following note might appear:

> Speech given before the 35th National Conference on Education, Chicago, Ill., March 1969.

If the reader is interested in gathering information for a speech that he is planning to make, this article may be particularly useful. On the other hand, if he needs lots of statistical data, a speech may not be of interest. In either case, the descriptive note may be helpful. Most abstracting services include descriptive notes in the body of the abstract.

4.1.10   Alternative Sources for Obtaining the Document

Identical material may be published in more than one place. For example, if the original document was a RAND publication, it may be available as a journal article, as a document in the ERIC system, or as a RAND Report. It is worthwhile listing this information. Here is an example:

> Available from RAND Corp., 1400 Main Street, Santa Monica, Calif. 90406
> ($2.00)

Generally, reports and articles are abstracted before they have appeared in two or more places. This policy improves promptness of the abstracting service. When the report appears later as an article in a journal, a brief abstract and a cross-reference to the abstracted report may be used. An example is, "Some comments on the construction and operation of a gas density balance. E. A. Johnson, D. G. Childs, and G. H. Beaven (Med. Research Council Lab., London). *J. Chromatog.* 4, 429–34 (1960). The balance of Martin and James (*CA 50*, 13660g) is discussed."

4.1.11   Price

If the abstract publication lists documents that are available from ERIC or NTIS (National Technical Information Service), the document is for sale in either microfiche or in hard copy, and the price should be given (see Figure 4.1).

Note that, in ERIC abstracts, the EDRS (ERIC Document Reproduction Service) price is printed in boldface. This serves to highlight the ERIC service and price; it is done to improve sales and apparently works. The boldface print also serves a secondary function in that it divides the reference portion from the body of the abstract.

4.2   BODY SECTION

The body of the abstract is usually the second of the three parts of the abstract. It contains the subject matter derived from the original work, and in a few instances is divided into two portions—the descriptors and the abstract proper.

4.2.1   Descriptors or Index Terms

The word *descriptor* was coined about 1960 by Calvin N. Mooers, president of the Zator Company. It originally meant a general subject-heading suitable for categorizing documents, but *descriptor* is now interchangeable with *subject heading* and *keyword*. Some A&I services publish a list of descriptors as a part of the abstract, but most do not.

Four purposes are served by including a list of descriptors in the abstract:

1. Descriptors provide the reader with additional guidance to the subjects discussed in the document. Descriptors listed separately, as in Figure 4.1, may be more specific than the words used in the body of the abstract. If a separate list of descriptors is not given, words (or their synonyms) suitable for indexing the abstract should appear in the abstract.

2. Descriptors provide the reader with a list of terms useful for filing the abstract in a personal retrieval system. The reader simply makes as many copies of the abstract as there are descriptors and files the same abstract under each descriptor to give a useful collectanea of abstracts.

3. Descriptors provide the reader with a list of terms for use in a search for related documents.

4. A block of descriptors at the start or end of the body of an abstract can be identified by a computer from machine-readable media and used to index the abstract for Boolean search, i.e., by logical combinations of terms.

These advantages can occur only if appropriate index terms are assigned to the document. Poor indexing is worse than useless; it is misleading. Indexing requires the use of trained personnel; it is time-consuming and expensive. The cost of preparing the list of descriptors can be justified only if the abstracting service is doing more than simply publishing abstracts—if it is also providing a retrieval service for current awareness and for search. Abstracts, even categorized, soon become a pile of wastepaper without indexes.

One other disadvantage in publishing a list of index terms is a semantic one. An unconnected list of index terms, even if properly selected, may mislead and confuse the reader because the words are out of context. At best, the list will require the reader to spend time to read and integrate the list into meaningful concepts. Thus some publishers omit a list of descriptors on the ground that the user would be better served by reading an abstract that includes descriptors as parts of sentences, rather than guessing at the meaning from the list of descriptors.

Whether to list the descriptors before or after the abstract proper is optional. Those who believe that a list of index terms is a brief guide to the contents of the document place the list first. They feel that the list often helps the user to decide whether to continue reading the abstract. Those who believe the list to be distracting or used mainly for indexing place the list last or omit it.

The ERIC system (Figure 4.1) provides each abstract with two lists of words. The *descriptors* are terms that are printed in the subject index. They are preceded by an asterisk. The *identifiers* are terms that are not subject headings but which may be used in formulating a computer search. Identifiers include acronyms, proper names, names of organizations, trade names, project names, and the like, which are generally much more specific than are descriptors or subject headings. Occasionally, words that were originally used as identifiers qualify for use as descriptors.

4.2.2 Abstract Proper (Body of the Abstract)

The outstanding feature of an abstract is that it is shorter than the original article; that is, it contains fewer words. Assuming that the article was written reasonably well and contained little redundancy, it is obvious that the abstract must be less informative than the original. There is no getting around this fact; it is in the nature of the abstract. Abstracts are not meant to serve the same purpose as the original article. Original research reports are designed to be complete descriptions of the project and should contain enough information about the background, purposes, methods, and results that the work can be duplicated or checked by other investigators without the necessity of consulting the author(s). Abstracts, by contrast, carry principally results and conclusions. Each serves different and important functions, and neither can be eliminated. They supplement each other in knowledge transfer.

Selection of Content

A number of policies, rules, and techniques can be used to achieve the desired degree of brevity. Once the function of the abstract is understood, it becomes clear that certain data in the original can and should be eliminated from the abstract. Abstracts omit history, introductions, old information, redundancy, summaries, and details of procedure. These items often constitute a large part of the original document.

Abstracts usually do not contain all the data reported in the original. At most, the abstract contains samples and examples of the data; it states the principal results and conclusions. The abstract may report the values of the processed data as minima, maxima, means, medians, and modes rather than raw data or tables of data. For example, in reporting the height of male college students in a sample, the data may be summarized in the abstract as follows:

> Students ranged in height from 4′ 10″ to 7′ 5″; the median was 5′ 8″; the mean was 5′ 9½″; and the mode was 5′ 7″.

Results can sometimes be summarized more tersely by words than by numbers. An example is the statement, "There was no significant correlation between the academic rank of the teaching staff and the rank by number of publications."

Omission of what readers are expected to know is still another way of shortening abstracts. A particular publication, for example, *Chemical Abstracts,* is designed for a designated class of users with a specified background knowledge, graduate chemists and chemical engineers. Thus background information is assumed and need not be stated. The abstract carries only what is expected to be novel or original to these selected readers.

Only what the author has done and the results obtained are abstracted. What the investigator tried to do but did not accomplish, and what he intends to do next, while perhaps important in the original article, are generally omitted from the abstract as a matter of policy.

All these policies and rules help the abstractor to achieve brevity. They enable selection of only significant material.

Achieving brevity is not automatic; it is maintained by the vigilance of abstractors, editors, proofcheckers, proofreaders, and users. Rules and policies for abstracting control brevity, and such policies and rules need to be established, applied, and kept up to date. Style is particularly important. Several sentences from an original article can often be condensed into one sentence. Note the following example:

> Television has become very popular as a source of entertainment and thus now competes with entertaining reading matter provided by the public library and its branches. It is impossible to read and to watch at the same time. It is the book that suffers.

The paragraph can be rewritten,

Television competes with the public library in entertainment.

This is a condensation of from 38 to 8 words; clarity is enhanced.

Whenever possible, the words in the abstract should be the words of the author. Exceptions are made when there are ambiguities in the original terminology. Abstractors must respect the author's choice of terminology, for authors choose their words with care, and no substitutions should be made without good reason. Another exception is that abstracts may use standardized abbreviations, acronyms, initialisms, and symbols. Large abstracting services use lists of approved abbreviations. Individuals abstracting for their personal collections of abstracts may find it simplest to avoid abbreviating.

Arrangement of Content

The body of the abstract can be arranged to save the reader's time. Conclusions placed first may satisfy the reader and save further reading. (S)he may accept or reject the conclusions without needing to know the findings upon which the conclusions were based. Amplifying information should be placed last. Labeling each part of an abstract as, for example, *conclusions, results,* or *procedures,* has been found to be unnecessary; readers understand what part they are reading. The arrangement of parts of the body of an abstract is done for the same purpose that parts of an item in a newspaper are organized—to communicate more information more rapidly.

Paragraphing is not desirable. The abstract is short; it should express a homogeneity of thought, and should be written as a single paragraph.

When the abstractor has completed the writing of the abstract, he checks it to see if he has made any errors, if any important information has been omitted, and if it has been written according to policies and rules.

A well-written abstract must convey both the significant content and the character of the original work. If the reader of the abstract is surprised by what he finds in the original, he can be sure that the abstract is not a good one. If novel or important data are omitted, it is not a good abstract. If the original is a spoof, or if it is a piece of original research, and the abstract does not indicate this, a disservice is done the reader.

Although one should not set a definite length for abstracts, it is possible to calculate an average length for abstracts in a given field and at a given period of time. The average abstract is calculated to be about one-tenth the length of the original or approximately 200 words. This is an arithmetical average and it is not a determiner of abstracting practice. Good abstracts vary from a few to a few thousand words. Averages can be used for guidance and not as arbitrary limits that might lead to the omission of significant material. The desired length of an abstract may be a guideline set by abstracting services that do not rely entirely on policies and rules to control length. Large abstracting services have found that they can rely upon stated policies and rules to control length.

4.3   SIGNATURE SECTION

The third part of abstracts, the signature, follows the body. The signature identifies the abstractor to give him credit, place responsibility upon him, and to indicate authority.

Very few abstractors are professional abstractors who earn their living by abstracting. Most abstractors are subject experts who abstract part-time as a contribution to their profession. They may be outstanding men or women in their field, and their names give authority to the abstracts they write. Giving credit for an abstract is also important. Abstractors value receiving this credit. Often they have no financial reward for their work or only a small honorarium. Acknowledgment, via their signatures, that they have written an abstract is a reward for their work. Abstractors enjoy the prestige of working for a large and successful publication and want their abstracts to be published in it.

Errors do occur in abstracts. It is economically impossible for abstract publications to check all statements made by their contributors. Abstractors appreciate this and do their best to ensure that abstracts above their signatures are as error-free as possible. Without signatures, it is difficult to associate an abstract with a given abstractor.

Signatures may be full names or initials only. Full names are preferable as a means of positively identifying the abstractor and of rewarding him. Regardless of whether initials or full names are used, the journal should always publish a list of names of abstractors.

It may be claimed that the use of the full name adds a line to the abstract. If this is a true concern rather than a rationalization on the part of the publisher, the matter can be taken care of by authorizing the typesetter to use the abstractor's full name where space is available, and to use initials when this will avoid adding another line to the abstract. The signature is an important part of the abstract, and it should be treated as such. It is not an appendage to be included only if space permits.

Even abstracts made for personal collections should be signed. Abstractors other than the owner may, at a later time, contribute abstracts to the collection. Again, the signature should always be part of the abstract.

5 | Editing

Fewer than 1% of the abstracts prepared or received at an abstracting service are suitable for publication without editing. This is not to imply that the abstracts are full of mistakes, although abstractors, like everyone else, forget rules and make errors. The elimination of errors is of the greatest importance, but there is more to editing than correcting mistakes. Editing seeks to establish consistency and uniformity in style and presentation and to provide cross-references when necessary. These tasks can be performed by the abstractor; however, they are primarily an editorial function, and thus virtually all abstracts need to be edited.

In describing the editorial function, it is important to make a distinction between *checking* and *editing*. Checking precedes editing; it is essentially a function of nontechnical personnel and does not require subject knowledge. Thus, checking can be done by one person and editing by another. The checker compares the abstract with the original document, paying particular attention to the bibliographic data—for example, the proper recording of the citation. In essence, the checker examines the abstract, looking for the type of information that can be checked for accuracy by direct comparison with the original article. The checker neither adds to nor modifies the meaning of the abstract; these are functions of the editor.

Editing is commonly done in colored pencil (blue or red) so that it can easily be distinguished from the author's corrections. It should be noted that blue-pencil corrections may not appear on Xerox copies. Abstracts are typed double-spaced with large margins to permit extensive changes. Changes made by the editor are written directly on the typescript rather than carried into the margin, as in the correcting of proof. Words are crossed out. New words, expressions, and even sentences are written on the typescript; carets are used to show location. Transpositions are made by serpentine lines. Symbols or terms are underlined to denote italics or given a wavy underline to denote boldface for emphasis. Proofreaders' marks are shown in Figure 5.1.

5.1   ELIMINATION OF ERRORS

The editorial goal of the abstracting service is to reduce the number of errors in the final publication to the barest minimum. Since the approach toward zero error seems asymptotic, the cost of achieving it is probably infinite. A more realistic goal needs to be identified and a practical compromise made between perfection and cost. Duplicate abstracting and editing to achieve fewer errors is economically unfeasible. Quality control needs to be obtained by training the abstractors, checkers, and editors so that they can identify and correct the common errors of content and format.

5.1.1   Errors of Format

Editing an abstract begins by checking the elements in the heading for factual accuracy and for form. These elements include the full title of the document, the authors and their affiliations, and the citation of the journal or book in which the article appeared. This work is generally done by a checker, who compares the abstract with the original for accuracy. He also checks that the form of the heading is correct and in accordance with the rules and procedures established by the service.

The body of the abstract is reviewed to ensure proper grammar and diction. Since abstractors are subject specialists, they may not have adequate training in English grammar or may have become careless in its use. In all fairness, it should be pointed out that nearly all abstractors are excellent and demanding grammarians. They fully believe the writer's

PROOFREADERS' MARKS

Mark	Meaning	Mark	Meaning
ℐ	Take out	bf	Bold face type
⊙	Turn character	‿	Bold face type
tr	Transpose	wf	Wrong font
X	Defective letter	s.c.	Small caps
[	Move to left	=	Small caps
]	Move to right	• • •	Let it stand
□	Em quad space	stet	Let it stand
#	Insert space	⅟m̅	One em dash
∧	Insert at this point	⅟n̅	One en dash
ℐ	Take out, close up	?	Interrogation point
⊙	Period	!	Exclamation mark
,/	Comma	⟍2⟋	Superior character
˅/	Apostrophe	/2⟍	Inferior character
˅˘ ˅˘	Quotations	[/]	Insert brackets
|=|	Hyphen	(/)	Insert parentheses
:/	Colon	˅	Push down
;/	Semicolon	&	Ampersand
caps	Capital letters	¶	Paragraph
=	Capital letters	no ¶	No paragraph
lc	Lower case	(?ok)	Query to author
rom	Roman type	(sp)	Spell out
ital	Italic type	⌐	Raise
—	Italic type	⌐	Lower
		(P)	Verify
		//	Straighten lines
		ld >	Insert leading
		=	Straighten type
		⌒	Close up entirely
		less #	Remove some space
		ﬀ	Ligature
		⊬	End

Figure 5.1 Proofreaders' marks. [Reprinted from separate by Mack Printing Company, Easton, Pa., n.d.]

dictum, "The English language is the most important tool in your possession; learn to use it with precision."* Nevertheless, it is nearly always possible to polish and improve an abstract. First, one must correct all errors. Singular subjects with plural verbs, or the reverse, must be changed. The word *data* is plural, and is used with a plural verb. Split infinitives and dangling expressions, mainly participles, need to be corrected. Spelling of all questionable words should be checked by referring to a dictionary.

Punctuation in abstracts is the same as in any good prose form. Editors learn to correct punctuation almost automatically. Complete sentences and abbreviations (except those of units of measurement) have periods. Commas are used to separate members of a series, and a comma is placed just before the conjunction connecting the last two members of a series. Semicolons are used for combining closely related sentences into one sentence and for separating parts of series in which commas are used within one or more of the parts. Parentheses, brackets, and braces are kept complete (as pairs). Restrictive clauses are not set off by commas— for example, "The method that gave best results was too costly," is correct. Nonrestrictive clauses are set off by commas—for example, "The method, which had not been used previously, was found to be too costly," is also correct.

A telegraphic style is undesirable. A few beginning abstractors may write this way in the hope of saving space. Complete sentences and only authorized abbreviations should be used. The standard, approved list of abbreviations is often forgotten or ignored by the abstractors. The editors, however, soon memorize this list, and they notice and correct deviations almost automatically.

Editors concentrate on eliminating all discovered serious errors. An undue amount of editorial time can be spent on trying to improve already correct grammar and style and to shorten the abstract just a bit more. Excessive editing, in an effort to achieve perfection, needs to be avoided, for it is not economical.

5.1.2   Errors of Content

Among the most serious abstracting errors are the invisible errors of content—for example, the omission of abstractable material. Detecting an omission is obviously difficult. However, editors seem to develop the

* This statement by Charles W. Foulk is framed in front of the main chemistry lecture hall of The Ohio State University.

ability to find clues that indicate missing data. Generalization is a common indicator of omissions. The abstractor may generalize and give no specific examples, yet it seems to the editor that the author must have provided some specific instances. And on checking the original document to verify a point suspected of being in error, the editor often notices information that has been omitted by the abstractor.

Nomenclature is a special problem in editing. Chemists, for example, deal with millions of organic compounds, and designations had to be devised for these compounds. Rules of nomenclature are designed to enable chemists, authors, abstractors, editors, and indexers to name all structural formulas. Nomenclature constitutes a principal language of organic chemists and must be used correctly. Unfortunately, these standard rules of nomenclature are not observed by all chemists. As an aid, molecular-formula indexes (formula indexes) were devised. Organic chemists can count the number of times each element occurs in a structural formula and write the symbols in order (C, then H, and all others alphabetically). For example, the following structural formula,

gives the molecular formula, $C_8H_9NO_2$. Search of a formula index gives the names of these compounds having this molecular formula. The name *methyl anthranilate*, which corresponds to this structural formula, may be found in this list. Thus, chemists are led, with only small effort on their part, to the standard name used in the index. Without proper nomenclature, chaos would reign. Everyone would invent his own chemical name and the number of cross-references required in the index would soon exceed the number of reference entries.

There are nomenclatures for electron tubes, bacteria, viruses, polymers, and so on. Use of these nomenclatures consistently in abstracts is the responsibility of both the abstractors and the editors. For organic-compound nomenclature, the name given by the author, rather than by the indexer, may be used in the abstract. The editor may not have time to change these names, and the users of abstracts might find themselves inconvenienced in going from the abstract to the original if the chemical names differ. Editors can prevent the inconsistent use of names in abstracts and should do so to avoid confusing the user.

5.2   CLASSIFYING AND INDEXING ABSTRACTS

The editorial function does not stop with the editing of individual abstracts. The abstracts need to be categorized and cross-referenced, and indexes must be prepared. Abstracting publications are organized and not just put together, and planning the publication is an editing responsibility.

5.2.1   Adding Categories and Cross-References

Since the scope of most, if not all, abstract journals is far greater than that of even the most omnivorous reader, abstracts are classified into major categories and subcategories to save the user's time. The main categories are normally very broad and fairly stable. These major categories are published as a table of contents in the abstract journal so that users can become acquainted with them. Subcategories provide narrower groupings without specific designations; they are more fluid and tend to be ad hoc. Despite the fact that the subcategories remain undesignated, users report them to be helpful in grouping like abstracts and in saving time for those who have time to read original documents in only a few subcategories.

Disciplines develop in ways that are unpredictable, and so categories and subcategories need to be created empirically from the existing abstracts and not according to a preformulated pattern. Actual changes made in categories through the years can be seen by examining bound volumes of an abstract journal. These changes reflect major developments in the field. Examples of categories and subcategories of abstracts in the field of psychology are shown in Figure 5.2, which is a partial table of contents from *Psychological Abstracts*. The main categories, in capital letters, have page numbers leading to the first abstract in that category. The subcategory name in the table leads to the first abstracts in the specific subcategory.

Tables of contents in abstract journals show the organization of the abstracts and provide a useful overview of a very practical classification for the entire field covered by the journal. In this case, the classification is based upon psychology as it is actually encountered in abstracts from works in the field. It is not a hypothetical classification based upon how the classifier believed that psychology should be. It is not difficult for the user of an abstract journal, if he knows the subject field of the journal, to select those categories and subcategories that are most relevant to his interests of the moment. For search in the current literature, these categories provide the most important access. Categories display, issue by issue, the only abstracts that are available at the time. Since the categories

TABLE OF CONTENTS

	Abstract Number	Page Number
GENERAL	1	1
PSYCHOMETRICS AND STATISTICS	41	5
Test Construction & Validation	51	6
Mathematical Models & Statistics	68	8
PERCEPTION AND MOTOR PERFORMANCE	118	13
Perceptual Processes	130	14
Auditory Perception	167	19
Visual Perception	198	24
Motor Processes & Performance	262	32
COGNITIVE PROCESSES AND MOTIVATION	278	34
Learning & Thinking & Conditioning	297	37
Attention & Memory	354	44
Motivation & Emotion	419	53
NEUROLOGY AND PHYSIOLOGY	432	56
Neuroanatomy & Electrophysiology	438	56
Physiological Processes	466	60
Genetics	499	64
PSYCHOPHARMACOLOGY AND PHYSIOLOGICAL INTERVENTION	515	67
Brain & Electrical Stimulation & Lesions	535	70
Drug Effects	588	77
ANIMAL PSYCHOLOGY	641	84
Learning & Motivation	668	87
Social & Sexual Behavior	749	98
Sensory Processes	786	103
DEVELOPMENTAL PSYCHOLOGY	802	105
Cognitive & Physical Development	840	110
Emotional & Personality Development	903	118
Social Behavior & Family Relations	914	120
Adult Development & Aging	941	123

Figure 5.2 *Partial table of contents of* Psychological Abstracts *showing categories and subcategories [Reprinted from* Psychological Abstracts, *Vol. 55, No. 1, July 1974, by permission of the American Psychological Association. © 1974 by the American Psychological Association.]*

and even subcategories are fairly broad, the display of abstracts will include surprises. Surprises are important in serendipity, creativeness, and stimulation.

A subject index built to maximum specificity provides for high search precision. But if only headings are searched such an index discourages browsing and reduces the chances for serendipitous findings. Recall will be affected if related headings are not also searched. The table of contents, organized into categories and subcategories, encourages browsing and serves as a valuable guide in keeping up with the newly published literature in a field, and this is the forte of an abstract journal

Since mutual exclusivity is a goal seldom if ever realized, many abstracts are related to several categories. The customary solution to this problem has been to place the abstract into the most appropriate category, write a rule that includes telling why it is placed there, and make one or more "see also" cross-references to it from the other related categories. The alternative to using cross-references is to place copies of the abstracts in all appropriate categories and to omit the cross-references. This is too costly and is not generally done.

It is the responsibility of the editor to place the abstract in the proper category or to approve or change the abstractor's placing and to add cross-references from other categories or to approve or change the abstractor's cross-referencing. Physically, categorization is carried out by writing the category number (or other symbol) in the upper right of the first typescript page and writing category number(s) of the cross-references to the abstract just below, each following an X (meaning *cross-reference*). For example,

$$12$$
$$X \; 7$$
$$X \; 28$$

means that the abstract will be published in category 12. Cross-references to this abstract will be published in categories 7 and 28; they will direct the reader to category 12. These category and cross-reference numbers will not appear with the published abstract.

5.2.2   Indexing

Abstracts without indexes soon become of little value. Without indexes, it would be necessary—and too time-consuming to be feasible—to go through years of back issues of an abstract journal in order to locate a specific subject, author, or abstract. Efficient literature searching is dependent upon indexes, the most important of which are the subject index and the author index, in that order. Title indexes have never been popular for abstract journals, because it is difficult to remember titles verbatim. Titles may be edited, sometimes to remove the first word(s); and the first alphabetized word could be critical in finding the abstract. Other special indexes include molecular-formula, organic-ring, Hetero-Atom-in-Context

(HAIC), Permuterm (*term-pair*), patent-number, patent-concordance, geographical, and corporate-author indexes. Special indexes can be, and are, designed to meet special needs.

Indexes to each issue of an abstract journal must be prepared quickly, because delays in the appearance of the issue must be avoided. This time pressure may result in indexes that are not so complete, or so error-free as they should be. Deficiencies are corrected in the annual or semiannual collective indexes, which are cross-referenced and edited to ensure high quality. Decennial and quinquennial indexes are generally edited to produce indexes of even higher quality; these are far superior to issue indexes. *Cumulative* indexes, in which the entries of individual indexes are alphabetically merged, are of special value in saving search time. *Collective* indexes are those in which the indexes in each issue are bound side by side without merging the entries; they are of considerably less value than are cumulative indexes.

5.2.3 Author Indexes

The author index provides a means for grouping all works written by a single author. The author's name generally serves as a significant search tool, and therefore the author index is an important part of the abstract publication. The checker is responsible for ensuring that all author names are included in the index, that they are spelled correctly, and that they are printed in a consistent format with uniform punctuation.

The task of ensuring uniformity is not so simple as it would seem, for many variations are possible:

> Smith, John Howard
> Smith, J. Howard
> Smith, John H.
> Smith, J. H.
> Smith, JH
> Smith, (J.H.)

Clearly, some policy guidance is needed, but even policy cannot be applied mechanically. Most indexes print only the surname and initials. However, if there are two *J. H. Smith*'s, then the editor must supply the given names. If there are two *John Howard Smith*'s, the names are differentiated by address, affiliation, and so on—for example, *John Howard Smith* (*Harvard*) and *John Howard Smith* (*UCLA*). On author-index cards that are used for printing the author index, it is customary to carry author names verbatim and then edit them to initials. This practice saves expensive lookup of author names during editing.

Another policy decision must specify which authors are to be included in the index—the first author or all authors. The simplest and perhaps best policy is to include all authors no matter how many are listed on the work. This policy is more expensive, but it is also more useful. Another policy, frequently followed, is to cross-reference all coauthors to the name of the first author. Cross-referencing saves duplication of entries under all co-authors, but it may require a double lookup on the part of the user.

An example of a cross-referenced author index is shown in Figure 5.3.

Eighth Collective Author Index: Chemical Abstracts

The sample page from the Eighth Collective (actually a *cumulative* index) Author Index of *Chemical Abstracts* (Figure 5.3) shows the structure of, and can be used to define the content of, this useful type of index.

Structure. The running head at the top left of the sample page names the first author printed on the page—in this case a corporate author, "American Standard Inc." This author is the assignee of the patents for which entries are listed below the author name. The centered running head, "Chemical Abstracts–8th Coll.," informs the index user that he is using the eighth cumulative index of *Chemical Abstracts;* on the right, "304 A" means page 304 of the author index. The three columns on the page are made up of author-index entries; for example, "**Amero, Clifford L.** Anaerobic digestion of sludge, **71: P** 116371s." The author name, "**Amero, Clifford L.,**" is the heading of the entry. The name is in boldface type to make it stand out and is inverted to aid alphabetization and location of the name in the index. The modification (modifying phrase), "Anaerobic digestion of sludge," is the title of the patent. The modification is indented to make the heading more prominent and to differentiate between heading and modifications. The "**71:**" refers to the *CA* volume number. The "**P**" stands for "patent": the abstract is that of a patent rather than that of an article or book. The "116371s" is the serial number of the abstract. This patent apparently relates to the digestion of sewage sludge in the absence of oxygen.

There are "see" cross-references. An example is "**Ameriks, J.** See Wallin, V. W." This means that Ameriks is a coauthor of a work by Wallin. Whether the work is a paper or a patent is part of the modification of the *main* entry, to be found under "**Wallin, V. W.**" In this index, "see" cross-references (for example, in the entry, "**Amerio, A.** See Padolecchia, N.") are used in place of "see also" cross-references. Below the just-mentioned entry is a dash, used to represent "**Amerio, A.**" the principal or first-named author. The coauthors of the first entry are "De Benedictis, G.; Leondeff, J.; Mastrangelo, F.; Coratelli, P." The modification for this entry is "Apiol nephropathy." (This refers to study of the pathological effect on the kidney of the natural chemical substance, apiol.) The "**69:**" is the volume number of *CA;* "75296j," the abstract number. This abstract is not that of a patent. The modification is the title of the work; however, the original title may have been edited and may have read, "A Study of Apiol Nephropathy."

Content. Some author indexes simply list the author name and then the abstract reference number. Thus, all entries become "maybes"—"Maybe I want to look up the entry." Use of the title as the modification in this *CA* index reduces the number of "maybes." The modification saves the user from looking up many entries only to find them irrelevant to his present interests. Thus, the modification takes a load off the user. Lightness of load on the user can be taken as a valid measure of index quality. Thus, this author index is of higher quality than is one in which modifications are omitted. As the letter "**P**" stands for "patent", so the letter "**B**" stands for "book." No letter preceding the reference number means that the work abstracted is an article or paper. Author names are carried verbatim. This policy reduces editorial changes and confusion about authors with the same last name and initials. The modifications are placed on a new line following the name(s) of author or coauthor(s) to make printing easier and less costly. The extra white space on the page is less expensive than is the extra effort to remove the white space. Use of Monotype and other printing methods would save the white space by converting it to printing, but extra keyboarding and time would be involved.

The listing of names of assignees of patents in the author index enables users to find patents owned by organizations. The "see" cross-references enable users to find the names of primary authors from the names of their coauthors. Using "see" cross-references also saves space, in that it is not necessary to repeat each entry under the name(s) of the coauthor(s). Titles of articles and books in the disciplines of chemistry and chemical engineering are usually highly informative and well coined. Titles express tersely the general subject studied. However, titles of patents may be more vague than are titles of papers, reports, and theses. A patent might be titled "Composition of Matter"—which could mean any kind of matter. An examination of the titles on the sample page shows that most are highly specific, therefore effective guides to the abstracts.

Author indexes are helpful guides to subjects mainly because authors and organizations often specialize in subject areas. The subject index is a more specific guide, but to use the author index effectively, one simply needs to note the names of authors in a given field and then search for their names in the latest author index. Many chemists and chemical engineers try to follow certain authors who regularly publish material of

1971 Annual Book of ASTM Standards, Pt. 13:
Refractories, Glass, and Other Ceramic Materials;
Manufactured Carbon and Graphite Products, 75: B
39918d

1971 Annual Book of ASTM Standards, Pt. 11:
Bituminous Materials for Highway Construction,
Waterproofing, and Roofing; Soil and Rock; Peats,
Mosses, and Humus; Skid Resistance, 75: B 39975v

1971 Annual Book of ASTM Standards, Pt. 32:
Chemical Analysis of Metals; Sampling and
Analysis of Metal - Bearing Ores, 75: B 44636q

1971 Annual Book of ASTM Standards, Pt. 27:
Plastics: General Methods of Testing;
Nomenclature, 75: B 64820v

1971 Annual Book of ASTM Standards, Pt. 26:
Plastics: Specifications; Methods of Testing Pipe,
Film, Reinforced, and Cellular Plastics; Fiber
Composites, 75: B 64821z

1971 Annual Book of ASTM Standards, Pt. 7
Nonferrous Metals and Alloys (Including Corrosion
Tests); Electrodeposited Metallic Coatings; Metal
Powders; Surgical Implants, 75: B 66918k

1971 Annual Book of ASTM Standards, Pt. 29:
Electrical Insulating Materials, 75: B 68811u

Energy Dispersion X - Ray Analysis: X - Ray and
Electron Probe Analysis (Special Technical
Publication 485), 75: B 71089v

1971 Annual Book of ASTM Standards, Pt. 30, 75: B
89625b

1971 Annual Book of ASTM Standards, Pt. 6:
Die -Cast Metals; Light Metals and Alloys
(Including Electrical Conductors), 75: B 90800m

1971 Annual Book of ASTM Standards, Pt. 5:
Copper and Copper Alloys (Including Electrical
Conductors), 75: B 90801n

1971 Annual Book of ASTM Standards, Pt. 31:
Metals: Physical, Mechanical, Nondestructive, and
Corrosion Tests, Metallography, Fatigue, Effect of
Temperature, 75: B 90802p

1971 Annual Book of ASTM Standards, Pt. 22:
Sorptive Mineral Materials; Soap; Engine
Antifreezes; Polishes; Halogenated Organic
Solvents; Activated Carbon; Industrial Chemicals,
75: B 94424q

1971 Annual Book of ASTM Standards, Pt. 28:
Rubber; Carbon Black; Gaskets, 75: B 110900z

1971 Annual Book of ASTM Standards, Pt. 16:
Structural Sandwich Constructions; Wood;
Adhesives, 75: B 111093a

ASTM Manual for Rating Motor, Diesel, and
Aviation Fuels, 75: B 111467a

1971 Annual Book of ASTM Standards, Pt. 4:
Structural Steel; Concrete Reinforcing Steel;
Pressure Vessel Plate; Steel Rails, Wheels, and
Tires; Bearing Steel; Steel Forgings, 75: B 112040t

1970 Annual Book of ASTM Standards, Pt. 3: Steel
Sheet, Strip, Bar, Rod, Wire, Chain, and Spring;
Wrought Iron Bar and Sheet; Metallic Coated
Products; Ferrous Surgical Implants, 75: B 132223h

Separation of solvent from a solution by reverse
osmosis, 75: P 9793s

Osmotic or semipermeable membrane, 75: P 25184z

Molded, multi -ply, flexible laminates, 75: P 64958z

Surface treatment of porous unfired chinaware, 75: P
143570v

Supporting member for an osmotic or semipermeable
membrane, 75: P 152651z

American Sterilizer Co.
Process for preventing boiler scale formation, 66: P
98414y

Water still, 69: P 107867q

Filtration and distillation process, 70: P 79566r

Process and apparatus for removing amines from
steam vapors, 70: P 98329g

Electrolytic process for producing pyrogen -free
deionized water, 71: P 6463r

American Sugar Co.
Tabletting sugar, 66: P 86860c

Compressed sugar cubes, 68: P 31323r

Dry sugar product, 69: P 42913e

Granular, free -flowing brown sugar, 70: P 79358z

Apparatus for crystallizing sugar as fine particles,
71: P 114435s

Separation of the solid and liquid components of a
suspension, 73: P 38332e

Apparatus for continuously separating finely divided
solids suspended in liquids, 75: P 22924e

American Synthetic Rubber Corp.
Liquid carboxylated polymers useful as binders for
solid propellants, 67: P 117581q

American Tank and Steel Corp.
Apparatus for reconcentrating glycol and other
desiccants, 71: P 40796m

American Tansul Co.
Chill - proofing beer with water - soluble alkyl
cellulose ethers, 66: P 36609g

Amine modified clay, 66: P 48938b

Treatment of swelling, gelling, cation -exchangeable
clay ores, 67: P 25075z

American Thermocatalytic Corp.
Refractory cement compositions, 66: P 31752p

Ceramic fiber combustion elements for flameless
radiant gas heaters, 66: P 31768y

Combustion elements containing aluminum, 69: P
45038j

American Thread Co.
Rapid bleaching of cotton yarn, 68: P 106034h

American Tobacco Co.
Flavor -enhanced cigarets and cigars, 69: P 84239v

Tobacco smoke filter with encapsulated liquid, 70: P
94077a

Tobacco smoke filter with activated carbon and
encapsulated liquid, 70: P 94078b

Reconstituted tobacco, 70: P 103601m

American Water Works Association, Inc.
Water Quality and Treatment: A Handbook of
Public Water Supplies, 3rd ed, 75: B 40206b

American Zinc, Lead and Smelting Co.

Polyvinylcycloalkanes), 73: P 56613b

-; Ivanyukov, D. V.; Kleiner, V. I.; Krentsel, B. A.;
Petrova, V. F.; Yakobson, F. I.; Stotskaya, L. L.;
Shteinbak, V. Sh.

Crystalline block mixture polymer from propylene
and vinyl monomer units, 73: P 121218t

-; Ivanyukov, D. V.; Kleiner, V. I.; Krentsel, B. A.;
Petrova, V. F.; Stotskaya, L. L.; Yakobson, F. I.

Polyvinylcycloalkanes), 74: P 23221q

-; Kleiner, V. I.; Ivanyukov, D. V.; Krentsel, B. A.

Crystalline propylene -vinyl block copolymers, 74 P
142662u

-; Yakobson, F. I.; Ivanyukov, D. V.; Petrova, V. F.

Cold -resistant polyolefins, 69: P 87601t

-; Yakobson, F. I.; Krentsel, B. A.

Polyallomers, 71: 92090w

Amerik, Y. See Guillet, J. E.

Amerik, Yu. B. See Golova, L. K.; Krentsel, B. A.;
Nechitailo, N. A.; Orlova, O. V.; Shaltyko, L. G.;
Tsvetkov, V. N.

-; Konstantinov, I. I.; Krentsel, B. A.

Polymerization of p -(methacryloyloxybenzoic acid

I. Polymerization of p -(methacryloyloxy)benzoic
acid in the liquid phase, 68: 13456g

-; Konstantinov, I. I.; Krentsel, B. A.; Malakhaev, E.
M.

Polymerization of p - methacryloyloxybenzoic acid.
II. Polymerization of p -methacryloyloxybenzoic
acid in the liquid crystalline state, 68: 50145a

-; Konstantinov, I. I.; Krentsel, B. A.

Polymerization of p - methacryloyloxybenzoic acid in
mesomorphic and in liquid states, 69: 77776q

-; Krentsel, B. A.

polymerization of certain vinyl monomers in
liquidcrystals, 67: 44128k

-; Reynolds, W. F.; Guillet, J. E.

Influence of monomer concentration on the structure
of poly(methyl methacrylate) polymerized by
butyllithium, 74: 142460b

Amerikov, V. G. See Boreskov, G. K.

-; Boreskov, G. K.; Kasatkina, L. A.

Catalytic activity of iron, cobalt, and nickel oxides
with respect of isotope exchange in carbon dioxide
molecules, 67: 76621g

-; Kasatkina, L. A.

Isotopic exchange of oxygen in molecules of carbon
dioxide on a zinc oxide surface, 70: 118572m

Infrared spectra of carbon dioxide adsorbed on the
surfaces of iron and copper oxides, 74: 117725j

-; Kasatkina, L. A.; Popova, G. Yu.

Kinetics of carbon dioxide isotope exchange on a
chromium oxide surface, 69: 2243v

Ameriks, J. See Wallin, V. W.

Amerine, Maynard A. See Esau, Paul; Kunkee,
Ralph E.; Ough, Cornelius S.

-; Kunkee, R.

Microbiology of winemaking, 70: 18866s

-; Ough, C. S.

Fermentation of grapes held under anaerobic

Lubricating Oils, Cutting Oils, Lubricating Greases; Hydraulic Fluids. 75: B 142530v
1971 Book of ASTM Standards. Pt. 18: Petroleum Products, Measurement and Sampling; Liquefied Petroleum Gases; Light Hydrocarbons; Plant Spray Oils, Aerospace Materials, Sulfonates; Crude Petroleum; Petrolatum; Wax; Graphite. 75: B 142531w
Miscellaneous ASTM Standards for Petroleum Products. 10th ed. 75: B 142532x
The Theory and Properties of Thermocouple Elements (Special Technical Publication 492). 75: B 145303j
Serial Number List of Compound Names and References to Published Infrared Spectra, Suppl 14 (Atomic and Molecular Data Series, 32–S14). 75: B 146127s
1971 Annual Book of ASTM Standards, Pt. 10: Concrete and Mineral Aggregates; Manual on Concrete Testing. 75: B 154638z
Molecular Formula List of Compounds, Names, and References to Published Infrared Spectra, Suppl 14 (Atomic and Molecular Data Series, 31–S14). 75: B 156943u

American Standard Inc.
Carbon equivalence of hypereutectic cast iron. 68: P 97992q
Recovery of sulfur compounds and heat from combustion gases. 69: P 29960v
Brass casting alloys for cast plumbing fixtures. 69: P 109364x
Coating precoated graphite surfaces with uniform defect–free silicon deposits. 70: P 101100h
Enamelware article with patterned surface. 71: P 53161a
Polyurethane –polysiloxane graft copolymers. 71: P 82404n
Osmosis membrane. 71: P 102622n
High –temperature bonding to germanium. 71: P 106868v
Compositions for wash basin and draining board. 71: P 125661p
Roughening vitreous enamel surfaces. 72: P 35325y
Pressed wood articles overlaid with paper. 73: P 36794h
Corrosion resistant refractory ceramic coatings. 73: P 101694s
Corrosion resistant silicon nitride coated steel surfaces. 73: P 126479p
Enamelware produced by firing dry enamel powder in contact with a glass fiber fabric. 74: P 45175e
Optical pH indicator comprising aromatic aminoazo dye and inert polymer containing carbonyl radicals. 74: P 60641x
Perlitic –martensitic transformation of iron –containing material. 74: P 114929t
Marbleized ceramic sanitary fixtures. 74: P 115349r
Apparatus for manufacturing sink and vanity top combinations of a thermosetting synthetic plastic composition. 74: P 142955s

Crystalline silica lamellae as a thickening agent. 67: P 45667x
Electrophotographic zinc oxide coatings. 70: P 92290r
Photoconductive zinc oxide. 70: P 101092g
Zinc recovery from zinc – and iron –containing solutions. 73: P 27848b
Recovery of zinc from solutions containing iron and zinc. 74: P 1516dh

Americo Gil, Benito See Paez, Dora M.
Amerik, B. K. See Dorogochinskii, A. Z.; Kazanskii, B. A.; Oprishko, A. A.; Zinov'ev, V. R.
–, Drozdova, E. I.; Svetozarova, O. I.; Zhdanova, V. V.; Antoshkina, R. A.; Frid, M. N.
Contact pyrolysis of low –sulfur distillates. 68: 97225a
–, Kalita, L. A.; Bliznyukova, R. A.; Maidebor, L. K.; Dorogochinskii, A. Z.
Experimental apparatus for study of dehydrocyclization of n –hexane in a fluidized –catalyst bed. 66: 97221w
–, Kalita, L. A.; Zinov'ev, V. R.; Votlokhin, Yu. Z.
Development of a reactor for the process of preparing benzene by the dehydrocyclization of –n –hexane in a fluidized catalyst bed. 69: 66999p
–, Kutsenok, L. Z.; Uspenskii, G. I.; Konina, V. F
Contact coking of coal pitches. 70: 108110v
–, Mutovin, Ya. G; Korovin, N. G.
Determination of the amount of circulating catalyst by a heat balance method. 66: 87271v
–, Mutovin, Ya. G.; Sapon, M. F
Distributing device for delivery of gas –catalyst stream into reactors with a fluidized bed. 66: 97222x
–, Ryazantsev, Yu. P.; Bolotov, I. T.; Uspenskii, G. I.; Prokhorenko, V. I.; Galeeva, K. S.; Zhdanova, V. V.
Vacuum distillation of cracking residues. 70: 21543q
–, Svetozarova, O. I.; Maidebor, L. K.; Romankova, I. K.; Levashova, E. P.; Golorenko, A. M.
Production of export automobile gasoline by the single –stage catalytic cracking of distillates. 66: 87274b
–, Svetozarova, O. I.; Romankova, I. K.; Golovenko, A. M.; Levashova, E. P.
Catalytic cracking of vacuum distillate from Uzen crude. 70: 98443q
–, Svetozarova, O.].; Ryazantsev, Yu. P.; Mataeva, B. V.; Romankova, I. K.
Processing of high –sulfur petroleum residues. 68: 61192q
–, Zinov'ev, V. R
Effectiveness of sectionalizing of a reactor for n –hexane dehydrocyclization. 68: 114175v
Amerik, V. V. See Abasova, S. G.; Glavati, O. L.; Gorodetskaya, N. N.; Paushkin, Ya. M.; Sirota, A. G.; Yakobson, F. I.
–, Ivanyukov, D. V.; Kleiner, V. I.; Krentsel, B. A.; Petrova, V. F; Stotskaya, L. L.; Yakobson, F. I.
Polyvinylcyclohexane). 73: P 4395n

II White grapes, with some further tests on red grapes. 72: 99104h
Acidification of grapes from region. IV. 72: 99105j
Effect of pre – and postfermentation addition of acids on the composition and quality of the wines produced. 74: 63148c
Amerine, Charles F. See Russell, Harold Daniel
Amerio, A. See Padolecchia, N.
–, De Benedictis, G; Leondeff, J.; Mastrangelo, F.; Coratelli, P.
Apiol nephropathy. 69: 75296j
Amerio, Alessandro
Reading an isotope table. II. Energy. 66: 7171x
Amerio, Pier L. See Rusciani, Luigi
Ameripol, Inc.
Catalytic condensation of 1,3 –butadiene with ethylene. 73: P 67042r
Catalytic olefin polymerization. 74: P 13991b
Vulcanizable elastomeric compositions containing a reaction product of an organic acid and a polyamide or polyamine. 74: P 43331d
Diolefin –olefin catalytic condensation. 75: P 48391d
Improved dehydrogenation process for converting olefins to diolefins. 75: P 49880z
Amerkhanov, I. M. See Gil'manshin, A. F.
Analysis of the hydrocarbon composition of stratified petroleums. 68: P 61400f
Amero, Clifford L.
Anaerobic digestion of sludge. 71: P 116371s
Amero, John J. See Jones, Cecil Moore
Crystalline abrasive alumina. 70: P 99317p
Impregnated sintered bauxite grains. 71: P 53137x
Sintered α –alumina and zirconia abrasive product. 71: P 73678c
Vitrified, bonded wheel for electrochemical grinding, containing conductive metal and a thermoset polymer filler. 74: P 32441p
–, Gerry, R. J.
Electrically conductive grinding tool. 71: P 53171d
Amero, R. C.
Fuels for transportation. 75: 142449a
Amerson, G. Malcolm See Hays, Sidney B
Effects of four chemosterilants on reproduction of the tobacco hornworm, Manduca sexta. 71: 37867e
Amerson, J. Richard See Humphrey, L. J.;
Zollinger, Robert M.
Amery, A. See Claeys, H.; Verstraete, Marc
Amery, Antoon See Hannon, Robert C
–, Claeys, H.
Review of the literature on the in vitro activation of the human plasma fibrinolytic system with streptokinase. 74: 122224z
Changes in biochemical parameters during streptokinase infusion. 72: 65272w
–, Verstraete, M; Bossaert, H.; Verstreken, G
Hypotensive action and side effects of clonidine –chlorthalidone and methyldopa –chlorthalidone in treatment of hypertension. 74: 41023f

Figure 5.3 Collective author index: Chemical Abstracts. [Reprinted from the 8th Collective author index of Chemical Abstracts, p. 304A, by permission of the Chemical Abstracts Service.]

interest. For these users, the author index provides the most rapid access to information desired. In checking for duplication of abstracts, the author index is invaluable. It is more difficult to find duplicates in the subject index and it is much more costly for the searcher.

5.2.4   Subject Indexes

The subject index is the most used feature of an abstract publication. Rarely do users have enough time to browse through the entire publication, even if it is categorized. The more common practice is to seek and read abstracts on particular topics. The subject index enables highly selective searching. The indexer is responsible for providing a subject index for each issue of the abstract publication. He also is responsible for the preparation of cumulative subject indexes.

There are many variations of subject indexes and many ways of constructing them. We will discuss in detail the following subject indexes:

1. subject index for *Historical Abstracts;*
2. keyword index for *Chemical Abstracts;*
3. keyword-in-context index for *Biological Abstracts,* B.A.S.I.C.;
4. biosystematic index for *Biological Abstracts;*
5. cross-index for *Biological Abstracts;*
6. formula index for *Chemical Abstracts;*
7. ring index for *Chemical Abstracts;*
8. patent concordance for *Chemical Abstracts;*
9. numerical patent index for *Chemical Abstracts;*
10. continuity index for *Information Science Abstracts.*

Author, Biographical, Geographical, and Subject Index for Historical Abstracts

A sample page from the index to an issue of *Historical Abstracts* (*Part A,* **19,** p. 511 [1973]) is shown in Figure 5.4.

Structure. Pages have the running heads, "INDIA: Christianity" and "INTERNATIONAL ECONOMICS." The rest of the page is made up of entries, such as "Indians, Bolivia, 2190." There are both "see also" and "see" cross-references such as, "Indonesia, By Place (See Also Topics)" and "Inflation, See 'Business Cycles.'" Glosses or notes are included; for example, "Societies and Meetings (in the Social Sciences and Humanities)" and "Finland (including periods under Sweden and Russian Empire)." Supergeneral cross-references are given also: "Indonesia, By Topic (See Also Places)."

Most of the index entries are made up of subject heading, modification or subheading, and reference number. For example, in the index entry,

Industry, Industrialization and Industrial Revolution
    Czechoslovakia, 2749, 2761

the terms, "Industry, Industrialization, and Industrial Revolution" constitute the subject heading; "Czechoslovakia" is the modification or subheading; and "2749" and "2761" are reference numbers that lead to the two abstracts in *Historical Abstracts,* Part A.

Content. In general, fewer prepositions are used in the modifications in this index than are used in some other subject indexes. *By, in, of, on,* and *to* are examples of prepositions used. The conjunction *and* is used, and the article *the* used sparingly. In other subject indexes, articles are never used, and prepositions are used more freely than in this index. Omitting prepositions may introduce ambiguity, as is shown by the index entry, "Infantry, Belgium, 1729," which could mean Belgian infantry or infantry of other nations in Belgium.

Subject headings consist of names of places, such as "Indonesia"; events, such as "Indian Mutiny (1857)"; classes of events, such as "Indian Wars"; ethnic groups, such as "Indians"; classes of organizations, such as "Industry"; social processes, such as "Industrialization"; organizational subunits, such as "Infantry"; and so on. It should be noted that some ambiguity is permitted. For example, in "Indian Mutiny" and "Indian Wars" Indians of India or of the Western Hemisphere are not specified.

Cross-references lead from the more-specific to the more-general term ("Infantry, See Also 'Military Ground Forces'") and from the more-general to the more-specific term ("Insurgency, See 'Guerrilla and Irregular Warfare.'"). They are used within subject headings, as in "Indonesia, By Place (See Also Topics)", and they refer to headings related by rhetorical tropes, such as synecdoche ("International Economics, See 'Trade'"). Modifications are often omitted, as in "Inkster, Ian, 2823." The reader is left to wonder whether he should or should not look up the abstract. Popular terminology is employed: the cross-reference, "Interest Groups, See 'Lobbies'" could have read, "Interest Groups, See 'Legislative Representation.'" The specificity of modifications is minimal. For example, in the index entry "Institutes, Great Britain, 2441," the index user is not told the exact relationship between "Institutes" and "Great Britain." A few more words in most of the modifications would have been helpful.

Dictionary definitions, such as "(Dutch Guiana)," the parenthetical synonym of Surinam, are commonly omitted from entries, such as "Surinam (Dutch Guiana)," as a way of saving space and of reading time.

Military-Civil Relations 460
Military History 2092 2103
Military Strategy 3138 3481
Missionaries 456 465 481 2095 2104 2108 3489 3493
Modernization 460
Napoleonic Era and Wars 3138
National Security, Armament and Disarmament 3138 3481
Nationalism 109 457 483-4 2093 2100 2105 2107 3480 3483 3487-8 3490
Nepal 453
Pacifism and Peace Movements 484
Political Parties 481 2096 3488
Political Reform and Reformers 461 475 2110
Political Theory 2107
Politics 2099
Population 2095 2109 3480 3484
Provincial and Colonial Government 461 463 470 473-5 479-80 2101 3483 3490
Public Administration 456 889 2097
Public Finance 480 2097
Real Property 459 3492
Religions and Churches 483-4
Revolutions, Revolutionary Movements, and Rebellions 177 457 466 468 473 478 2092 2103 2105
Rural Settlements 2112
Science and Society (including Scientific and Technical Advancement) 2015
Science and Technology 2015

Provincial and Colonial Government 3497
Spain 982
United States 1678 3555
Venezuela 682 2265
Indonesia
By Place (See Also Topics)
Delhi 3486
By Topic (See Also Places)
Imperialism 3498
Military History 3486 3496
Politics 3496
Provincial and Colonial Government 3498
Urbanization, Founding and Development of Cities, Urban Renewal, and Housing 3486
Industrial Revolution See "Industry, Industrialization and Industrial Revolution"
Industrialization See "Industry, Industrialization and Industrial Revolution"
Industry, Industrialization and Industrial Revolution 346 829
Austria, Republic 1223 4181
Belgium 3202
Czechoslovakia 2749 2761
Denmark 1111
Europe 339 1945 3058
Finland (including periods under Sweden and Russian Empire) 1119
France 2326 3703
Germany 1060 1072 1077 1082 1087 1104-5 3186 4061-2 4065 4097 4208
Great Britain 357 776 827 852

Great Britain 2441
Italy 49
Rumania 1334
Spain 3949
Instituto Español (Spain) 1036
Instituto Español de Oceanografia 4001
Instituto Geográphico y Catastral 3949
Instituto Municipal de Historia (Spain) 3031
Insurance
France 713
Great Britain 344
Spain 713
United States 344
Insurgency See "Guerrilla and Irregular Warfare"
Intellectual Life and Ideas 68 299 314 378 1842 1875 1909 1916 3244 3254
Argentina 2216 3576
Austria, Republic 3225 3283 4179
Balkans and Balkan States 330
China 426
Cuba 389
Czechoslovakia 2755
Denmark 4136
Egypt 2856
Europe 292 389 3217
France 295 757 1731 1884 1923 2383 2393-4 3225 3283 3704
Germany 295 1081 1089 1910 3110 3283
Great Britain 313 2408 2487 2500 2540 3110 3832 3850 3870 3900 3906
Habsburg Empire (to 1918)

France 2030 2298
Germany 2809 4221
Ghana (Gold Coast) 3441
Great Britain 808
Habsburg Empire (to 1918) 3105
Hungary (since 1867) 185
Israel 1369
Italy 3105
Ivory Coast 3441
Ottoman Empire (to 1918) 2030
Poland 2809 4221
Rumania 3087
Russian Empire (to 1918) 3087
Silesia 4221
Spain 2298
Surinam (Dutch Guiana) 1696
Tunisia 2030
United States 808
Uruguay 2192
Venezuela 1696
Yugoslavia and Antecedents (from 1918) 185
International Commission for Intellectual Cooperation 1916
International Congress of Maritime History (1966) 336
International Coooperation in History of Technology Committee 3023
International Council on Archives 3019
International Economic Integration
Denmark 1111
Latin America 3533
International Economics See "Trade"

Figure 5.4 Author, biographical, geographical, and subject index: Historical Abstracts. [Reprinted from Historical Abstracts, Part A, Vol. 19, 1973, p. 511, by permission of ABC–Clio, Inc. © 1973 by American Bibliographical Center–Clio Press.]

Keyword Index for Chemical Abstracts

Figure 5.5, a sample page from *Chemical Abstracts'* keyword index, shows details of this type of subject index.

Structure. The letter *K* is added to the page number to signify *keyword* —thus, "46K." The running heads are "Chemical Abstracts Vol. 79, No. 25, 1973" and "Biochem. 1–20 142709–145449, Org. 21–34 145450–146859." This informs index users that they are consulting *Chemical Abstracts,* Volume 79, Issue number 25, which was published in 1973. Entries from the Biochemical Sections of *Chemical Abstracts* numbered 1–20 are included in this index; the abstracts for these sections are numbered from 142709 through 145449. Also included in this index are entries for Organic Sections 21–34, abstracts 145450 through 146859.

The rest of the page is made up of four columns of index entries, set in about 5.5-point type, derived from keywords that have been selected by editors at Chemical Abstracts Service. An example of an index entry is "Zinc copper blood cow 144453d." "Zinc" is the subject heading; "copper blood cow" is the modifying phrase; and "144453d" is the reference number, which in this case is the abstract number in this particular issue of *CA.*

Prepositions and conjunctions, commonly used in indexes, are omitted from this index. As is customary in subject indexes, articles, verbs, and adverbs are omitted from this index.

There are no cross-references, glosses (explanatory notes), italicized names of organisms, or punctuation after the heading and end of the entry. Headings and genus names are capitalized. Headings are repeated, as are first words of modifications, and indentations are not used.

Content. The index entry "Zinc copper blood cow 144453d" informs the reader that abstract number 144454d deals with zinc in relation to something about copper, something about blood, and something about cow. The precise relationships are left unspecified. The following are conjectures as to the meaning of this entry:

- Zinc effect upon copper in blood of cow.
- Copper effect upon zinc in blood of cow.
- Zinc mutual interaction with copper in blood of cow.
- Existence of zinc and copper in blood of cow.
- Quantity of zinc and copper in blood of cow.
- Effect of zinc supplements.
- Effect of copper supplements.
- Toxicity of zinc and (or) copper in blood of (from) cow.
- Effect of zinc and copper on blood of cow.
- Unspecified relationships to blood from cow.
- Unspecified relationships to blood in cow.

The index user is helped by a specific description of what is in the abstract. The use of prepositions, conjunctions, and other words contributes to specificity, often saving users from looking up entries only to find that the abstract is unrelated to their interests.

Use, in this example, of an index entry of the four words, zinc, copper, blood, cow, aids the reader better than had fewer words been used. Thus, "Zinc cow" is less informative than "Zinc blood cow" or "Zinc copper cow." And any entry that contains terms relevant to the abstract is better than no entry at all. The ideal entry enables the index user to say, "Yes, I want to look up the entry," or "No, I do not want to look up the entry," rather than, "Maybe I want to look up the entry."

In this index, synonyms are scattered. For example, there is an entry for "Vitamin C apple juice 145025c" on the same page. Earlier in the same index there is an entry for "Ascorbic acid." The burden of bringing synonyms together is placed on the index user. Guidance is normally provided by cross-references and glosses within indexes.

The subject headings, except for scattering among related headings, are about the same as those that would be used in regular subject indexes. The modifications are less precise than those used in other subject indexes, such as those to be found in the volume indexes to *Chemical Abstracts*. The references are to abstracts as units rather than to sections of abstracts. Abbreviations used in the index entries have no periods. The entries seem generally to be related to subjects rather than to words. Thus, it seems to be a subject index rather than a word index.

Keyword-in-Context Index for Biological Abstracts, B.A.S.I.C.

The sample page of *Biological Abstracts'* keyword-in-context (KWIC) concordance, B.A.S.I.C., (the twice-monthly subject index to *Biological Abstracts*) (Figure 5.6), shows important details of this specific concordance and of KWIC concordances in general. (Concordances are word indexes that display, in their entries, words in context).

Structure. The sample page is numbered "E275." The running heads "Substances" above the first column and "Succinate" above the second column show the first alphabetized word in the central part of the two columns. The date of issue is given in the running head on the far left. Running heads inform the concordance user where he is in this index. Each of the two columns of entries is divided into three columnar parts. The right-hand part is made up of reference numbers that lead to the abstract from which the entry was derived. The first word of the center columnar part, e.g., "substantia" in the left column, controls the alphabetical position of the entry. The words to the right of the alphabetized word are also from the same title and are generally words that follow the

Vinylchlorosilane 146646t
Vinylcyclobutane heat formation 145797f
Vinylcyclopropane torsional barrier review 145457v
Vinylgermanium metal carbonyl 146605d
Vinylidenephosphorane triphenyl addn fluorenone 146603b
Vinylpyridine picoline 146407r
Vinylpyridine polymer silicosis prevention 143278p
Vinylpyridine ylide condensation 146340p
Vinyltetrahydronaphthol dihydroresorcinol condensation 146734v
Vinylthiooxazolidone deriv goiter 143112e
Vinyltoluene 146150b
Vinyltoluene dehydrogenation ethyltoluene 146157j
Viomycin redn product antimicrobial 143191e
Viremin interferon inducer fungi 144862m
Virucide benzamide 146255cq
Virus acid inactivation 144156j
Virus adeno assocd DNA 143595q
Virus aerosol inactivation 143195j
Virus antigen 144761c
Virus canine distemper buoyant density 144146f
Virus cell interferon 144820w
Virus chemotherapy BAYf1123 142837h
Virus disinfection 143187h
Virus DNA degrdn endonuclease 143618z
Virus DNA replication rolling circle 144124x
Virus DNA UV damage 144129c
Virus DNP hapten antibody 144794r
Virus hemagglutinin 144759h
Virus hepatitis antigen 144737z
Virus herpes DNA polymerase purifn 143760q
Virus infection prevention viremin 144862m
Virus influenza 144755d
Virus influenza infection polypeptide 144575v
Virus irradn DNA 143894m
Virus mammary tumor pH 146689k
Virus murine leukemia antiserum 144746b
Virus polyoma cell transformation 144691e
Virus prodn corticosteroid 143180a
Virus protein formation formylmethionine 143684t
Virus respiratory actinomycin D 144116w
Virus RNA tumor cancer 146892f
Virus sarcoma peptide glycoprotein 146061z
Virus tumor function review 144560m
Virus tumor steroid 143126n
Viscosity charge transfer absorption 145769y
Viscosity chocolate coating 145023a
Viscosity dependent phosphorescence benzoylnaphthalene 145563g
Viscosity molten alk acetate 145750k

Walnut fat detn magnesium 144948u
Washing solonchak soil sulfuric acid 145205m
Waste fat refining 144925j
Waste polyester fiber amination 146254p
Waste water potato protein 145015z
Water analysis nitrate 145406c
Water chlorination benzopyrene carcinogen= esis 143355m
Water demethylation toluene pressure 146070a
Water drinking atropine hypothalamus 142964x
Water drinking brain angiotensin 143146u
Water drinking methemoglobinemia nitrate 143336f
Water drinking nitrate methemoglobinemia 143335e
Water ecosystem carbon cycle 145361j
Water flea atrazine toxicity 143398c
Water fluoride dental cavity 143019e
Water fluoride detn serum 143981n
Water Krasnodar Territory boron 145178e
Water level corn amino acid 144249s
Water methane simulation optimization 145893j
Water microorganisms insecticide 143385w
Water oxygen methane simulation 145892h
Water PMR tissue 144391g
Water pollutant Federal Register 144599f
Water pollution fish phthalate 144983b
Water purifn styrene dehydrogenation 146158k
Water radium polonium Japan 143931w
Water sodium bone rachitism 142816a
Water soil boron fluorine 145171x
Water soil salinity tomato 145223v
Water stress metab plant 144247q
Watermelon cotyledon chlorophyll synthesis 145202w
Wave function LCAO methane fluoromethane 145172u
Wavelength light monochromic slit width 145404a
Wax chloroplast fir needle fluorine 143353j
Wax coating fruit vegetable 145057q
Wax removal sunflower oil 145004x
Weed control corn Latrin 143489h
Weed control herbicide review 143453s
Weed control mercaptoketothiazole deriv 143522p
Weed control methylphenoxypyridazine thiocarbamate 143518s
Weed control methylphenylthiocarbamate 143520m
Weed control oxazolidone 143519t
Weed control propionamidothiazole wheat 143521n
Weed control rice 143452r 143517t
Weed control sunflower Treflan 143486e
Weed control vegetable review 143454t
Wettability contact angle detn 145413c

X ray formaldehyde mutation 143208r
X ray nucleotide review 143538y
X ray spectral fluorescence micronutrient 145158y
X ray tungsten chelate 146622g
Xanthan gum dispersant insecticide 143526t
Xanthane hydride acetylation formylation 146468m
Xanthate triazole herbicide 143523q
Xanthenedione dinaphtho 146473j
Xanthine dehydrogenase induction Asper= gillus 144135b
Xanthine oxidase dissocn detergent 143851v
Xanthine oxidase inhibitor benzothiadiazine 146566s
Xanthomonas metab genetics 144133z
Xanthophyll ester grapefruit 145012w
Xanthophyll ester orange tangelo 145013x
Xanthopurpurian macrosporin Alternaria 144079m
Xenopus protein initiation estradiol 143067u
Xenopus transfer RNA gene 143598t
Xenopus 143599u
Xylan degree polymerization 146761b
Xylan sulfate pectin substitute 145051h
Xylanase Penicillium purifn 143758c
Xylaric acid aliph amide complex 145933x
Xyleborus bacterial symbiosis 144291z
Xylene 146148g
Xylene alkylation propylene 146155g
Xylene chloro NQR 145509p
Xylene dehydrocyclization dimethylhexene 146146e
Xylene isomer sepn adsorption 146140v
Xylene oxidn kinetics 146679u
Xylene oxidn phthalic anhydride 146241g
Xylene oxidn recovery 146225e
Xylene solvation assocn acid amine 145820h
Xylidide aminoaceto local anesthetic 146258t
Xylidide haloalkylamino anesthetic 142783n
Xylidine conformation dipole moment 145851u
Xylose absorption protein 145108g
Yam dough starch retrogradation 145000r
Yangonin deriv NMR 145519s
Yeast fermn charcoal contact 144898c
Yeast fermn continuous surfactant 144995z
Yeast formose synthetic carbohydrate 144114u
Yeast glutathione fermn 144900x
Yeast glutathione metal chelate 144906d
Yeast glycolysis review 144048a
Yeast hydrocarbon fermn kinetics 144859r
Yeast lytic enzyme cell membrane 144891v
Yeast mapping ribosome RNA genetic 144143c

Zinc 65 mussel 143906s
Zineb food heat 144973y
Zipromat Antracol fungicide 143471w
Zipromat Phytophthora tomato 143475a
Zipromat toxicity Alternaria 143472x
Zirconium neopentyl 146619m
Zollinger Ellison syndrome secretin gastrin 143178f
Zwitterion polypeptide pH 146836e

Viscosity sedimentation DNA 143622w
Viscosity thermal cond alkene equation 145821j
Visible spectrum benzoquinone 145502f
Vision photoreceptor rhodopsin 143716e
Vitamin A acid mucopolysaccharide prodn 142817b
Vitamin A deficiency skin 144437b
Vitamin A serum kwashiorkor 145135p
Vitamin A stereoisomer 146702h
Vitamin anemia therapy review 142730t
Vitamin B legume Rhizobium 144097r
Vitamin B soil root secretion 145208c
Vitamin B12 absorption intestine 144523b
Vitamin B12 enzyme reaction 143824p
Vitamin B12 food Hungary 145048n
Vitamin B12 hepatitis oxygen 144635n
Vitamin B12 hyperchromic anemia 142864q
Vitamin B12 manuf stillage 144923q
Vitamin B12 Methanobacillus acetic acid 144094n
Vitamin B12 Propionibacterium medium 144861k
Vitamin B6 analog carcinoma 142786r
Vitamin B6 ferrm microorganism 144870n
Vitamin B6 pregnancy 145096b
Vitamin C apple juice 145025c
Vitamin C oxidn copper ion 145684s
Vitamin D bone sodium 142816a
Vitamin D calcium mechanism kidney 143557d
Vitamin D hypophosphatemia review 144340q
Vitamin D metab review 144330m
Vitamin D skeleton review 144337u
Vitamin D toxicity overdose 142962v
Vitamin D2 irradn ergosterol 146736x
Vitamin E antagonist cresyl phosphate 143279q
Vitamin E feed review 144907e
Vitamin E pig fat 144996h
Vitamin Rhizopus cultivation 144849n
Vitamin tissue aminoisobutyrate uptake 143135q
Vitamine E swine nutrition 145090v
Vobasine methylaminoethyl ester antiviral 146722q
Vol wt soil cotton conditioner 145275j
Volatile compd Curculio pheromone 144281w
Volatile compd mushroom cooking 145011v
Volatile compd tobacco 144246p
Volatile compds food chromatog 144956v
Volatile fatty acid detn 144032r
Volatile flavor compds beer stopper 144826c
Volatile odor compd beer 144844g
Vole blood esterase irradn 143924w
Voltammetric redn organochlorine detn 143466y
Von Willebrand disease factor 144676d
Von Willebrand disease factor VIII 146678f

Wagnerite defluorination fertilizer 143349m

Wheat boron toxicity nitrogen compost 145238z
Wheat flour storage thiamine 145019d
Wheat grain phosphine residue 143964w
Wheat isoenzyme Puccinia resistance 143748s
Wheat organ formation dichlorophenoxyace= tate 143770u
Wheat phenol drought stress 145168q
Wheat phosphorus soil 145295r
Wheat protein compn 144197y
Wheat protein electrophoresis 144942n
Wheat root CCC 143498k
Wheat root secretion vitamin B 145208q
Wheat soft detn macaroni 145034e
Wheat variety nitrogen fertilizer 145322x
Wheat weed control propionamidothiazole 143521n
Wheat yield transpiration silicon 145259g
Wheat zinc soil fertilizer 145282j
Whetzelinia oxalate metab pathogenesis 144091i
Whey buttermilk concn membrane 144378c
Whey buttermilk protein food 145062n
Whey potassium cheese 144943p
Whey sulfhydryl disulfide fluorometry 144944q
Whitefish acid oxidn kinetics 144995g
Wine amine content pharmacol 144837g
Wine artificial color detection 144824a
Wine clarification EDTA addn 144845h
Wine colorimetry test strip 144045x
Wine fungicide Botrytis fermn 144835e
Wine prodn thermal 144881s
Wine putrefaction benzaldehyde deriv 144880c
Wine putrefaction phenoxyacetate deriv 144879z
Wine red fermn continuous mixing 144846j
Wine stabilization diethyl pyrocarbonate 144845?
Withaferin A immunol antiinflammatory 142880s
Wittig reaction solvent effect 145749s
Wood decompn forest ecol 145357n
Wood decompn fungicide review 143443p
Woodlandic soil nitrate detn 145168b
Woodward Hoffmann phosphine acetylene 144580d
Wool quality sheep 144378h
Wool triplet state 144501t
Workshop chem information 145427k
Worm tussocid Hb irradn 143903p
Wort amino acid diacetyl acetoin 144842e
Wort beer nonalc beverage 144878w
Wound slab cerebrum glycogen 144593z
X irradn heart sialate 143912r
X irradn lactate dehydrogenase 143921t
X irradn lymphopenia 144817a
X ray analysis electron microscopy
X ray crystallog thiobinupharidine 146713s
X ray diethyldithioacetal ethylthiomannose conformation 146753a

Yeast methionine accumulation 144584v
Yeast microsome desaturase 144104r
Yeast molasses fermn pH 144838h
Yeast nonfoaming sake 144882l
Yeast prodn methanol aliph alc 144896a
Yeast respiration cytochrome analysis 144663g
Yeast Rhizobium fodder compn 145038j
Yeast ribosomal RNA cistron 143577k
Yeast sporulation repression reversal 143193g
Ylide cumulated phosphorus 146603b
Ylide phosphorus aldonic acid 146772f
Ylide phosphorus Group VIB 146623h
Ylide selenonium rearrangement stereochem 146688h
Ylide sulfonium sulfide transalidation 145590h
Ylide vinylpyridine condensation 146340p
Yogurt acidity formate 145064q
Yogurt powd lactic acid 145063p
Yohimbine beta adrenolytic 142969c
Yolk pigment carotenoid 145128p
Zea carbofuran metab 143505a
Zeazin corn herbicide 143489h
Zeolite adsorption alkylbenzene xylene 146140v
Zeolite catalytic alkylation xylene 146155g
Zeolite nickel hydrogenation activity 146071b
Zeolite palladium ethynyldimethylcarbinol hydrogenation 145910n
Zimanat Pseudoperonospora cucumber 143474z
Zinc acetate soil amendment 145365m
Zinc Agrostis uptake 145310s
Zinc barley protein 145234v
Zinc benzamidothiophenate rubber plasti= cizer 146247p
Zinc blood hemorrhage 144592x
Zinc cadmium distribution liver 143322y
Zinc copper blood cow 144453d
Zinc deficiency behavior 145086y
Zinc deficiency iron 145091w
Zinc deficiency rice 145230r
Zinc fungicide 143471w
Zinc iron milk Austria 144979e
Zinc liver enzyme 142850g
Zinc pancreas insulin diabetes 129932k
Zinc phosphorus rice fertilizer 145254b
Zinc poisoning gastroenteritis review 143244z
Zinc propylenebisdithiocarbamate Alternaria 143472x
Zinc serum progesterone 143093z
Zinc sheep 145089b
Zinc soil phosphorus fertilizer 145196j
Zinc soil plant detn 145169c
Zinc sorghum genotype growth 145251y
Zinc subcellular prostate neoplasm 144684e
Zinc thiocyanato alkyl 146614f
Zinc uptake orange leaf 145287q
Zinc uptake Phaeodactylum 144253p
Zinc vegetable compost 145308x
Zinc wheat soil fertilizer 145282j
Zinc 65 benthic fish 144324n

Figure 5.5 Keyword index: Chemical Abstracts, Vol. 79, No. 23, 1973, p. 46K, by permission of the Chemical Abstracts Service.

SUBSTANCES

TION OF RADIOPROTECTIVE	CYSTAMINE AMINOETHYL THIU	16964
S DITCHES RANKS VISCOUS	FORMULAS/ A NEW METHOD TO	17278
CRAGEN GIBBERELLIN-LIKE	GERMINATION CHROMATOGRAPH	16636
NONSPECIFIC ANTI VIRAL	IN FRESH AND THERMALLY T	14242
THE ROLE OF ENDOGENOUS	IN MAKING AN ENHANCED RAD	15241
/ MOBILITY OF NUTRITIVE	IN RELATION TO EARTHWORM	17005
MUCIN SULFO MUCIN/ MUCO	IN THE HARDERIAN GLAND OF	13423
EFFEC OF RE TOXICATING	ISOLATED FROM EUCALYPTUS	17250
ACTIVITY OF PROTEIN	MEDICATED AND NON VALINE	12869
CN OF VOLATILE AROMATIC	OF SPARKLING APPLE WINE C	14801
TOPLASTIC FORM INDUCING	ON GROWTH PEAT QUALITY AN	14270
STUDIES ON BLOOD GROUP	ON MITOMYCIN C TREATED TR	16806
OILS QUALITY/ STUDY OF	PART 5 BLOOD GROUP SUBSTA	12943
ALENE ACETIC-ACID GROWTH	RESPONSIBLE FOR GRAPE ARO	14413
SUBSTANTIA	NHOR BERRIES FRUIT SET CR	14272
HE EFFECT OF UNILATERAL	NIGRA LESIONS ON APO MORP	14450
UCINOGENIC AGENT HEROIN	/ NARCOTIC ADDICTION WITH	16214
ENT-DEPRESS-DRUG HEROIN	IN BROILER RATION GROUNDN	16817
NGAL ACTIVITY SOME N	SUBSTITUTE ANTHRANILIC-ACID DERIVAT	17424
UTYL ESTER OF VARIOUS 5	CYSTEINES RELATIVE MOLAR	17922
COYNAMICS ALCOHOL ETHER	FORMAMIDES BENZENE WATR	12154
L UREA NADPH FORMATION/	SUBSTITUTED INDAMINES AS ELECTRON DO	12191
TO THE SYNTHESIS OF TRI	OLEFINS AND 2 ANT MANDIR	16759
ICOCHEMICAL PROPERTIES/	PYRIMIDINES PART 1 N-4 5	14852
LENT HISTIDINES 1 PH M 4	1 PHENYL QUINAZOLINE QUI	17901
NT MICROBIAL ACTION OF 4	2 THIO ADENOSINE 5 MONO	15592
N INHIBITORS PART 7 1-5	2 4 DI AMINO QUINOLINE M	12932
RENE METHANOL 6 SULFUR	6 CHLORO BENZOCAINONE	12932
S PART 7 SYNTHESIS 3F 3	/ CARAZINE PEPTIDASE 6	14105
RATES ACTIVE SITE METAL	CLOSTRIPAIN-SP REACTION	14101
CEMILSTROM ACCOMPANYING	SUBSTITUTION ETHYL SUBSTITUTION/ DI	12471
5 PACTERIOSTATIC METHYL	TYROSINE AA HISTIDINE P	14327
CSERU-5% THE AMINO-ACID	SUBSTITUTIONAL PROCESS/ STATISTICAL	14364
A DYNAMIC MODEL OF THE	SUBSTITUTIONS /A GENETIC METHOD OF E	14242
IN SRINE GLUTAMIC-ACID	SUBSTRATE ALIGNIN THERMOPHILITY R	14577
V BENE AP MERRILINGSIDE	SUBSTRATES OF RATTUS-NORVEGICUS STAR	14740
ALKALINE PHOSPHATASE/	SUBSTRATE /ACTION OF ETHIDIUM BROMID	14677
TAE NUCLEAR DNA GLUCOSE	AFFINITY CHROMATOGRAPHY MI	14213
FERENTIAL CENTRIFUGATION	ANALOG BY GLYCEROL 3 PHO-P	15416
NATION OF A PHOSPHONATE	ASSIMILATION GROWTH CELL A	15321
CELL PROTEIN PRODUCTION	ATTACHED GLYCO PROTEINS ME	14075
ACETIC-ACID TREATMENT/	BINDING AMINO-ACID CONST	16368
TIVE LECITHINYL-SN RESIDUE	BINDING MODEL/ ACTIN MC STU	14177
E SYNTHETASE EC-2.7.2.5	CARBON DI OXIDE PROPIONATE	12943
N METABOLISM COENZYME A	CONCENTRATION YIELD GAS NI	14083
DER LOW OXYGEN TENSIONS	CONCENTRATION/ EFFECT OF H	14177
ASE BIOMASS TEMPERATURE	DEPLETION USING THE TRAYSE	12743
RUN UPTAKE/ DIRECTION OF	DEPENDENCE PROPYL/ MODEL	17901
VITY CONCENTRATION OF T	GALACTURONIC-ACID GLUCOSE	14273
OF GRAPE SKIN AND JUICE	IN HUMAN AND ANIMAL PLASMA	13922
ACTION ATP AMMONIUM ION	INHIBITOR BINDING CONSTANT	14083
-GLUTAMIC-ACID NAD NADP	INHIBITORS PH/ DELTA-1 PYR	16563

SUCCINATE

	ELECTROSTATICS SURFACTANT	17230
M OI-2 ETHYLHEXYL SULFO	IN RABBIT 5 WITH EXPERIMEN	16423
E HYDROCORTISONE SODIUM	IN RABBITS WITH EXPERIMEN	12882
ITY OF PHOSPHATE ACETATE	SEROSAL MEDIUM SEROSAL GAS	13506
CNATF PHOSPHATE TICETATE	SEROSAL MEDIUM SEROSAL GAS	13299
RIC PLANDS OF MAN FETUS	SUCCINIC DEHYDROGENASE ALPHA NAPHTHY	11823
PARAMYXOVIRUS GLYCOGEN	DEHYDROGENASE MONO AMINE OX	15361
SP MAMMAL MYOSIN ATPASE	DEHYDROGENASE PHOSPHORYLASE	13427
0 HYDROXY GLUTARIC-ACID	SUCCINIC-ACID ALANINE ASPARTIC-ACC	14729
NCEPHALOPATHY ARGININO	SUCCINIC CHOLINE SKELETAL AUTONOMIC-D	16455
N PHOSPHATE ASPARTIC-AC	SUCCINIC COENZYME A ARSENOLYSIS/ MAL	14596
BY INITIAL RATE STUDIES	CONCANAVALIN A ON THE GROWT	15427
STRUM DEPRIVED NORMALLY	SUCKLED AND PASSIVELY IMMUNIZED LAMB	14570
METAB-DRUG/ EFFECTS OF	BEHAVIOR OF PIGS AND/ VOC	12046
THE SOW IN RELATION TO	SUCKLING BEHAVIOR AND MILK EJECTION	12046
NOSING/ THE NURSING AND	BEHAVIOR ELICKALING PHOSPHATASE	15832
ILEE PEPTIDE OR OLESES	SUCRASE MALTASE ALKALINE PHOSPHATASE	15904
ENCE INTESTINAL LACTASE	MALTASE PALATINASF ACID RFTA	15757
GLUCO AMYLASE TURANDSE	SUCROSE /ACID ALPHA GLUCOSIDASE FRM	13450
CTOSF 6 CNRYNO MYCELATE	/FRUCTOSE LIPIDS OF ARTHROBA	16368
FAL CALF PART 2 LACTOSE	AND FRUCTOSE NUTRITION BLOOD	11909
OR ALL PH ALE NODE AND	AS LUCLORNTTEDM SURVIVAL RA	16132
NEATING NADM GLUCOSE/	CONCENTRATION ON THE ACQUISI	16408
TYPE OF DEPRIVATION AND	CONCENTRATION ON THE ACQUISI	16081
OLESTEROL PHOSPHO LIPID	DENSITY GRADIENT/ ADENYL CYC	13503
LACTOFERRIN TRYPTOPHAN	ETHYLENE GLYCOL GLYCEROL DI	12225
CARBOHYDRATE STARVATION	FEEDING TRANSCRIPTION/DEVEL	13552
ASE IN NADH GLUCOSE	GLUCOSE SEMICARBAZIDE STUDIES	16341
CENE T N-4 5 ME FED DEPORT	GLUTAMATE SEMICARBAZIDE RIS	15432
GEN METABOLISM ALKALINE	GRADIENT ANALYSIS/ INHIBITIO	12534
LABIATAE 6-F GALACTOSYL	MISTOLOGY TAXONOMY/ PLANTEDS	13118
TPITIATED WATER LABELED	LARELED DEXTRAN ADENINE NUCL	16729
S GLYCOLATE POLY GLUCAN	MALATE/ PHOTOSYNTHETIC CARBO	14637
EEN METHYL ACRYLATE/	MONSACCHARIDE OXIDATION/	14447
RANVIER RANA-TEMPORARIA	SEDIMENTATION PROTEIN ALKYLA	15717
VALENCIA ORANGES STARCH	SODIUM CHANNEL POTASSIUM CON	14549
IN TECHNIQUES BILE FLOW	SUGAR FALL GROWTH/ EFFECT OF	13511
DAE AND MOSQUITOES FROM	SUCTION PRESSURE PUMPING PROTECTIVE	14980
NODITHE ANOMALY SOUTHERN	TRAPS CULEX-PIPIENS CULEX-TO	15867
GEN FROM GEON SOUTHERN	SUDAN RIOMHALARIS SUDANICA RIOMHALA	15180
NISM EXPEDITIONS TO THE	BRAIN LUNGS-SANSIBARICUS HISTO PATH	15094
AND MINERAL BALANCE IN	DIAPERASTICUS-SANSIRARICUS NEW	11713
HALICTOPHAGUS-PONTIFEX	GRASS AS INFLUENCED RY POTASSI	15096
US/ DERMAPTERA FROM THE	PRETORIA SOUTH AFRICA/ A NEW S	14939
SYNONMY ISRAEL GULF OF	ZOOLOGICAL CONTRIBUTION FROM THE	15047
LFEREBRAL INJURIES LEV	SUFF /MORTALITY AMONG GRAY MULLETS, I	16725
L CEREBRAL INJURE USE	SUFFICIENT ADMINISTRATION NEURO MODON	11849
TIVITY OF HAMPSHIRE AND	SUFFICIENT AND THE GLUCOS OF FICIENT	16769
ABOLITE RESPONSIBLE FOR	SUFFOLK EWES OUTSIDE THE RREFDING SE	16742
EA-MAYS DETACHED LEAVES	SUGAR ACCUMULATION IN CHLORELLA-VULG	13888
NST HEPPELATES-COLLUSOR	AMINO-ACID ORGANIC ACID FORMAT	16420
A RECTIPENNELYS CAUSING	RAIT DICHLORVOS INSECTICIDES/	16525
NULL ACRIDIDEMS/ CULTUR	REET LEAVES BOTH IN THE COURSE OF T	11791
ATIRLE RELATED LINES IN	REET SUGAR YIELD/ EFFECT OF SE	13854
D/ VARIETAL RESPONSE BY	REET TO NITROGEN SODIUM AND PO	14524
IFORNICUS INSECTICIDES/	REET WIREWORM CONTROL EXPERIME	
GES IN THE TITER OF THE	REET YELLOWS VIRUS IN SUGAR RE	
ITY OF AUTO POLY PLOIDS	REET/ CELL SIZE AS A BIOLOGICA	

Figure 5.6 *Keyword in context index: Biological Abstracts, B.A.S.I.C. [Reprinted from Biological Abstracts, Vol. 59, No. 3, 1975, p. E275, by permission of Biosciences Information Service.]*

alphabetized word in the title. The alphabetized word is used only for the first entry of a series of entries with the same word. A virgule (oblique line) indicates that the preceding word is the last word of the title. Words following the virgule start the title of the same abstract. The first part of the column (of the three parts, the left-hand part of the column) gives those words in the title of the abstract that precede the alphabetized word. This part of a column has been called the *wraparound feature*. The KWIC concordance provides words in context; the wraparound feature provides more words of the title in context than does the center part. These additional words give the concordance user a better idea of the complete title than does the rest of the title alone. From the sample page, it can be seen that most of the entries have been abridged at the right side of the center part and at the left of the left part of a column. Abridgment by deleting all letters after a given letter or before a given letter is done to provide a uniform column width. All letters, numbers, and punctuation marks and spaces more than the 57 required for the column are omitted. If the title has 57 or fewer keystrokes (characters and spaces), then the title may appear complete as an entry in the concordance. For an example of a complete title, consider the entry on the sample page under the heading *sugar*. This entry reads,

mellitus/true blood   level a simple method diabetes   12246

The virgule indicates that "true" starts the title. The space to the left of "mellitus" is permitted because there were not enough keystrokes in the title to fill the line. The computer has been programmed to move the symbols remaining in the title as far to the right as is necessary to give a uniform space between left and center columns. This aids the index user in easily locating the center-part words that are alphabetized and control the position of the entry in the column. The purpose (explained to Bernier by Hans. P. Luhn, of IBM, the inventor of the KWIC concordance) of the seemingly odd arrangement of entries in the concordance is to allow the eye as it skims the alphabetized words in the center part also to pick up adjacent words that provide context for the alphabetized word. This context, according to Luhn's hypothesis, enables the user to decide better, faster, and more conveniently whether or not to look up the abstract corresponding to the entry. Just how much context the normal eye picks up as it skims the first word of the center part would be an interesting subject for research, as would the effect of the context picked up upon decision to look up the entry. It was Luhn's contention that if the alphabetized word were removed from context and placed to the left, as is done in KWOC (keyword out of context) concordances, then the bene-

fits of immediate context would be lost. The omission of some words from
most titles makes them more difficult to understand. However, it is often
possible to guess as to what the complete title meant. If the guess is
wrong, then the user may be inconvenienced by looking up an entry that
is irrelevant to his interests.

It is possible to modify titles to aid users of KWIC concordances. One
modification is the separation of prefixes and suffixes or the artificial
division of words so that the computer program will create an additional
entry following the space that has been created. For an example of the
separation of a prefix, consider the first entry of the right-hand column of
the sample page alphabetized by the word *succinate*. The complete entry
reads,

       m di-2 ethylhexyl sulfo   electrostatics surfactant 12230

The person keyboarding this entry has introduced a space between the
letters o and s in "sulfosuccinate" in order to cause the program to produce an entry at "succinate." This is done in the expectation that some
users of this concordance might look under "succinate" rather than
under "sulfosuccinate."

Another kind of title modification is the addition of words thought by
the editor to be useful guides to the abstract. These words, taken from
the body of the abstract, are usually added at the end of the title. This
process has been called *title enrichment*. Yet another way to modify the
title is the editing of the title so that insignificant words (words believed
by the editor or keyboard personnel to be unlikely to be of use in search)
will not be printed at the beginning of the central part of the column.
Thus, they will not be found by, nor distract, the searcher. One way of
accomplishing this is to delete terms, usually at the start of titles, that
seem to be poor guides to the subject of the abstract. Examples of such
terms are *study of, introduction to*, and *contribution to*. Terms like these
are also removed from titles of abstracts before the abstracts are published. Another way to prevent words thought to be insignificant from
appearing at the start of the central part of the column is to hyphenate
them. An example taken from the sample page is "Rana-temporaria" in
the left-hand part of the right-hand column under "sucrose." The purpose
of the hyphen is to prevent "temporaria" from becoming an alphabetized
word in the center part of a column in the T's. That is, the editor has
decided that species names are not to appear as alphabetized words in
the concordance. The computer program treats a hyphenated word as one
word that starts with the first letter of the first word. Still another way of
modifying titles is to use an "artificial title" in addition to the regular title

as a way of adding entries that may be found to be useful by the searcher. Or a new title may be substituted. All these ways of modifying titles require human thought and action. The KWIC concordance was designed by Luhn to eliminate editorial thought and action, and substitute for it less skilled effort.

The typography is that of computer printout reduced in size. Use of all-capital letters makes necessary the spelling out of what might otherwise be given as symbols, such as the chemical elements and Greek letters. Keypunch operators can be trained to do this.

Content. The content of KWIC concordances is often derived from complete references of abstracts. The title (perhaps edited, enriched, artificial, or substituted) appears, usually in part, as the entry in the concordance. Thus, guidance to the abstract or article hinges on the adequacy of the title or modified title. In the field of chemistry, titles supply about one-third of the entries in indexes (Bernier, 1961, p. 26). R. K. Maloney has found an average loss of 73% of the potential output to the chemist using an SDI system based (as they usually are) on titles (Maloney, 1974, p. 370). Thus, KWIC concordances derived from titles to abstracts of a chemical nature omit at least two-thirds of the valid entries. For example, if the title is "Thermodynamic properties of 27 hydrocarbons," the specific thermodynamic properties that have been measured will be omitted as well as all 27 specified hydrocarbons. Thus, the user of a chemical concordance is obliged to look, not only under synonyms, but also under more generic headings.

There is scattering among synonyms. This is illustrated on the sample page by some of the entries under "SUCROSE," "SUGAR," and "SUG–ARS." The average drug name has six synonyms, so the pharmaceutical researcher must look, on the average, under six headings in a KWIC concordance if he is not to miss entries about a specific drug. There is scattering among singular and plural words; for example, "SUBSTRATE" entries are separated from "SUBSTRATES" entries on the sample page. In some cases, e.g., *fur* and *furs* or *mouse* and *mice*, singulars and plurals may be several pages apart. The concordance user should be aware of this scattering. Many of the alphabetized words in concordances are not effective guides to subjects reported by authors. Examples from the sample page are "SUBTOTAL," "SUBUNITS," and "SUCCESSES." Also, many of the entries under words that would seem to be good subject headings are not useful as guides to subjects reported by the author.

There are no cross-references displayed on this sample page. There could have been. Cross-references are put into KWIC concordances by human thought. If cross-references are not to be dangling, then even more human thought must go into checking the entry to which they refer.

Again, KWIC concordances were originally designed to avoid this kind of human participation in their construction.

Although concordances are inadequate substitutes for subject indexes, they provide a valuable start into indexing for new services. Their use eliminates the expenditure of time required to edit subject indexes. They are far better than no guidance at all. For organizations starting to provide subject guidance to their new abstracts, the KWIC concordance should prove to be attractive, especially from the viewpoint of economics and speed of publication. This was Luhn's hope. Substitution of KWIC concordances for existing subject indexes is a way of reducing costs by placing on the user the responsibility for looking up synonyms, rejecting irrelevant material, and locating more generic headings.

Biosystematic Index for Biological Abstracts

Figure 5.7 is a sample page of the biosystematic index of *Biological Abstracts*. Biologists and others who are interested in organisms can use this index to locate abstracts indexed by names of specified organisms.

Structure. The categories of organisms are listed as headings, with subcategories, brief modifications, and the abstract reference number following. The page is divided into three columns and each column into three parts. The first part of each column is the systematic name, the second part of the column has the modification, and the third part of each column has the reference number (locator).

The running heads give the page number, in this case "B16," which means biosystematic index, page 16, and the volume and issue numbers. The category and subcategory names are alphabetized, as are the modifications. For the same modification under the same subcategory, the reference numbers are placed in numerical order.

Content. The content is largely self-explanatory. Abstracts about organisms are found through the organisms' systematic names.

Cross-index for Biological Abstracts

The sample page in Figure 5.8 is from the cross-index to *Biological Abstracts*.

Structure. The page is divided into two main columns of postings of reference numbers. Placing reference-number postings into ten columns by their last digits as was done in earlier cross-indexes is a convenience for users in locating matching numbers under different subject headings. This format for posting reference numbers is described by Taube, Gull, and Wachtel (Taube *et al.*, 1952). The subject headings (or categories of subject headings) on the sample page have under them the reference

CTENOPHORA

HELMINTHES

	CTENOPH EXPT	14879

PLATYHELMINTHES

	AN PROD FEED	11928	
	AVES SYST	12983	
	CHEMO PARAST	12942	
	IMMUN GEN	14611	
	PH COMM DIS	16937	
	SYMPOSIA	14321	
CESTODA	BEHAV ANIMAL	12047	
CESTODA	SYMPOSIA	14313	
CESTODA	IMMUN PARAST	14718	
CESTODA	IMMUN PARAST	14725	
CESTODA	PARAST GEN	15847	
CESTODA	PARAST GEN	15851	
CESTODA	PARAST GEN	15861	
CESTODA	PARAST GEN	15863	
CESTODA	PARAST MED	15878	
CESTODA	PARAST VET	15886	
CESTODA	PARAST VET	15894	
TREMATODA	PLATYHM SYST	15123	
TREMATODA	BEHAV ANIMAL	12018	
TREMATODA	CHEMO PARAST	12935	
TREMATODA	DIGEST PATH	13488	
TREMATODA	ECOL ANIMAL	13597	
TREMATODA	PARAST GEN	15850	
TREMATODA	PARAST GEN	15851	
TREMATODA	PARAST GEN	15853	
TREMATODA	PARAST GEN	15854	
TREMATODA	PARAST GEN	15861	
TREMATODA	PARAST MED	15873	
TREMATODA	PARAST MED	15882	
TREMATODA	PARAST VET	15884	
TREMATODA	PARAST VET	15885	
TREMATODA	PARAST VET	15886	
TREMATODA	PARAST VET	15889	
TREMATODA	PARAST VET	15894	
TREMATODA	PARAST VET	15895	
TREMATODA	PARAST VET	15896	
TREMATODA	PH VECT ANIM	16898	
TREMATODA	PLATYHM SYST	15125*	
TREMATODA	PLATYHM SYST	15126	
TREMATODA	PLATYHM SYST	15127*	
TREMATODA	PLATYHM SYST	15128*	
TREMATODA	SYMPOSIA	14322	
TURBELLARIA	WILDLIFE TER	13792	
TURBELLARIA	ECOL ANIMAL	13645	
TURBELLARIA	ECOL ANIMAL	13651	
TURBELLARIA	OCEANOGRAPHY	13704	
TURBELLARIA	PLATYHM SYST	15124*	

NEMATODA	PL DIS CONT	16387
NEMATODA	SYMPOSIA	14322
ROTIFERA	ECOL ANIMAL	13660
ROTIFERA	LIMNOLOGY	13695
ROTIFERA	OCEANOGRAPHY	13704
ROTIFERA	OCEANOGRAPHY	13714

ECTOPROCTA

	ECOL GEN	13687
	ECOL GEN	13688
	ECTOP SYST	15107*
	ECTOP SYST	15108
	ECTOP SYST	15109
	PALEOZOOLOGY	15843
	SYMPOSIA	14313

BRACHIOPODA

	PALEOZOOLOGY	15842
	PALEOZOOLOGY	15843

MOLLUSCA

CEPHALOPODA	ECOL ANIMAL	13637
CEPHALOPODA	LIMNOLOGY	13695
CEPHALOPODA	MOLLUSC SYST	15113
GASTROPODA	MOLLUSC SYST	15116
GASTROPODA	OCEANOGRAPHY	13704
GASTROPODA	PALEOZOOLOGY	15842
GASTROPODA	PARAST GEN	15851
GASTROPODA	ENZYMES CHEM	14051
GASTROPODA	NERV PHYSL	14713
GASTROPODA	PALEOZOOLOGY	15842
GASTROPODA	PALEOZOOLOGY	16310
GASTROPODA	ANTHROPOLOGY	12018
GASTROPODA	BEHAV ANIMAL	12023
GASTROPODA	BEHAV ANIMAL	14944
GASTROPODA	CRUSTAC SYST	13178
GASTROPODA	CYTOL PLANT	13618
GASTROPODA	ECOL ANIMAL	13636
GASTROPODA	ECOL ANIMAL	13640
GASTROPODA	ECOL GEN	13684
GASTROPODA	ECOL GEN	13689
GASTROPODA	IMMUN DEMAT	14647
GASTROPODA	IMMUN PARAST	14700
GASTROPODA	LIMNOLOGY	13700
GASTROPODA	MOLLUSC EXPT	14884
GASTROPODA	MOLLUSC EXPT	14886
GASTROPODA	MOLLUSC EXPT	14887
GASTROPODA	MOLLUSC EXPT	14888
GASTROPODA	MOLLUSC SYST	15110*
GASTROPODA	MOLLUSC SYST	15114*
GASTROPODA	MOLLUSC SYST	15115
GASTROPODA	MOLLUSC SYST	15117
GASTROPODA	MOLLUSC SYST	15118*

POLYCHAETA	ANNELID EXPT	14761
POLYCHAETA	ANNELID SYST	14908
POLYCHAETA	ANNELID SYST	14910
POLYCHAETA	ANNELID SYST	14912
POLYCHAETA	ECOL ANIMAL	13617
POLYCHAETA	OCEANOGRAPHY	13718
POLYCHAETA	WILDLIFE AQU	13780

LINGUATULIDA

	DIGEST PATH	13488

ARTHROPODA

CRUSTACEA		BEHAV ANIMAL	11992
CRUSTACEA		ECOL ANIMAL	13591
CRUSTACEA		EVOLUTION	14167
CRUSTACEA		BEHAV ANIMAL	12015
CRUSTACEA		BEHAV ANIMAL	12021
CRUSTACEA		ECOL ANIMAL	13613
CRUSTACEA		OCEANOGRAPHY	13704
CRUSTACEA		OCEANOGRAPHY	13715
CRUSTACEA		PARAST GEN	15851
CRUSTACEA	BRANCHIOPODA	CRUSTAC EXPT	14775
CRUSTACEA	BRANCHIOPGCCA	ECOL ANIMAL	13627
CRUSTACEA	BRANCHIOPODA	ECOL PLANT	13732
CRUSTACEA	BRANCHIOPODA	LIMNOLOGY	13695
CRUSTACEA	CIRRIPEDIA	CRUSTAC EXPT	14781
CRUSTACEA	CIRRIPEDIA	CRUSTAC EXPT	14785
CRUSTACEA	CIRRIPEDIA	OCEAN LIMNOL	13720
CRUSTACEA	CIRRIPEDIA	PALEOZOOLOGY	15794
CRUSTACEA	COPEPODA	CRUSTAC EXPT	14980
CRUSTACEA	COPEPODA	CRUSTAC EXPT	14928*
CRUSTACEA	COPEPODA	CRUSTAC SYST	14939
CRUSTACEA	COPEPODA	CRUSTAC SYST	14934
CRUSTACEA	COPEPODA	ECOL ANIMAL	13627
CRUSTACEA	COPEPODA	ECOL PLANT	13732
CRUSTACEA	COPEPODA	LIMNOLOGY	13699
CRUSTACEA	COPEPODA	LIMNOLOGY	13711
CRUSTACEA	COPEPODA	OCEANOGRAPHY	13713
CRUSTACEA	COPEPODA	OCEANOGRAPHY	13715
CRUSTACEA	COPEPODA	WILDLIFE AQU	13765
CRUSTACEA	MALACOSTRACA	BEHAV ANIMAL	12012
CRUSTACEA	MALACOSTRACA	CRUSTAC EXPT	14772
CRUSTACEA	MALACOSTRACA	CRUSTAC EXPT	14773
CRUSTACEA	MALACOSTRACA	CRUSTAC EXPT	14774
CRUSTACEA	MALACOSTRACA	CRUSTAC EXPT	14776
CRUSTACEA	MALACOSTRACA	CRUSTAC EXPT	14777
CRUSTACEA	MALACOSTRACA	CRUSTAC EXPT	14778
CRUSTACEA	MALACOSTRACA	CRUSTAC EXPT	14782
CRUSTACEA	MALACOSTRACA	CRUSTAC EXPT	14783

RHYNCHOCOELA

ACANTHOCEPHALA

ASCHELMINTHES

GASTROTRICHA
GASTROTRICHA
KINORHYNCHA
NEMATODA
NEMATODA
NEMATODA
NEMATODA
NEMATODA
NEMATODA
NEMATODA
NEMATODA
NEMATODA
NEMATODA
NEMATODA
NEMATODA
NEMATODA
NEMATODA
NEMATODA
NEMATODA
NEMATODA
NEMATODA
NEMATODA
NEMATODA
NEMATODA
NEMATODA
NEMATODA
NEMATODA
NEMATODA
NEMATODA
NEMATODA
NEMATODA
NEMATODA
NEMATODA

SIPUNCULOIDEA

ANNELIDA

Figure 5.7 Biosystematic index: Biological Abstracts. [Reprinted from Biological Abstracts, Vol. 59, No. 3, 1975, p. B16, by permission of Biosciences Information Service.]

```
12838  13297  13305  13363  13366  15004  15031  15564  15618
17149  17436
```

CARDIOVASCULAR SYSTEM- BLOOD VESSEL PATHOLOGY

```
11798  11816  11823  12391  12392  12394  12625  12627  12628
12629  12630  12631  12632  12633  12634  12636  12637  12638
12639  12640  12651  12652  12653  12654  12645  12647  12648
12649  12650  12660  12661  12662  12663  12655  12657  12658
12659  12660  12671  12672  12673  12674  12665  12677  12668
12680  12684  12693  12699  12703  12704  12705  12707  12708
12709  12710  12711  12712  12716  12717  12718  12719  12721
12722  12723  12726  12728  12729  12731  12732  12733  12736
12737  12738  12739  12740  12744  12747  12749  12751  12752
12753  12755  12756  12757  12758  12760  12762  12766  12788
12770  12773  12774  12775  12778  12781  12782  12786  12788
12790  12791  12793  12794  12796  12801  12806  12844  13275
13286  13322  13329  13341  13347  13399  13400  13422  13426
13438  13445  13459  13499  13501  13519  13902  13921  14309
14677  14692  14695  14708  15176  15178  15223  15286  15311
15317  15397  15404  15416  15453  15467  15485  15534  15562
15604  15639  15640  15643  15656  15668  15669  15677  15779
15799  15829  15846  15871  15877  15880  15897  15947  15951
15959  15960  15972  15977  15978  15979  15981  15982  15992
15994  15996  16000  16003  16007  16016  16044  16111  16169
16200  16285  16857  16925  16933  16943  16947  16954  16972
16973  17016  17025  17071  17095  17161  17169  17221  17230
17342  17351  17415  17420  17426  17435  17441  17442  17443  17458
```

CARDIOVASCULAR SYSTEM- GENERAL; METHODS

```
11671  12277  12625  12628  12631  12632  12654  12668  12673
12678  12679  12680  12681  12682  12683  12684  12685  12687
12688  12689  12690  12691  12692  12693  12694  12695  12696  12697
12698  12699  12700  12701  12703  12706  12709  12710  12713  12714
12715  12718  12721  12722  12723  12726  12727  12736  12741
12742  12744  12745  12748  12754  12755  12757  12760  12761
12763  12764  12767  12777  12782  12783  12785  12786
12789  12794  12797  12799  12800  12803  12804  12812  12825  12840
17184  17187  17415  13290  13426  13568  15223  15641  17152
```

CARDIOVASCULAR SYSTEM- HEART PATHOLOGY

```
12633  12654  12656  12669  12670  12678  12684  12693
12694  12695  12702  12704  12705  12706  12707  12708
12700  12710  12711  12712  12713  12714  12715  12716  12717  12718
12719  12720  12721  12723  12724  12725  12726  12727  12728
12729  12730  12731  12732  12733  12734  12735  12736  12738
12739  12740  12741  12742  12743  12744  12745  12746  12747  12748
12749  12750  12751  12752  12753  12763  12764  12757  12758
12759  12760  12770  12771  12772  12773  12774  12766  12767  12768
12779  12780  12781  12782  12783  12784  12785  12786  12787  12788
```

```
11816  12169  12425  12428  12429  12430  12431  12432  12433  12434
12435  12436  12437  12438  13351  12630  12636  12708  13199  13200
13201  13203  13343  13351  13403  13412  13485  14664  14667  14468
14469  14641  14644  14675  14691  14695  14700  14731  14467  14741
15179  15196  15251  15283  15315  15380  15385  15422  15465  15453
15465  15466  15468  15474  15485  15475  15485  15490  15491  15499
15506  15510  15511  15529  15536  15551  15562  15581  15588  15594
15605  15608  15641  15663  15800  15832  15821  15825  15853
15871  15902  15911  16021  16024  16025  16104  16106  16212  16925
17087  17382  17444  17457
```

BONES, JOINTS, FASCIAE, CONNECTIVE AND ADIPOSE TISSUE- PHYSIOLOGY, BIOCHEM

```
11797  11824  11835  11837  11891  11917  11931  11934  11944  12737
12148  12223  12231  12255  12258  12305  12410  12434  12437  12439
12440  12451  12442  12443  12444  12445  12446  12448  12458  12449
12450  12451  12452  12453  12454  12455  12456  12457  12459  12459
12460  12461  12462  12463  13047  13136  13205  13217  13237  13238
13264  13253  13294  13304  13312  13320  13915  13919  13929  13973
13988  14018  14047  14423  14643  14644  14756  14757  14856
15304  15322  15324  15328  15705  15729  15759  15784  15789
15707  15800  15825  15826  16022  16374  16375  16971  17018
17013  17178  17217  17220  17255  17311  17337  17340  17456  17458
```

BOTANY, GENERAL AND SYSTEMATIC

BOTANY, GENERAL & SYSTEMATIC- ALGAE

```
12464  12465  12466  12467  12468  12469  12470  12471  12472  12473
12474  12475  12476  12477  12478  12479  12480  12481  12482  12483
12484  12485  12486  12487  12488  12489  12490  12491  12492  12539
12542  12542  13737  13743
```

BOTANY, GENERAL & SYSTEMATIC- ANGIOSPERMAE

```
12493  12494  12495  12496
```

BOTANY, GENERAL & SYSTEMATIC- BRYOPHYTA

```
12497  12498  12499  12500  12539  12542  12547
```

BOTANY, GENERAL & SYSTEMATIC- DICOTYLEDONES

```
12493  12494  12496  12501  12502  12503  12504  12505  12506  12507
12508  12509  12510  12511  12512  12513  12514  12515  12516  12517
12518  12519  12520  12522  12523  12524  12525  12526  12527
12528  12529  12530  12531  12532  12533  12534  12535  12536  12537
12538  12551  12552  12553  12554  12555  12558  13800  14169  14537
16519
```

BOTANY, GENERAL & SYSTEMATIC - FLORISTICS, DISTRIBUTION

```
12464  12465  12467  12468  12469  12470  12473  12477  12483  12489
12495  12497  12498  12520  12521  12523  12530  12513  12509  12517
12518  12519  12520  12521  12522  12530  12532  12535  12514  12516
12537  12539  12540  12541  12552  12553  12554  12555  12556  12557
12548  12549  12550  12551  12552  12553  12554  12576  12577  12580
12582  12585  12588  12593  12594  12598  12599  12604  12606  12611
13731  13737  13739  13747  13748  13749  13753
```

BOTANY, GENERAL & SYSTEMATIC - FUNGI

```
12539  12542  12547  12560  12561  12562  12563  12564  12565  12566
12567  12568  12570  12571  12572  12574  12575  12576
12577  12578  12579  12580  12581  12582  12583  12584  12585  12586
12587  12588  13837  16414  16419  16420
```

BOTANY, GENERAL & SYSTEMATIC - GENERAL, MISCELLANEOUS

```
12589  12590
```

BOTANY, GENERAL & SYSTEMATIC - GYMNOSPERMAE

```
12493  12591  12592  12593
```

BOTANY, GENERAL & SYSTEMATIC - LICHENES

```
12542  12547  12594
```

BOTANY, GENERAL & SYSTEMATIC - MONOCOTYLEDONES

```
11768  12493  12494  12495  12496  12540  12546  12557  12595  12596
12597  12598  12599  12600  12601  12602  12603  12604  12605  12606
12607  14169
```

BOTANY, GENERAL & SYSTEMATIC - PTERIDOPHYTA

```
12608  12609  12610  12611  12613  12614  12615  12616  12617  12618
12824
```

BOTANY, GENERAL & SYSTEMATIC - TRACHEOPHYTA

```
12543
```

CARDIOVASCULAR SYSTEM

CARDIOVASCULAR SYSTEM - ANATOMY

```
11839  12394  12419  12612  12613  12614  12615  12616  12617
12619  12620  12621  12622  12623  12624
```

CARDIOVASCULAR SYSTEM - PHYSIOLOGY, BIOCHEMISTRY

```
12799  12790  12791  12792  12793  12794  12795  12796  12797  12798
12799  12800  12801  12802  12803  12804  12805  12806  12916  12970
13117  13286  13331  14309  14663  14676  15176  15194  15216  15223
15264  13265  13271  15967  15968  15969  15974  15981  15983  15989  15846
15872  15265  15243  15394  15968  15969  15974  15981  15989  15991
15993  15490  15967  15997  16005  16006  16009  16010  16011  16012
16014  16015  16020  16214  16501  16006  16943  16947  17002  17155
17183  17184  17348  17351  17393  17394  17401  17406  17415  17430
17433  17458
```

CARDIOVASCULAR SYSTEM - PHYSIOLOGY, BIOCHEMISTRY

```
11676  11686  11687  12001  12096  12277  12412  12415  12416  12417
12440  12617  12635  12640  12650  12661  12693  12696  12717  12753
12760  12785  12786  12787  12807  12808  12809  12810  12811  12812
12813  12814  12815  12816  12817  12818  12819  12820  12821  12822
12823  12824  12825  12826  12827  12828  12829  12830  12831  12832
12833  12834  12835  12836  12837  12838  12839  12840  12841  12842
12843  12844  12845  12846  12847  12848  12849  12850  12851  12852
12853  12854  12855  12856  12857  12858  12859  12860  13272  13283
12885  13288  13291  13305  13314  13320  13322  13331  13492  13501
13523  13528  13630  13903  13911  13930  13977  14047  14095
14109  14309  14405  14421  14530  14626  14733  14735  15240  15295
15302  15138  15511  15693  15709  15710  15736  15754  15754  15949
15950  15963  15966  15970  15971  15973  15975  15976  15980  15984
15985  15987  15988  15990  15995  15998  15999  16002  16006  16008
16017  16018  16019  16022  16147  16175  16194  16202  16210  16221
16231  16270  16294  16371  16374  16813  16857  16863  16864  16872
16875  16876  16885  17100  17173  17190  17200  17260  17307
17329  17330  17360  17361  17373  17378  17452
```

CHEMOTHERAPY

CHEMOTHERAPY - ANTIBACTERIAL AGENTS

```
12291  12861  12862  12863  12864  12865  12866  12867  12868  12869
12870  12871  12872  12873  12874  12875  12876  12877  12878  12879
12880  12881  12882  12883  12884  12885  12886  12887  12888  12889
12890  12891  12892  12893  12894  12895  12896  12897  12898  12899
12900  12901  12902  12903  12904  12905  12906  12907  12908  12909
12910  12911  12912  12913  12914  12915  12916  12917  12918  12919
12920  12950  12955  12962  12964  13583  13759  14172  14341  14351
16928  16935  15171  15179  15185  15195  15215  15216  16337  16927
```

CHEMOTHERAPY - ANTIFUNGAL AGENTS

```
12921  12922  12923  12924  12950  12956  12962  12966  14457  17264
```

CHEMOTHERAPY - ANTIPARASITIC AGENTS

```
12925  12926  12927  12928  12929  12930  12931  12932  12933  12934
12935  12936  12937  12938  12939  12940  12941  12942  12943  14668
15147  15873
```

numbers of abstracts that can be categorized by, or indexed under, these terms.

Since the index user would be puzzled as to which reference numbers to look up because none of the numbers has a modification to help him, the necessary discriminating power is supplied in the following way: Suppose that the user is interested in sucrose as a possible cause of heart disease. In use of the cross-index to find references to this more specific subject, the reader compares reference numbers that he finds under the subject heading, "CARDIOVASCULAR SYSTEM—HEART PATHOLOGY" with the reference numbers that he finds under the subject heading, "SUCROSE" (or equivalent term). Every reference number that he finds under both subject headings leads to an abstract that was indexed by both terms. There is a good chance that the two terms are related in the subject of the abstract. Of course, they do not have to be related. There might be an abstract dealing, for example, with cardiovascular diseases among workers in industrial sucrose plants.

Content. The subject headings (categories) used are rather broad. Indexing is not to the maximum specificity, as is common in subject indexes. The general terms used are subcategorized to make them much more specific. For example, "CARDIOVASCULAR SYSTEM" has five subcategories on this page—"ANATOMY," "BLOOD VESSEL PATHOLOGY," "GENERAL: METHODS," "HEART PATHOLOGY," and "PHYSIOLOGY, BIOCHEMISTRY." Since entry specificity is not provided by modifying phrases in this index, it is supplied by the effort of the user in correlating numbers under two or more headings. The cross-index is a correlative indexing scheme (Bernier, 1971, p. 189) designed to help the user locate references that have been indexed by several different indexing terms. With patience, it can be a valuable locating device. It is one of several indexes produced by *Biological Abstracts*, and it is recommended to be used in conjunction with the others.

Formula Index (Molecular-Formula Index) for Chemical Abstracts

The sample page in Figure 5.9 illustrates the structure of the *Chemical Abstracts'* Formula Index.

Structure. The page is divided into three columns of entries. The running heads show that this page is 622F (for formula index, page 622), that the reader is consulting *Chemical Abstracts,* Vol. 72, and that the first entry on the page in column 1 relates to chemical compounds with the molecular formula $C_{12}H_{22}O_{11}$. An entry in the formula index usually consists of a subject heading, which is the molecular formula of the chemical compound indexed, a modification, and a reference number to the abstract (locator). As an example of an index entry, sucrose (cane sugar, beet sugar, white sugar, sugar, etc.), which has the molecular formula, $C_{12}H_{22}O_{11}$, can be seen about a fourth of the way down the first column of the sample page. The first modification under this formula is "compd. with calcium hydroxide (1:3) [28251–54–9]," which is followed by the reference number, "68439s."

The molecular formula gives the symbols for the chemical elements contained in the molecule. It also gives the number of atoms of each element. The number follows the symbol for the element and is printed as a subscript. The number *one* (1) is understood and not used. For example, the molecular formula $C_{12}H_{23}NO_2$ in the third column means that all molecules under this subject heading have 12 carbon atoms, 23 hydrogen atoms, 1 nitrogen atom, and 2 oxygen atoms in them. It is easy to calculate molecular formulas from structural formulas, which may be presented to the librarian for search. For example, the structural formula for acetic acid, which is found in vinegar, is $H_3C—\underset{\underset{OH}{|}}{C}{=}O$. The molecular formula can easily be seen to be $C_2H_4O_2$.

Since all but the simplest molecular formulas apply to more than one chemical compound, a way must be provided to differentiate among these compounds. This way is by use of systematic names for the compounds in the modifications. For example, in the first column of the sample page, under the molecular formula, $C_{12}H_{22}O_{11}$, there are found the names of different chemical compounds generically called sugars, viz. lactose, maltose, mannobiose, melibiose, sophorose, sucrose, trehalose, and turanose. All eight of these sugars have the same molecular formula, $C_{12}H_{22}O_{11}$.

The modifying phrase may indicate polymers and compounds with other substances, as well as systematic names. There may be a *P* before the reference number to indicate that the abstract is that of a patent.

There are inorganic chemical compounds (those not containing organic carbon) as well as organic compounds in the formula index. Also, there are organometallic compounds ($C_{12}H_{22}Sn$) and compounds containing metal ions ($C_{12}H_{23}AlO_5$).

In molecular formulas of this formula index, the symbols for the chemical elements are arranged alphabetically by symbol letters except for carbon (C), which is placed first, and hydrogen (H), which is placed second. Another system for arranging the symbols is the Richter System, which is used in *Chemisches Zentralblatt*.

Within the formula index, the molecular formulas are arranged alphabetically by the symbol of the first chemical element (usually C for car-

-, 3 -O-α-D-glucopyranosyl- [497-48-3].
39200b
-, 4 -O-β-D-mannopyranosyl - [28072-80-2].
41926m
2,4,6,8,10,12,14 -Heptaoxapentadecane -1,15 -diol
diacetate [27969-34-2]. P 95310z
Inositol, 1-O-α-D-galactopyranosyl-
(1 R) - myo- [16908-86-4]. 39791v
isomaltose [499-40-1]. 39261x, 52957y, 53165a,
117992c
Lactose [63-42-3] See Subject Index
β-[5965-66-2]. 76345y
polymer with phthalic anhydride and propylene
oxide [26352-77-2]. P 91103m
Laminaribiose [497-47-2]. 51165b, 79355n, 79356p
41926m
Maltose [69-79-4] See Subject Index
α-, 39261x
β-[133-99-3]. 39261x
polymer with phthalic anhydride and propylene
oxide [27296-68-2]. P 91103m, P 112255e
Mannobiose [6799-60-6]. 41926m
Mannopyranose, 2 -O-α-D -mannopyranosyl-
-, 3 -O-α-D -mannopyranosyl -
-[23745-85-9]. 10079h
Mannose, 4 -O-β-D -glucopyranosyl -
β - [15761-61-2]. 3687b, 41926m
Melibiose [585-99-9]. 44062n, 63843j, 86550a,
90763g, 97914y
Phthalic anhydride
polymer with lactose and propylene oxide
[26352-77-2]. P 91103m
Sophorose [534-46-3]. 44062n, 79356p, 97652m
Sucrose [57-50-1]. See Subject Index
compd with calcium hydroxide (1:3)
[28251-54-9]. 68439s
polymer with acrylic acid [27553-47-5]. P
113483q
polymer with formaldehyde and melamine
[26763-42-8]. P 91190n
polymer with glycerol, phthalic anhydride and
propylene oxide [27437-08-7]. P 112255e
polymer with glycerol, propylene oxide and
tetrachlorophthalic anhydride [26445-91-0]. P
91103m
polymer with phthalic anhydride and propylene
oxide [26352-78-3]. P 91103m. P 112255e
Trehalose [99-20-7]. 937x, 9447v, 10314f, 40006a,
40230l, 44062n, 52104l, 63828h, 64054q, 74887c,
76086q, 97498r, 108139c, 118862x, 129572d
Turanose [5349-40-6]. 74937u, 75946h, 79355n,
117992c

C₁₁H₂₀O₁₂
Gluconic acid, 4 -O-β-D -glucopyranosyl-
D - [534-41-8]. 45208b
Lactobionic acid [96-82-2]. 41726w, 62538b
compd with erythromycin (1:1) [3847-29-8].
99009f
monosodium salt [27297-39-8]. 29143w
Melibionic acid [21675-38-7]. 62538b

C₁₁H₂₀ClN₂Si₂
o-Phenylenediamine, 4 -chloro -N,N-bis-
(trimethylsilyl) - [26682-08-6]. 90564a

C₁₁H₂₀ClO
Ether, butyl 3 -chloro -5,5 -dimethyl -2 -hexenyl
[26339-54-0]. 11986p
Lauroyl chloride [112-16-3]. P 7847m

C₁₁H₂₀ClO₂
Decanoic acid
2 -chloroethyl ester [15175-04-9]. 89711q
Hexanoic acid, 2 -butyl -5 -chloro -
ethyl ester [26826-03-9]. 2982g
-, 5 -chloro -2 -isobutyl -
ethyl ester [26826-05-1]. 2982g
Undecanoic acid, 2 -chloro -
methyl ester [26040-71-1]. 15998s
-, 11 -chloro -
methyl ester [17696-12-7]. 15998s

C₁₁H₂₀ClO₃
Malonaldehydic acid, chloro -
isopropyl ester, 3 -(diisopropyl acetal)
[27579-29-9]. 120974d

C₁₁H₂₀Cl₃NO₃P
Phosphonic acid, (2,2,2 -trichloro -1 -=
hydroxy -1 -morpholinoethyl) -
diisopropyl ester [24693-34-3]. 31930u

C₁₁H₂₀CoN₄O₃
Cobalt, aquamethyl[(3,3 -trimethylenedinitrilo =
)bis[2 -butanone oximato]](2-)] -=
[27073-11-6]. 108248n

C₁₁H₂₀F₃O
2 -Dodecanol, 1,1,1 -trifluoro - [26902-82-9].
110696a

C₁₁H₂₀F₄O₃Si₃
Trisiloxane, 1,3,5 -trimethyl -1,3,5 -tris(3,3,3 -=
trifluoropropyl) - [27703-86-2]. P 103722c

C₁₁H₂₀F₆O₃Si₃
1,5 -Trisiloxanediol, 1,3,5 -trimethyl -1,3,5 -tris =
(3,3,3 -trifluoropropyl) - [2802-54-2]. 31912q.
P 103722c

C₁₁H₂₁N
Bicyclo[2.2.2]octan -1 -amine, 4 -butyl -
hydrochloride [25899-27-8]. 89864s
-, 4 -tert -butyl -
hydrochloride [25344-98-3]. P 15761j, 89864s
-, 4 -methyl -N,N-dimethyl -
hydrochloride [26065-27-0]. 89864s
-, 4 -methyl -N-propyl -
hydrochloride [25899-36-9]. 89861s
Bicyclo[2.2.2]octane -1 -methylamino -4 -propyl-
hydrochloride [5567-68-2]. P 15761j, 89864s
-, N,N-4 -trimethyl -
hydrochloride [5567-67-1]. P 15761j, 89864s
-, N,α,4 -trimethyl -
hydrochloride [25907-41-9]. 89864s
-, α,α,4 -trimethyl -
hydrochloride [5561-76-2]. P 15761j, 89864s
2 -Bornanemethylamine, α -methyl-
hydrochloride, t - endo -(+) - [25221-89-0]. P
54896b

polyamide with hexahydro -2H-azepin -2 -one
[25191-04-2]. P 32466j. P 32466h. P 447x, P
67505v
polymer with cyclic ethylene ethyl phosph..te
[28206-73-7]. 133254u
polymer with cyclic ethylene phenylphosphonite
[28206-71-5]. 133254u
1 H -Azepine, 1 -hexanoylhexahydro - [IN494-57-0].
31583h
2 -Azetidinone, 3,3,4 -tripropyl - [25744-72-3].
90161s
2 -Bornanol, 3 -(dimethylamino) -
endo,endo - [21841-39-4]. 42600n
exo,exo - [26620-26-8]. 42600n
exo -2,endo -3 -(+) - [25050-46-8]. 42600n
54868u
hydrochloride, cis-exo - [25050-48-0]. 54868u
hydrochloride, endo,endo - [25050-54-8].
54868u
monopicrate, endo,endo - [25050-55-9]. 54868u
551900d
Cyclohexanol, 1 -(piperidinomethyl) - [25363-21-7].
551900d
oxalate (salt) (1:1) [25363-34-2]. 551900d
Cyclohexanone, 4 -butyl -4 -ethyl -
oxime [25923-64-2]. P 89885z
Cyclopentanol, 1 -(2 -piperidinoethyl) -
[25363-30-8]. 551900d
Formamide, N-[4 -(1 -methylbutyl)cyclohexyl] -. P
89895c
4 -Hepten -3 -one, 1 -(dimethylamino) -5,6,6 -=
trimethyl - [26072-68-4]. 31124j
2 -Heptyn -4 -ol, 1 -(diethylamino) -4 -methyl -
[17356-22-8]. 31134n. 66570d
Hexanamide, N-cyclohexyl - [10264-27-4]. 42899s
monopicrate [24863-14-7]. 42899s
p -Menth -1 -en -4 -ol, 8 -(dimethylamino) -
[26903-14-0]. P 10093n
p -Menth -8 -en -1 -ol, 2 -(dimethylamino) -
stereoisomer [6069-83-6 6069-84-2], 121716i;
picrate, stereoisomer [6069-85-N 28296-54-0].
121716h
p -Menth -8 -en -2 -ol, 1 -(dimethylamino) -
stereoisomer [6069-86-9], 121716h
2 -Naphthol, 3 -(dimethylamino)decahydro-
stereoisomer [25690-15-7], 78929r,115624k
-, 3α -(dimethylamino) -1,2α,3,4,4aα,5,6,7,8,-=
8aβ -decahydro -
(-) - [27935-05-3], 137521b
(+) - [27935-04-2], 137521b
3 -Octyn -2 -ol, 5 -(diethylamino) - [26981-16-2].
89880d
Piperidine, 1 -(2,2 -dimethylvaleryl) - [13146-38-8].
P 12150y
-, 1 -(2,3 -epoxypropyl) -2,2,6,6 -tetramethyl -
[23793-65-9]. P 31631x
4 -Piperidone, 3 -hexyl -1 -methyl-
hydrochloride [26822-36-6]. 42440k
Pyridine, 4 -butoxy -1,2,3,6 -tetrahydro -1 -propi-
[26493-38-9]. P 100685g
3 -Pyridinemethanol, 1 -hexyl -1,2,5,6 -tetrahydro-

C₁₂H₂₂S
Cyclohexyl sulfide [7133-46-2], P 31308x, 36891s
Hexenyl sulfide
  polymer with sulfur, P 4225m

C₁₂H₂₂S₃
Ethanethiol, 2,2'-(9-thiabicyclo[3.3.1]non-2,6-=
  dithio)di- [26034-29-7], P 43457h

C₁₂H₂₃NSi
Silane, [α-(dimethylsilyl)-m-tolyl]trimethyl-
  [30386-93-7], 120723w
-, [α-(dimethylsilyl)-p-tolyl]trimethyl-
  [27278-48-4], 120723w
-, m-phenylenebis[trimethyl-
  radical ion(1-), 127095b
-, o-phenylenebis[trimethyl-
  radical ion(1-), 127095b

C₁₂H₂₈Sn
Stannane, cyclopentylisopropyl)methylpropadienyl)-
  [26900-56-7], 132904u
-, cyclopentylisopropylmethyl-2-propynyl-
  [26900-55-0], 132904u

C₁₂H₂₇AlO₃
Aluminum, (hydrogen acetoacetato)diisopropoxy-
  ethyl ester [14782-75-3], 21441w, 121851y

C₁₂H₂₇AsSn
Arsine, phenylbis(trimethylstannyl)- [24385-37-3],
  12832x

C₁₂H₂₅BO₂
1-Butaneboronic acid
  cyclic 1,2-cyclohexyleneethylidene ester
  [24371-97-9], 12962q

C₁₂H₂₄BrNO₂P
Phosphonic acid, [1-bromo-2-(cyclohexylami-=
  no)vinyl]-
  diethyl ester [26654-87-3], P 32128a

C₁₂H₂₅BrO₂
Hexanoic acid, 3-bromo-2,2-dipropyl-
  [25744-80-3], 90161s
Propionic acid, 2-bromo-
  nonyl ester [26072-73-1], 31126m
Undecanoic acid, 2-bromo-
  methyl ester [26040-76-6], 15998s

C₁₂H₂₅ClGe
Germane, (1-chloromethyl)-3-methyl-1,3-=
  butadienyl]triethyl- [29023-57-2], 79174e

C₁₂H₂₅ClGeO
Germane, [(4-chloro-1,1-dimethyl-2-=
  butynyl)oxy]triethyl-, 79174c

C₁₂H₂₅ClHgO₂
Mercury, (10-carboxydecyl)chloro-
  methyl ester [27151-78-6], 132834w

C₁₂H₂₅ClNO₂P
Phosphoric acid
  diisopropyl ester, ester with 2-chloro-3-=
  hydroxy-N,N-dimethylcrotonamide
  [15289-80-2], 12002b

C₁₂H₂₆Cl₂N₃
3,9-Diazabicyclo[3.3.1]nonane, 9-(4-chlorobut=
  yl)-3-=
  dihydrochloride [27447-76-3], 132668v

Dicyclohexylamine [101-83-7], 6269c, P 32665y,
  36472f, P 67719w, P 69012j, 89404s, 117138d,
  117457g, 119751x
  nitrite [3729-91-7], P 4496a, 57419j, 81943w,
  102009p
  propenylphosphonamide (1:1), (Z)- [24349-89-1], P
  67093n
Glutamic acid, N-(4-nitro-7-oxo-1,3,5-=
  cycloheptatrien-1-yl)-
  compd with dicyclohexylamine (1:2), L-
  [25528-66-9], 67236m
-, N-[(piperidinooxy)carbonyl]-
  compd with dicyclohexylamine (1:2), L-
  [24730-67-4], 21934j
5-Hexenylamine, N,N-diethyl-1-vinyl-
  [26682-28-0], P 78373e
Hexylamine, N-cyclohexylidene-
  polymer with hexamethylene isocyanate
  [26298-75-9], 101170x
  polymer with methylenedi-p-phenylene
  isocyanate [26298-73-7], 101170x
  polymer with 4-methyl-m-phenylene
  isocyanate [26298-74-8], 101170x
5-Hexynylamine, N,N-diisopropyl- [3512-54-7],
  121894q
  hydrochloride [3512-55-8], 121894q
  monopicrate [3512-55-9], 121894q
Lauronitrile [2437-25-4], P 42851v
2-Norbornanamine, 3-isopropyl-N,N-dimethyl-
  hydrochloride [25220-16-0], P 42971j
2,7-Octadienylamine, N,N-diethyl- [25017-02-1], P
  78373e

C₁₂H₂₅NO
Acrylamide, N-(1,1-diethylpentyl)- [18452-90-9],
  3841x
  polymers [25280-98-2], 3841x
-, N-(1,1-dimethylheptyl)- [25269-99-2],
  3841x
  polymers, 3841x
-, N-(1,3-dimethyl-1-propylbutyl)-
  [25270-02-4], 3841x
  polymers [25280-99-3], 3841x
-, N-(1-methyl-1-propylpentyl)-
  [24345-71-9], 3841x
  polymers [25280-97-1], 3841x
3-Azabicyclo[3.2.2]nonane-3-butanol
  [26478-28-4], P 121387b
Azacyclotridecan-2-one [947-04-6], P 67705p, R
  9904u, P 110832a, P 121031f
  polyamides [26028-74-8], P 32846h, P 67474n, P
  79867f, P 91002c, R 111819e, R 11182lz,
  111832d, P 112259), P 112272h
  polyamide with adipic acid, 6-aminohexanoic
  acid and 1,6-hexanediamine [26659-07-4], P
  32769k
  polyamide with adipic acid and
  6-hexanediamine [26702-53-4], P 67705p
  polyamide with adipic acid, hexahydro-2H-=
  azepin-2-one and 1,6-hexanediamine
  [26777-62-8], P 68144s

[26721-25-5], P 90298s
1αH,5αH-Tropane, 3β-butoxy- [16487-35-7],
  90243v

(C₁₂H₂₃NO)ₓ
p-toluenesulfonate [16487-36-8], 90243v
Poly(iminocarbonylundecamethylene) [24937-16-4],
  P 32846h, P 67474n, P 67705p, 67816a, P
  79867f, P 91002c, P 101397b, R 111819e, R
  11182lz, 111832d, P 112259), P 112272h

C₁₂H₂₃NO₂
Acrylamide, N-methyl-3-)octyloxy)-
  [27657-49-4], P 110435v
Bicyclo[4.2.0]octane-7,8-dimethanol,
  1-dimethylamino)- [19244-87-2], P
  54874t, P 54875u
1,2-Cyclobutanedimethanol, 3,3-dimethyl-4-=
  1-pyrrolidinyl)- [18126-19-3], P 54874t, P
  54875u
Cyclododecanone, 2-hydroxy-
  oxime [26377-98-4], P 121083z
Cyclohexanecarbamic acid, 1-methyl-
  butyl ester [27701-09-3], 2986m
1,2-Dioxa-4-azaspiro[4.5]decane,
  3,3,7,9-pentamethyl- [24075-11-4], 4289r
  p-Menth-1-en-4-ol, 8-(dimethylamino)-
  oxide [26903-15-7], P 100934n
Methacrylic acid
  6-(dimethylamino)hexyl ester [26602-93-7], P
  3045r, P 54792q
2H-1,3-Oxazine, tetrahydro-3-octanoyl-
  [23047-75-4]. P 66929c
Oxazolidine, 5-methyl-2-pentyl-3-propionyl-
  [23047-54-3], P 66929c
-, 3-octanoyl-5-methyl- [23246-55-1], P
  66929c
4-Piperidineacetic acid, 3-ethyl-1-methyl-
  ethyl ester, cis- [21372-30-5], 12518z
  ethyl ester, trans- [21372-35-0], 12518z
4-Piperidinol, 1,2,2,6,6-pentamethyl-
  -1,3,5,5,5-pentamethyl-
  acetate (ester) [2764-29-7], 99855d
  acetate (ester) [27644-30-0], 99855d
Tetrolaldehyde, (diethylamino)-
  diethyl acetal [5799-78-0], 16223x

C₁₂H₂₃NO₃SSi
Benzenesulfonamide, N,N-bis(trimethylsilyl)-
  [1023-95-6], 132852a

C₁₂H₂₃NO₂S₂
Thiocyanic acid
  (decylsulfony1)methyl ester [24655-54-7], P
  21694f

C₁₂H₂₃NO₄S₂
Carbonic acid, dithio-
  S-butyl ester, S-ester with S-butyl
  2-mercaptoethyl)carbamate [28174-18-7],
  132261g

C₁₂H₂₃NO₄
Acetamide, N-[1-(tert-butyldioxy)cyclohexyl]-
  [24829-63-8], 42898r
Acetohydroxamic acid, 2-(p-menth-3-yloxy)-
  (1R,3R,4S)- [26252-28-8], 55667q

Figure 5.9 Formula index: Chemical Abstracts. [Reprinted from Chemical Abstracts, Vol. 72, p. 622F, by permission of Chemical Abstracts Service.]

bon). Then under the symbol for the first element, the entries are arranged by the number of that element in the compound, e.g., C_{12} comes before C_{13}. Within the group of molecular formulas starting, for example, with C_{12}, come those formulas having, say, H_{22}. Then, follow those formulas with C_{12} and H_{23}, and so on. Under a single molecular formula, the modifications are alphabetized, as in the list of sugars above, for the convenience of the searcher. For a given modification, the reference numbers are then arranged numerically.

Many of the systematic names in the modifications are inverted, just as they are in the subject index. An example under "$C_{12}H_{23}BrO_2$," is "Propionic acid, 2-bromo-." Inversion is done in the subject index and carried over into the formula index to guide users to related compounds better than if the names had not been inverted; for example, "2-Bromopropionic acid." Identical names in the subject and formula indexes have been used to aid the searcher in going from one index to the other.

There are many cross-references in the formula index that lead the user to the subject index. An example is "$C_{12}H_{22}O_{11}$ Sucrose [57–50–1]. See Subject Index." The number "57–50–1" in brackets is a serial code number for sucrose and is used in the Registry of Chemical Compounds.

Content. The formula index was invented at *Chemical Abstracts* to help chemists who had difficulty with systematic organic nomenclature. Many chemists had difficulty and many still do. Perhaps 85% of the names coming into abstracts must be translated into systematic, index names. It is relatively easy for chemists and others to count the number of each kind of chemical element in a structural formula of interest and then to find that structural formula in the formula index by means of its molecular formula. Finding the right name under the molecular formula may be a bit more difficult, but it is not impossible. It is easier to determine if the name under a given molecular formula is the right one than it is to name the compound from the structural formula.

The formula index guides users to references to chemical compounds of known, unknown, indefinite, and undetermined structure. Librarians can learn to use the Formula Index even if they are not chemists.

Indexable compounds—those that relate to subjects in abstracts—are indexed in the subject index and in the formula index unless there is no molecular formula calculable, and unless there is a cross-reference that guides the reader from the formula index into the subject index. Search for abstracts dealing with chemical compounds of definite structural formula is, without doubt, most rapid and easiest through the formula index unless the searcher also knows the systematic, index name of the compounds. If the searcher does know the systematic, index name, searching the subject index is best because the modifications found there will help to specify what was studied about the compound. Likewise, after the systematic, index name has been found in the formula index, it is best to turn to the subject index because of the modifications found there.

Since there are about 3 million chemical compounds known, the need for rapid, sure access to abstracts dealing with them is evident. The formula index provides this kind of guidance.

Ring Index for Chemical Abstracts

The sample page in Figure 5.10 shows the structure of the ring index of *Chemical Abstracts.*

Structure. The first running head shows the number of rings in the ring system entered on the page: "2-Ring Systems" means that all entries on the page are names of chemical compounds having two rings in their structures. The centered running head informs the user that he is looking at Volume 77 of *Chemical Abstracts.* The page number is "8R" (page 8 of the ring index). The entries are placed in three columns for economy and for ease of reading the short lines. The size of each ring of the two-ring systems carried on the page is set off to the left of each column in boldface. Thus, "5,30" means a two-ring system in which one ring has 5 atoms and the other ring has 30 atoms. Likewise, "6,6" means a two-ring system with 6 atoms in each ring. Next, indented under the pair of numbers indicating the size of each ring, comes the kinds of atoms and the number of each kind in each of the two rings. For example, "C_2N_4–C_2N_4" means that each ring of 6 atoms has 2 carbon atoms and 4 nitrogen atoms. Next indented is the systematic, index name or names for the chemical compound(s) that have such a ring system. These compounds can then be found in the subject index to Vol. 77 of *Chemical Abstracts.*

Content. Chemical compounds may contain rings of atoms. Such compounds are called *ring compounds.* The ring index was designed to help chemists name ring compounds, as the nomenclature has been found to be difficult for chemists to master. For example, in the third column under "C_6–C_6," there is the modification, "Naphthalene." This compound of two rings has been used as an insecticide and insectifuge and is commonly known as *moth balls.* It consists of two 6-membered carbon rings "fused" at two adjacent carbon atoms in this way:

$$\begin{array}{c}
\text{C} \diagup^{\text{C}} \diagdown \text{C} \diagup^{\text{C}} \diagdown \text{C} \\
\mid \quad \parallel \quad \mid \\
\text{C} \diagdown_{\text{C}} \diagup \text{C} \diagdown_{\text{C}} \diagup \text{C}
\end{array}$$

On each carbon atom outside of the two fused carbon atoms in the center, there is a hydrogen atom. Often this hydrogen is not shown in structural

1H,10H-Pyrrolo[2,1-j][1,2,5,8,11,14,17]=
dithiapentaazacycloeicosine

5,30
$C_4N-C_{20}N_{10}$
Tyrocidine A

5,39
$C_4N-C_{26}N_{13}$
Mycobacillin

6,6
$C_2N-C_2N_4$
[1,2,4,5]Tetrazino[1,2-a][1,2,4,5]tetrazine
$C_2OSi_3-C_2OSi_3$
9-Oxa-1,3,5,7-tetrasilabicyclo[3.3.1]nonane
$C_2O_2P-C_2O_2P_2$
2,6,7-Trioxa-1,4-diphosphabicyclo[2.2.2]octane
3,7,9-Trioxa-2,4,6,8-tetraphosphabicyclo[3.3.1]=
nonane
C_3AlO-C_6
4H-1,3,2-Benzodioxaluminin
$C_3AsO_2-C_6$
4H-1,3,2-Benzodioxarsenin
C_3BNO-C_6
2H-1,3,2-Benzoxazaborine
$C_3BN-C_3BN_2$
[1,3,2]Diazaborino[1,2-a][1,3,2]diazaborine
$C_3BO-C_3BO_2$
[1,3,2]Dioxaborino[5,4-d]-1,3,2-dioxaborin
D-Xylitol, cyclic 2,4,3,5-diboronate
C_3NOS-C_6
1,2,3-Benzoxathiazine
4,1,2-Benzoxathiazine
$C_3NOSi-C_6$
4H-3,1,2-Benzoxazasiline
$C_3NS_2-C_2N_2$
2,3-Dithia-5,7-diazabicyclo[2.2.2]octane
$C_3N_2O-C_3N_2O$
[1,2,4]Oxadiazolo[6,5-e]-1,2,4-oxadiazole
$C_3N_2O-C_6$
1H-4,1,2-Benzoxadiazine
$C_3N_2P-C_3N_2P$
1,3,7-Triaza-5-phosphabicyclo[3.3.1]nonane
2,6,7-Triaza-1-phosphabicyclo[2.2.2]octane
$C_3N_2S-C_4N_2$
2H-Pyrimido[4,5-e]-1,2,4-thiadiazine
2H,8H-Pyrimido[2,1-b][1,3,4]thiadiazine
$C_3N_2S-C_5N$
2H-Pyrido[4,3-e]-1,2,4-thiadiazine
4H-Pyrido[2,3-e]-1,2,4-thiadiazine
$C_3N_2S-C_5$
6-Thia(6-S^{IV})-1,5-diazaspiro[5.5]undecane
$C_3N_3S-C_6$
1H-2,1,3-Benzothiadiazine
2H-1,2,3-Benzothiadiazine
2H-1,2,4-Benzothiadiazine
4H-1,2,4-Benzothiadiazine
$C_3N_3-C_3N_3$
1,3,5,7-Tetraazabicyclo[3.3.1]nonane
$C_3N_3-C_3NO$
[1,4]Oxazino[3,4-c][1,2,4]triazine
$C_3N_3-C_2N_2$

2H,8H-Pyrimido[2,1-b][1,3]thiazine
4H-Pyrimido[4,5-b][1,4]thiazine
7H-Pyrimido[4,5-b][1,4]thiazine
4H-Pyrimido[2,1-b][1,3]thiazin-5-ium
C_3NS-C_5OS
2-Oxa-7-thia-5-azabicyclo[2.2.2]octane
C_3NS-C_5N
Pyrido[2,1-c][1,4]thiazine
3H-Pyrido[2,3-b][1,4]thiazine
4H-Pyrido[2,1-b][1,3]thiazinium
1-Thia-5,9-diazaspiro[5.5]undecane
C_3NS-C_6
1H-1,2-Benzothiazine
1H-2,1-Benzothiazine
1H-2,3-Benzothiazine
2H-1,3-Benzothiazine
2H-3,1-Benzothiazine
4H-1,2-Benzothiazine
4H-3,1-Benzothiazine
C_3NSe-C_6
1-Selena-5-azaspiro[5.5]undecane
$C_4N-C_2N_2$
1,5-Diazabicyclo[3.3.1]nonane
1,4-Diazabicyclo[2.2.2]octane
Pteridine
6H-Pyrazino[1,2-c]pyrimidine
Pyridazino[1,2-a]pyridazine
Pyridazino[4,5-d]pyridazine
Pyrimido[4,5-c]pyridazine
Pyrimido[4,5-d]pyrimidine
Pyrimido[5,4-d]pyrimidine
2,4,6,8-Tetraazabicyclo[3.3.1]nonane
C_4N-C_5N
1,2-Diazabicyclo[3.3.1]nonane
3,9-Diazabicyclo[3.3.1]nonane
1,2-Diazabicyclo[2.2.2]octane
Pyrido[2,3-b]pyrazine
2H-Pyrido[3,4-b]pyrazine
4H-Pyrido[1,2-a]pyrazine
Pyrido[2,3-c]pyridazine
Pyrido[3,4-d]pyridazine
1H-Pyrido[1,2-b]pyridazine
Pyrido[2,3-d]pyrimidine
Pyrido[3,2-d]pyrimidine
2H-Pyrido[1,2-a]pyrimidine
3H-Pyrido[1,2-c]pyrimidine
4H-Pyrido[1,2-a]pyrimidine
2,4,9-Triazaspiro[5.5]undecane
C_4N-C_5O
1H-Pyrano[3,2-d]pyrimidine
1H-Pyrano[2,3-d]pyrimidine
C_4N-C_5S
2H-Thiopyrano[2,3-d]pyrimidine

2,3-Benzodithiin
$C_4Si_2-C_4$
2,3-Disilabicyclo[2.2.2]octane
C_5As-C_5As
1-Arsabicyclo[2.2.2]octane
C_5B-C_5B
9-Borabicyclo[3.3.1]nonane
C_5B-C_6
2-Borabicyclo[3.3.1]nonane
3-Borabicyclo[3.3.1]nonane
C_5N-C_5N
1-Azabicyclo[3.3.1]nonane
9-Azabicyclo[3.3.1]nonane
1-Azabicyclo[2.2.2]octane
Cinchonan
3,7-Diazabicyclo[3.3.1]nonane
2,5-Diazabicyclo[2.2.2]octane
2,6-Diazabicyclo[2.2.2]octane
1,9-Diazaspiro[5.5]undecane
10,11-Dinorcinchonan
1,5-Naphthyridine
1,6-Naphthyridine
1,7-Naphthyridine
1,8-Naphthyridine
2,6-Naphthyridine
2,7-Naphthyridine
2H-Quinolizine
4H-Quinolizine
C_5N-C_5O
1H-Pyrano[3,4-c]pyridine
1H-Pyrano[4,3-c]pyridine
2H-Pyrano[3,2-b]pyridine
2H-Pyrano[3,2-c]pyridine
3H-Pyrano[3,4-c]pyridine
4H-Pyrano[2,3-b]pyridine
4H-Pyrano[4,3-c]pyridine
6H-Pyrano[3,2-c]pyridine
7H-Pyrano[2,3-b]pyridine
C_5N-C_5S
3-Thia-7-azabicyclo[3.3.1]nonane
C_5N-C_6
3-Azabicyclo[3.3.1]nonane
2-Azabicyclo[2.2.2]octane
1-Azaspiro[5.5]undecane
2-Azaspiro[5.5]undecane
3-Azaspiro[5.5]undecane
Cinchonan
10,11-Dinorcinchonan
Emetan
Isoquinoline
11-Norcinchonan
Quinoline
C_5O-C_5O
2,5-Dioxabicyclo[2.2.2]octane
1,7-Dioxaspiro[5.5]undecane
9-Oxabicyclo[3.3.1]nonane
Pyrano[3,2-b]pyran
1H,3H-Pyrano[3,4-c]pyran
1H,5H-Pyrano[2,3-b]pyran
2H,5H-Pyrano[4,3-b]pyran

Figure 5.10 Ring Index: Chemical Abstracts. [Reprinted from Chemical Abstracts, Vol. 77, p. 8R, by permission of Chemical Abstracts Service.]

4H-Pyridazino[1,6-a]-1,3,5-triazine
Pyrimido[4,5-e]-1,2,4-triazine
Pyrimido[5,4-e]-1,2,4-triazine

C_3N_3-C_2N
Pyrido[3,2-d]-1,2,3-triazine
4H-Pyrido[1,2-a]-1,3,5-triazine
4H-Pyrido[2,1-c][1,2,4]triazine

C_3N_3-C_6
1,2,3-Benzotriazine
1,2,4-Benzotriazine
1,3,5-Triazaspiro[5.5]undecane

C_3OSSn-C_6
4H-3,1,2-Benzoxathiastannin

C_3OS-C_6
2,1,4-Benzoxadithiin

C_3O_3P-C_3O_3P
2,4,8,10-Tetraoxa-3,9-diphosphaspiro[5.5]undecane
2,6,7-Trioxa-1-phosphabicyclo[2.2.2]octane

C_3O_3P-C_3N
4H-1,3,2-Dioxaphosphorino[4,5-c]pyridine

C_3O_3P-C_6
4H-1,3,2-Benzodioxaphosphorin

C_3O_3S-C_6
2,4,1-Benzodioxathiin

C_3O_3Si-C_4
4H-1,3,2-Benzodioxasilin

C_3Si-C_3Si_3
1,3,4a,6,6-Pentasilanaphthalene
1,3,5,8-Tetrasilabicyclo[2.2.2]octane

C_4NO-C_2N_2
4H-Pyrazino[2,3-d][1,3]oxazine
6H-Pyrimido[5,4-b][1,4]oxazine

C_4NO-C_3N
1-Oxa-5,9-diazaspiro[5.5]undecane
Pyrido[2,1-c][1,4]oxazine
2H-Pyrido[4,3-b]-1,4-oxazine

C_4NO-C_6O
2H,5H-Pyrano[4,3-b]-1,4-oxazine

C_4NO-C_6
1H-2,3-Benzoxazine
2H-1,2-Benzoxazine
2H-1,3-Benzoxazine
2H-1,4-Benzoxazine
2H-3,1-Benzoxazine
4H-1,2-Benzoxazine
4H-1,3-Benzoxazine
4H-1,4-Benzoxazine
4H-3,1-Benzoxazine
3,1-Benzoxazin-3-ium

C_4NO-C_2N_2
2-Oxa-3-azabicyclo[2.2.2]octane
1-Oxa-2-azaspiro[5.5]undecane
1-Oxa-5-azaspiro[5.5]undecane
3-Oxa-1-azaspiro[5.5]undecane

C_4NS-C_2N_2
2H-Pyrazino[2,3-b]-1,4-thiazine
2H,6H-Pyrimido[2,1-b][1,3]thiazine
2H,6H-Pyrimido[6,1-b][1,3]thiazine

Cinnoline
2,3-Diazabicyclo[2.2.2]octane
Phthalazine
Quinazoline
Quinoxaline

C_2OP-C_6

C_2OS-C_2OS
9-Oxa-3,7-dithiabicyclo[3.3.1]nonane

C_2OS-C_2N
1,4-Oxathiino[3,2-b]pyridine

C_2OS-C_6
1,2-Benzoxathiin
1,4-Benzoxathiin
4H-1,3-Benzoxathiin
4H-3,1-Benzoxathiin

C_2O-CO_2
4,10-Dioxa-2,8-dioxoniaspiro[5.5]undeca-2,8-diene
[1,3]Dioxino[5,4-d]-1,3-dioxin
[1,4]Dioxino[2,3-b]-1,4-dioxin
4H,5H-[1,3]Dioxino[4,5-d]-1,3-dioxin
Glucitol, 1,3:2,4-di-O-methylene-
Ribitol, 2,4:3,5-di-O-methylene-
2,4,8,10-Tetraoxaspiro[5.5]undecane
2,6,7-Trioxabicyclo[2.2.2]octane

C_2O-C_3N
1,5-Dioxa-9-azaspiro[5.5]undecane
4H-1,3-Dioxino[4,5-c]pyridine
4H-1,3-Dioxino[5,4-b]pyridine
4H-1,3-Dioxino[5,4-c]pyridine

C_2O-C_6O
Glucopyranose, 4,6-O-methylene-
Hex-2-enopyranose, 4,6-O-methylene-
Hexopyranose, 4,6-O-methylene-
Mannopyranose, 4,6-O-methylene-
Pyrano[3,2-d]-1,3-dioxin
Pyrano[3,4-d]-1,3-dioxin
6H-Pyrano[2,3-b]-1,4-dioxin
Streptamine, O-4,6-O-ethylideneglucopyran-osyl-(1→6)-
Talopyranose, 4,6-O-methylene-

C_2O-C_6
1,4-Benzodioxin
2,3-Benzodioxin
4H-1,3-Benzodioxin
1,4-Dioxaspiro[5.5]undecane
1,5-Dioxaspiro[5.5]undecane
2,4-Dioxaspiro[5.5]undecane

C_2P-C_2P_2
1,4-Diphosphabicyclo[2.2.2]octane

C_2P_2-C_6
1,4-Benzodiphosphorin

C_2S-C_3S_2
1,5,7,11-Tetrathiaspiro[5.5]undecane
2,4,8,10-Tetrathiaspiro[5.5]undecane

C_2S-C_6
1,4-Benzodithiin

C_5O-C_6
1H-2-Benzopyran
2H-1-Benzopyran
3H-2-Benzopyran
4H-1-Benzopyran
5H-1-Benzopyran
7H-1-Benzopyran
8aH-1-Benzopyran
1-Benzopyrylium
2-Benzopyrylium
2-Oxabicyclo[3.3.1]nonane
3-Oxabicyclo[3.3.1]nonane
2-Oxabicyclo[2.2.2]octane
1-Oxaspiro[5.5]undecane

C_5P-C_3P
9-Phosphabicyclo[3.3.1]nonane

C_5S-C_5S
9-Thiabicyclo[3.3.1]nonane
Thiopyrano[3,2-b]thiopyran
2H,5H-Thiopyrano[4,3-b]thiopyran

C_5S-C_6
1H-2-Benzothiopyran
2H-1-Benzothiopyran
4H-1-Benzothiopyran
1-Benzothiopyrylium
2-Thiabicyclo[2.2.2]octane

C_5Se-C_6
4H-1-Benzoselenin
2-Benzoseleninium

C_5Si-C_5Si
1-Silabicyclo[2.2.2]octane

C_5Si-C_6
2-Silabicyclo[2.2.2]octane
2-Silanaphthalene

C_6-C_6
Bicyclo[3.3.1]nonane
Bicyclo[2.2.2]octane
Naphthalene
Spiro[5.5]undecane

N_4P_2-N_4P_2
2,3,5,6,7,8-Hexaaza-1,4-diphosphabicyclo[2.2.2]octane

O_3Si-O_3Si_3
Spiro[5.5]pentasiloxane

Si_6-Si_6
Bicyclo[3.3.1]nonasilane
Bicyclo[2.2.2]octasilane

6,7

C_2N_7-C_2N_2
9H-1,2,4-Triazino[5,6-e][1,4]diazepine

C_2N-C_6N
[1,2,4]Triazino[4,3-a]azepine

C_2N_2-C_3N_3
2,3,4-Trithia-6,8-diazabicyclo[3.2.2]nonane

C_2N-C_2N_2
5H,7H-Pyrimido[2,1-b][1,5,3]dithiazepine

C_2N_2-C_2NO
Pyrimido[4,5-e][1,4]oxazepine

formulas. Hydrogen, shown or not, must be used in calculating the molecular formula for the compound. Under the heading "C_6–C_6" there are three other ring compounds also studied in this volume of *Chemical Abstracts*. The four ring compounds found under this heading may be studied as named or may be studied as derivatives or addition compounds in the abstracts of the volume.

The ring index is especially useful if the chemist does not know the systematic, index name of the ring compound in which he is interested.

Patent Concordance *for* Chemical Abstracts

The sample page in Figure 5.11 shows the structure of this unique concordance. The use is comparatively simple.

Structure. The running head informs the reader that he is viewing page 5 of a patent concordance ("5 pc"). The page is divided into four columns, and each column is divided into four parts. The first part gives the name of the country and the number of the patent issued there. The second part of the column gives the name of the country issuing the identical or closely related patent of the same patentee or assignee. The third part of the column gives the patent number of the identical or closely related patent. The fourth part of the column gives the *CA* volume number and abstract number.

Content. In patent search and other work it may be useful or even vital to discover if the same patent has been issued in another country. The patent concordance is a convenient way of discovering this.

This particular patent concordance covers abstracts related only to chemistry and chemical engineering.

Numerical Patent Index *for* Chemical Abstracts

Figure 5.12 is a sample page from the numerical patent index of *CA*. The user is simply guided from the name of the people in the country in which the patent was issued and the number of the patent to the abstract for the patent.

Structure. The sample page has a running head that lets the user know that he is using *Chemical Abstracts*, Volume 79, Issue 25, and that he is looking at the first (and only) page. The name of the people of the country issuing the patent heads the list of patents. The patent number is followed by the reference number of the abstract—a serial number attached to the abstract and used to identify it in the indexes. For some countries, references to abstracts of patent applications are separated from patents issued in the index. References to abstracts of additions to existing patents are also listed separately in the index.

The numerical patent index is invaluable if one is given only a patent number with which to search.

Continuity Index for Information Science Abstracts

Figure 5.13, a sample page from the Continuity Index of *Information Science Abstracts* (*ISA*), can be used to illustrate the structure and content of this experimental index.

Structure. The running head carries the name of the journal, the month and year of issue, and the page number. This index has eight columns. At the head of segments of each column are the volume and year numbers for earlier issues of *ISA*. Following these headings are, on the left of the column, boldfaced, serial numbers of abstracts that have appeared in the volume and year indicated above. Indented under this are abstract numbers in the current issue or in issues subsequent to the issue of the heading in the column. Following the indented abstract number is a code letter indicating the relationship between the two abstracts. For example, under the column heading "Vol. 1, 1966" appears the first index entry, "0047, 68–0815 M." This means that the abstract numbered 0047, which appeared in Volume 1 in 1966 is a work continued by the work reported in the abstract in *ISA* that appeared in Volume 68, and was serially numbered 815. (The code "M" indicates that the second abstract reports work that is a continuation of the work reported in the earlier abstract.)

Content. The entries in the continuity index specify the relationship that exists between two abstracts, by means of a code that is explained in a section entitled "key" on the page in Figure 5.13.

Thus, the continuity index is a combination of an erratum sheet and a citation index. Because the entries lack modifications, there is some uncertainty on the part of the user as to whether or not the abstract cited will actually be found useful when examined.

5 pc

JULY–DEC. 1973—PATENT CONCORDANCE

PATENT NUMBER	CORRESPONDING PATENT	CA REF. NUMBER	PATENT NUMBER	CORRESPONDING PATENT	CA REF. NUMBER	PATENT NUMBER	CORRESPONDING PATENT	CA REF. NUMBER	PATENT NUMBER	CORRESPONDING PATENT	CA REF. NUMBER

1285800	SWISS	512556	78,125846X
	US	3755343	
1285813	GER	2013506	
1285829	GER	2042450	
1285830	GER	2060668	
1285836	GER	2013506	
1285860	US	3751259	78, 10199W
1285917	GER	1955522	
1285961	GER	1938606	
1285992	FR	2015806	
1286030	GER	2024604	
1286161	GER	2102631	
1286183	GER	2057239	
1286216	GER	2061507	
1286225	GER	2106620	
1286232	GER	1900898	
	GER	1927908	
1286307	US	3770606	77,119849P
1286516	GER	1954119	
1286528	GER	1953582	
1286560	GER	2063312	
1286572	GER	1955065	
1286573	GER	2015063	
1286734	FR	2061574	
	FR	2080840	
1286741	GER	1900349	
1286755	GER	2031288	
1286798	GER	2007603	
1286856	GER	1947178	
1286885	FR	2065117	
1286886	GER	2048548	
1287177	S AFR	70 06222	78, 31584H
	US	3758331	
1287240	GER	2126893	
1287243	GER	2103592	
1287251	GER	2027452	
1287317	GER	2052256	
1287329	GER	2045428	
1287500	GER	2064810	
1287547	GER	2112530	
1287621	GER	1937439	
1287672	GER	2033642	
1287701	GER	2105260	
1287898	GER	1943975	
1287899	GER	1943915	
1287944	GER	1949023	
1287978	GER	2131455	
1287999	US	3748126	78, 10171F
1288005	GER	2041151	
1288010	GER	2046689	
1288082	GER	1949575	
1288111	GER	2129171	
1288117	GER	2032418	
1288138	S AFR	70 08448	
1288168	GER	2010049	
1288367	GER	2056782	
1288480	GER	1935567	
1288540	GER	1943915	
1288583	GER	1959649	
1288652	GER	2044281	
1288666	FR	2083778	
1288699	GER	2042829	
1288706	FR	2085023	78,147348P
1288738	GER	2100499	
1288806	GER	1949590	
1288833	FR	2037973	
1288872	GER	2118918	
1289003	GER	2062613	
1289042	GER	2005393	
1289057	GER	2062025	
1289137	GER	1961326	
1289182	GER	2046597	
1289197	GER	2048239	
1289215	GER	2040091	
1289265	GER	2024302	
1289283	GER	2109910	
1289643	GER	2018362	
1289650	US	3764396	78, 9409H
1289740	GER	2060333	
1289755	GER	2008791	
1289791	GER	2102203	
1289850	GER	1960917	
1289852	GER	1807585	
1289876	GER	2052397	
1290080	FR	2072984	
1290291	GER	2102889	
1290301	GER	2118692	
1290384	GER	1952585	

1293427	GER	2059916	
1293443	GER	2023428	
1293483	GER	2101866	
1293500	GER	2107698	
	GER	2107699	
	GER	2107774	
1293507	GER	2111775	
1293565	GER	2021195	
1293569	FR	2023340	
1293632	GER	2010827	
1293744	GER	2161570	
1293833	S AFR	70 07944	
1293857	GER	2128465	
1293870	GER	2034682	
1293887	GER	2126588	
1293982	FR	2064940	78,153681H
	US	3707375	
1294116	GER	1954284	
1294141	GER	2021307	
1294171	GER	2001903	
	GER	2001904	
1294172	GER	2001904	
1294205	GER	2040207	
1294214	GER	2041487	
1294272	GER	2100584	
1294335	GER	1954205	
1294430	GER	2132900	
1294455	GER	1960267	
1294467	GER	1956496	
1294474	FR	2026091	
1294582	GER	2002815	
1294613	GER	2117906	
1294614	GER	2019431	
1294703	GER	2124105	
1294711	GER	2004276	
1294734	GER	2040554	
1294763	GER	2005134	
1294768	GER	1953344	
1294771	GER	2003421	
1294812	GER	2128730	
1294889	GER	1812556	
1294975	GER	2005937	
1295063	FR	2023568	
1295145	FR	2057914	
1295235	GER	2060912	
1295338	GER	2110635	
1295366	GER	2047427	
1295371	GER	2063247	
1295403	FR	2076724	78, 96449M
	GER	2103595	
	S AFR	71 00460	
	US	3761445	
1295496	GER	2036668	
1295561	FR	2061484	
	GER	2104570	
1295565	GER	2123433	
1295605	S AFR	71 03575	
1295678	GER	1959400	
	GER	1965968	
1295679	GER	1965968	
1295696	GER	2006215	
	GER	2017651	
1295721	GER	2004899	
1295722	GER	2046204	
1295798	GER	2130338	
1295829	GER	2021795	
1295932	GER	2025781	
1295962	GER	2010685	
1295992	GER	2000127	
1296100	GER	2032873	
1296133	GER	1909272	
1296159	GER	2048812	
1296167	GER	2006776	
1296276	FR	2074836	
	GER	2021070	
1296319	GER	2015157	
1296331	GER	2123123	
1296373	GER	2009965	
1296383	GER	2038240	
1296425	GER	2045095	
1296447	GER	1919228	
1296458	GER	2031205	
1296481	GER	2107467	
	GER	2107468	
	GER	2107469	
1296504	GER	2123319	
1296510	GER	2126533	78, 88617A
	S AFR	71 05734	

1298309	GER	2125965	
1298311	GER	2003144	
1298313	GER	2106510	
1298318	GER	2114300	
1298407	GER	2136478	
1298504	GER	1920246	
1298563	GER	1961927	
1298583	GER	2036250	
1298595	GER	2010418	
1298596	GER	2010418	
1298603	US	3746325	78, 97701A
1298607	FR	2070210	
1298644	GER	2013393	
1298657	FR	2075755	78,160502D
	GER	2102512	
1298682	GER	1957903	
1298683	GER	1957903	
1298786	GER	2118390	
1298800	GER	1816841	
1298821	GER	2038168	
1298895	GER	2041420	
1298955	GER	2049754	
1299041	GER	2125926	
1299107	S AFR	70 01486	
1299120	GER	2050085	
1299155	US	3759985	78,135965M
1299180	US	3716329	78,137853K
1299198	GER	1965304	
1299245	BELG	767195	
1299246	NETH	7108386	
1299275	GER	2012533	
1299333	GER	2101869	
1299406	GER	1921464	
1299416	GER	2118917	
1299542	GER	1913097	
	GER	1926538	
1299553	GER	2111735	
1299561	GER	2000468	
1299570	S AFR	71 04255	
1299650	GER	2059190	
1299669	GER	2027077	
1299670	GER	2027077	
1299746	US	3764298	78, 75121J
1299801	GER	2002208	
1299950	GER	2043192	
1299994	GER	2002371	
1300134	GER	2010550	
1300137	GER	2011982	
1300223	GER	2010179	
1300252	US	3657111	
1300266	GER	2025817	
1300307	GER	2050534	
1300308	GER	1945967	
1300445	GER	2010494	
1300450	GER	2014276	
1300496	GER	2035558	
1300514	GER	2139563	
1300558	GER	2017898	
1300722	GER	2101926	
1300839	GER	2142427	
1300846	JAP	73 7913	78, 73245D
	JAP	7323830	
1300880	GER	2128296	
1300964	GER	2010760	
1300970	GER	2036936	
	GER	2064918	
1301052	GER	2124525	
1301058	GER	2111668	
1301145	GER	2023475	
1301152	GER	2030653	
1301158	GER	2038782	
1301174	GER	2009338	
1301175	GER	2009338	
1301187	GER	2020518	
1301238	GER	2136508	
1301278	GER	2007947	
1301287	GER	1961552	
1301295	GER	1954252	
1301296	FR	2150552	78, 99975S
1301298	GER	2058942	
1301310	GER	2056718	
1301390	GER	2052114	
1301403	GER	2018233	
1301418	GER	2128046	
1301465	GER	2040708	
1301492	GER	1945053	
1301505	GER	1964996	
1301676	GER	1811657	

1304825	GER	2139627	
1304836	GER	2004012	
	GER	2004048	
1304864	GER	2043746	
	S AFR	70 05709	
1304865	GER	2042367	
1304871	GER	2009390	
1304965	GER	2126478	
1304966	GER	2129788	
1304987	FR	2084344	
	GER	2110665	
1305009	GER	2108459	
1305036	GER	2004048	
1305037	US	3770484	78,142450F
1305071	GER	2033677	
1305128	GER	2057942	
1305133	GER	2025377	
1305136	GER	2058317	
1305144	FR	2095076	
1305157	GER	2149740	
1305160	GER	2165396	
1305250	GER	2104615	
1305260	GER	2035231	
1305262	GER	2044405	
1305323	GER	2030509	
1305370	US	3759792	78,122669F
1305376	US	3756458	78,161281T
1305413	GER	2021306	
1305510	GER	2143816	
1305518	GER	2139288	
1305569	GER	2063269	
1305611	GER	2024345	
1305618	GER	2059614	
1305621	GER	2022216	
1305636	GER	2126129	
1305661	GER	2125037	
1305678	FR	2131156	79, 32490G
1305724	GER	2027287	
1305748	US	3743538	78,103639E
1305752	GER	2110523	
1305772	FR	1597514	
1305793	GER	1923990	
1305794	GER	1963188	
1305795	GER	2013431	
1305807	GER	2143986	
1305810	FR	2066134	
1305842	GER	2133472	
1305846	GER	2132665	
1305855	S AFR	71 03575	
1305985	GER	1928129	
1306000	FR	2155884	79, 19907D
1306093	GER	2021728	
1306243	GER	2042192	
1306263	GER	2024859	
1306283	GER	2015586	
1306309	GER	2155919	
1306313	GER	2122633	
1306332	GER	2114190	
1306374	GER	2000793	
1306401	GER	2014895	
1306446	FR	2100345	79, 3841S
	GER	2133906	
1306449	GER	2041360	
1306558	GER	2140601	
1306619	GER	2109010	
1306638	GER	2142916	
1306665	GER	2141918	
1306693	GER	2025723	
1306721	FR	2042588	
	GER	2020510	
	GER	2020560	
	GER	2023401	
1306722	FR	2042588	
	GER	2020510	
	GER	2020560	
	GER	2023401	
1306724	FR	2042588	
	GER	2020510	
	GER	2020560	
	GER	2023401	
1306725	FR	2042588	
	GER	2020510	
	GER	2020560	
	GER	2023401	
1306726	FR	2042588	
	GER	2020510	
	GER	2020560	
	GER	2023401	

***Figure 5.11** Patent concordance:* Chemical Abstracts. [*Reprinted from* Chemical Abstracts, *July–Dec. 1973, p. 5 pc, by permission of Chemical Abstracts Service.*]

NUMERICAL PATENT INDEX

AUSTRIAN

NO.	REF.
308760	146538j

BELGIAN

NO.	REF.
787258	145366q

BRITISH

NO.	REF.
1307041	144898c
1323555	146379h
1325900	146170h
1326013	145988u
014	146000c
015	145940x
302	144884v
327	146272x
443	146184r
780	145959k
999	146255q
1327315	145968n
331	146532c
483	146507y
542	146205y
581	146201a
707	146217d
1328205	146565r
1329140	145956q
387	144867s
612	145065r
956	146265u
1330135	146416t
209	145146t
248	145957h

CZECHO-SLOVAKIAN

NO.	REF.
148770	146289c
926	145061m
149061	146807w
207	145970g
270	146295c
278	146292z
279	146061y
293	146251k
763	146250j
803	146197x
822	145991q
831	146404n
839	146198y

FRENCH DEMANDE

NO.	REF.
2210189	146661u
401	145050g
544	146857n
604	146856m
620	146646t
623	145949g
633	145368s
650	146658y
667	146180m
672	146426w
687	146519d
762	146402k
799	146411p
836	146410m
838	146420q
916	146704k
2211101	146428y
863	146655r
2212188	146653t
218	146208b
263	146851f
340	145951b
600	146263s
642	145968m
674	146664x
695	144878w
929	146385g
2213233	146177r
271	146650q
408	146205y
483	146201a
505	146217d
568	146565r
785	145956q
799	144867s
864	145065r
2214058	146259u
059	146657x
405	146850e
608	146419w
610	145909a
611	146807w
627	146012h
2215089	146045x
549	146189w
955	146253n
2216115	146168p
116	146250j
117	146251k
293	146197x
763	146252k
803	146197x
822	145991q
831	146197x
839	146198y
2239504	145991q
2253031	146404n
483	145950a
2262626	148465q
2300327	146214a
2301527	145517b
2302057	146382d
386	146186t

GERMAN

NO.	REF.
1518931	145962f
1542681	145370m
1593472	146027s
1688031	145975n
1768256	146024p
781	145980k
1793565	146005h
1957008	145449u
2221736	145983p
2244234	146011g

GERMAN (EAST)

NO.	REF.
92913	146016n
93164	146182u
95225	145953d
226	145954e
351	145994t
365	146017p
371	145978r
374	145939d
839	145971h
96062	145067t
393	145671
727	144895z

ISRAELI

NO.	REF.
36022	146376e
023	146373b

JAPANESE

NO.	REF.
72 43807	143514n
808	143520m
809	143515p
810	143519t
033	146429z
753	146391f
757	146852g
73 27306	146383e
307	146392q
73 28402	145947e
403	145948f
409	145961e
413	145969p
414	145973k
415	145981m
417	146019r
419	146003f
420	146020j
425	146185a
427	146261p
429	146066d
430	146201n
431	146215b
432	146296d
73 32115	145972j

JAPANESE KOKAI

NO.	REF.
72 39698	144864p
73 22618	143525s
73 32811	146703j
836	146236j
73 40729	146150h
730	146150b
733	146157j
734	146160e
739	146151c
742	146225e
744	146232e
73 43290	144890u
73 48383	145079y
418	146370y
463	146396m
73 49701	146153e
776	146551h
781	146399q
782	146558r
783	146568u
73 52552	146510u
775	145372p
783	146421r
73 54064	146535f
085	146514y
096	146530a
099	146569v
73 56603	146560k
607	146589q
612	146226f
615	146001d
616	146845g
618	146844f
620	146210w
621	145984q

NETHERLANDS APPLICATION

NO.	REF.
72 01502	145060k
673	146220z

ROMANIAN

NO.	REF.
49844	146173m
52806	146238m

SOUTH AFRICAN

NO.	REF.
72 04486	146846h
72 05136	144888z

SPANISH

NO.	REF.
403003	146389m

SWISS

NO.	REF.
538295	145054m
451	145983g
539636	146424u
637	146423t

USSR

NO.	REF.
215992	146649w
322999	146737y
326862	146371z
332738	146655v
360844	144861k
366739	146213z
382628	146525c
629	146539k
633	146381c
634	146513k
637	145974m
638	145979q
383728	144866r
396946	146235h
389970	146152d
092	146395k
099	146647u
103	146656w
105	146652s
390078	146228h
079	146230c
083	146203w
096	146648v
103	146662v
391124	146204x

UNITED STATES

NO.	REF.
083	146523a
3761354	144873r
356	144896x
530	146293a
3762998	144887y
3763037	146139e
148	146417u
149	146738z
163	146540d
181	146515z
181	146567t
184	146502t
194	146470u
199	146247p
213	146135a
237	146252m
238	146165k
243	146191r
3764522	146137c
597	146644r
629	146183q
3766197	146650q
198	146663w
209	146136b
244	146239n
250	146270r
276	146231d
280	146196w
287	146643q
290	146414g
290	146149g
291	146147f
3767704	146146e
722	146143b
723	146145d
3769238	146138d
317	146142a
324	146256r
325	146222b
327	146240f
349	146221a
351	146144c
359	146182p
360	146141z
427	146268w
431	146237k

2124347 145063p
2151132 144881s
2157683 145369t
692 146414r
818 145073s
819 145076v
2158055 145070p
403 146219f
404 146218e
2160479 145062n
2161007 146415s
776 146413q
2162438 146242h
562 146387j

FRENCH

2149674 144259v
2157086 146140y
132 146188v

FRENCH
(ADDITION)

2162696 146289d

GERMAN
(OFFEN.)

1966666 146808x
695 145992r
2065461 146705m
465 146172k
477 145982n
2141468 146511v
2149586 143532s
2202007 145952c
205 145364n
734 145987t
2203326 146006j
2205065 146512w
565 146659z
745 146548n
814 146505w
2206300 146163h
385 146503u
861 143516q
862 146002e
2207020 146263r
098 146374c
235 146571q
460 146166m
856 146418v
922 145371n
2208368 146271s
437 146562n
757 146660t
917 145363m
2209298 146742w
312 146741v
528 146202v

567 146573s
2303118 146008m
170 145995u
2304414 145266u
780 144897b
963 145955f
2305404 146004g
495 146248q
870 146847j
2306222 146179t
306 145993s
433 145942z
738 146264s
739 146267v
2307233 146167n
263 146858p
2308305 146531b
494 146216c
731 146739a
816 146265t
831 146533d
858 146546k
2309023 146258t
108 144863n
160 146425v
379 146378g
768 146194u
794 144044w
983 143526t
2310285 146813v
287 146504v
302 146814w
329 146811t
330 146022m
331 146021k
334 146549p
544 144260p
741 146724s
827 146848k
985 145996v
2311006 144893x
059 144262r
099 146853h
277 146014k
391 146526d
524 146817z
597 146534e
778 146725t
786 146854j
822 146368d
828 144883u
2312256 146516a
284 146723r
373 145964h
374 145965j
422 146386h
452 146722q
696 144874s
728 146211x
750 146192s
2313017 146062z
068 145941y
191 144261q
227 146393h

812 143522p
815 143521n
816 143517r
820 143518s
826 143531r
72 46792 146809y
72 47588 145051h
72 48662 143523q
72 50365 143033e
379 143513m
337 145059s
389 144876u
392 144892w
73 00054 143524r
073 144899d
075 144870n
078 144885w
946 145057q
73 01165 146269x
194 144905c
199 144880r
200 144879x
499 143535v
500 143534u
501 143533t
73 02780 145075u
781 145066s
782 145074t
790 144891v
792 144872q
800 144877v
73 05899 146556p
918 144906d
73 12990 144896a
73 14042 145052j
075 144903a
077 144862m
078 144868t
73 16178 145053k
179 145058r
181 145055n
183 145072r
73 17596 145056p
73 19626 146390e
73 20535 145976p
543 146067e
544 146063a
547 146394j
73 21935 146249r
73 22682 145944b
683 145945c
684 145946d
685 146009n
699 146384f
702 146007k
704 146406q
705 146405p
710 146408s
711 146407r
73 23425 146023n
73 25182 146521y
199 146570p
200 146559s
73 26020 146554m

623 146018q
625 146025q
626 146026r
629 146377f
630 146158k
633 146171j
637 146195v
641 146176q
692 146564q
73 57910 146806v
948 146246n
949 146229j
950 146260n
951 146233f
960 146816y
962 146294b
963 146290x
73 58121 143509q
122 143508p
123 143507n
124 143527u
73 59087 145365p
73 61614 146175p
630 143528v
633 143529w
634 143530q
638 143510h
689 144900x
693 144882t
73 62708 145967m
709 145966k
718 146015m
722 145985r
723 145989v
729 146174n
731 146244k
732 146227g
733 146223c
747 146291y
760 146520x
761 146524b
770 146552j
775 146547m
776 146553k
777 146541e
778 146542f
779 146545j
780 146543g
781 146544h
782 146537h
783 146536g
784 146427x
928 143511j
930 143512k
971 145064q
992 144902z
995 144875t
73 64064 146369e
074 146401j
079 146815x
73 68597 146561m
600 146810s
73 75560 146013j
563 146375d

392059 146161f
060 146162g
063 146178s
070 146654u
393272 146366b
273 146367c
274 146010f
275 146403m
278 146380b
394347 146154f
348 146155g
349 146297e
350 145960d
351 146159m
352 146200t
353 146199z
354 145998x
355 146234g
356 146245m
357 146299g
359 145990p
360 146300a
361 145986s
362 146298f
363 146212y
364 146181n
365 146028t
366 146744y
367 146363y
368 146365a
370 146372a
371 146364z
372 146411n
373 146501s
380 146209c

UNITED STATES

3741871 143885j
876 143884h
3748231 144901y
319 145069v
3753859 144869u
3755118 146397n
376 146241g
479 146642p
577 145071q
3756951 146206z
3758540 145367r
559 146849m
568 146257s
3759687 145373q
714 145077w
715 145078x
911 146563p
933 146522z
940 146527e
951 146528f
952 146529g
956 146398p
976 146555n
3760014 146164j
082 146518c

***Figure 5.12** Numerical patent index:* Chemical Abstracts. [*Reprinted from* Chemical Abstracts, *Vol. 79, No. 25, 24 Dec. 1973, by permission of Chemical Abstracts Service.*]

Continuity Index to Volume 4

This index is intended to be a convenient guide to some of the important relationships between abstracts which have appeared in *Information Science Abstracts*. It is called a "continuity" index because such relationships may continue to arise or become apparent long after the initial publication of an abstract. The index design is experimental. Comments from users are earnestly invited. This listing supplements, but does not replace, the three-year cumulation which appeared on pages 223-227 of the 1968 December issue. The listing below contains only relationships identified during 1969.

KEY

Code letters indicate relationships between lightface abstract and the boldface (left justified) abstract under which it is listed. ("AUIN" indicates annual author index, rather than an abstract; "CNIN" indicates continuity index; "ABBR" indicates list of standard abbreviations.)

A — an application of (the boldface reference)
C — corroborates or affirms
D — rebuts or rejects
E — erratum, corrects the original text of
F — erratum, corrects the abstract of
G — provides availability data on
M — a work continued by
N — a continuation of
R — reviews, discusses, or compares
S — part of the same series or collection as
U — abstract is replaced by
V — a different published version of

0341
69-1080 G
69-2638 C
0368
69-0010 N
0481
65-2638 G
0748
69-1358 N
0760
69-1358 N
0779
68-1409 U
0789
69-1735 N
0806
69-1102 M
0815
66-0047 N
69-1766 G
0835
69-1167 R
0845
69-1815 N
0846
69-0099 N
0873
69-1080 F
0876
69-0524 G
0881

1107
69-1080 G
1124
69-1080 FG
1129
69-1080 G
1130
69-1080 G
1136
69-1080 G
1138
69-0243 D
1160
69-1072 V
1166
67-1208 V
1175
65-2638 G
1203
69-1080 G
1245
69-1766 G
1305
69-0089 U
69-0524 G
1306
69-0545 VY
1358
69-0524 G

VOL. 4 1969

ABBR
69-1080 E
0001
69-1080 G
0004
69-0010 Y
0007
69-0008 X
69-0012 X
69-0018 X
69-0019 X
69-0020 X
69-0026 X
69-0027 X
69-0030 R
69-0031 X
69-0033 X
69-0054 X
69-0056 X
0008
69-0007 Y
0010
68-0368 M
69-0004 X
69-0017 X
69-0029 M
69-0079 X
69-0437 X
69-0443 X
69-0444 X
69-0449 X
69-0474 X
69-0476 X
69-0490 X
69-0521 X
0012
69-0007 Y
0014
69-0207 X
69-0226 X
69-0227 X
69-0235 X
69-0262 X
69-0281 X
69-0295 X
69-0296 X
69-0297 X
69-0298 X
0017
69-0010 Y
0018
69-0007 Y
0019
69-0007 Y
0020
69-0007 Y
65-2638 G
0021
69-0492 X
69-0494 X
69-0495 X
69-0500 X
69-0501 X
69-0502 X
69-0503 X
69-0506 X
69-0508 X
69-0509 X
69-0511 X
69-0514 X
69-0515 X
69-0519 X
69-1080 F
0026
69-0007 Y
0027
69-0007 Y
0029
69-0010 AN
69-0119 A
0031
69-0007 Y
0033
69-0007 Y
0034
67-0483 M
69-0199 X
69-0201 X
69-0202 X
69-0471 X
69-0482 X
69-0486 X
69-0493 X
0035
69-0037 X
69-0038 X
69-0039 X
69-0040 X
69-0042 X
69-0043 X
69-0044 X
69-0046 X
69-0048 X
69-0050 X
69-0051 X
69-0053 X
69-0055 X
69-0057 X
69-0058 X
69-0059 X
69-0062 X
69-0063 X
69-0064 X
69-0068 X
69-0555 V
0037
0038
69-0035 Y
0039
69-0035 Y

W — a replacement or supplemental abstract of
X — a portion of
Y — a composite work containing

VOL. 1
1966

0047	0892		
68-0815 M	69-2638 G		
69-1766 G	0895		
0367	65-1361 N		
0973	0901		
69-0833 N	67-0595 W		
0819	69-0374 V		
69-0921 N	1065		
0838	69-0528 R		
69-1588 N	1073		
0960	69-1048 N		
0989	1208		
69-1766 F	68-1166 V		
	1211		
	69-0528 R		
	1275		
	69-1080 G		

VOL. 2
1967

VOL. 3
1968

0358	AUIN
69-1791 R	69-1080 E
0371	69-1766 E
65-0524 G	CNIN
0452	69-1080 E
65-0644 N	0094
0521	0096
69-1080 G	0293
0595	0327
67-C901 U	0330
0702	0837
66-0960 M	0883
69-0099 N	0330
0786	
69-0639 V	
0837	
69-1280 N	
0883	
0330	

69-0736 A
65-0736 N
69-1080 G
65-1248 N
69-0940 M

0892	69-0651 N
0893	69-2638 G
0894	0891
0895	69-1080 G
0896	0892
C901	69-1080 C
0902	0893
0903	69-1C80 G
0905	0894
0908	69-1766 G
0909	0895
0928	69-1C8C G
0933	0896
0948	67-C41C R
0957	1065
1029	69-108C G
1043	0902
1047	69-1080 G
1049	0903
1091	69-1080 G
	0905
	69-1080 G
	0908
	69-1C80 G
	0909
	69-1C80 G
	0928
	69-1CE0 G
	0933
	69-1080 F
	0948
	65-1C80 C
	0957
	69-1C80 FG
	1029
	69-15E8 M
	1043
	69-0524 F
	1047
	69-1248 N
	1049
	69-0940 M
	1091
	69-1C80 F

1359	69-0100 X	69-0047 X	69-C2C3 X
69-1080 G	69-0119 X	69-0060 X	69-0204 X
69-2638 G	69-0133 X	69-0146 X	69-0205 X
1360	69-0148 X	69-0229 X	69-0206 X
69-0559 F	69-0159 X	69-0247 X	69-C208 X
69-1080 G	69-0165 X	69-0263 X	69-C209 X
1363	69-0174 X	69-0266 X	69-0210 X
69-0559 N	69-0180 X	69-0273 X	69-0212 X
69-0560 N	69-0189 X	69-0282 X	69-C213 X
69-1C8C G	69-0198 X	69-0283 X	69-0215 X
69-2638 G	69-0200 X	69-0286 X	69-0216 X
1387	69-0223 X	69-0299 X	69-0217 X
69-0524 G	69-0253 X	69-0301 X	69-0218 X
1393	69-0254 X	69-0305 X	65-0219 X
69-0312 U	69-0256 X	69-0307 X	69-C220 X
1404	69-0258 X	69-0308 X	69-0221 X
68-0775 W	69-0265 X	69-0309 X	69-0222 X
1409	69-0267 X	69-0316 X	65-0224 X
68-0779 W	69-0279 X	69-0353 X	69-0225 X
1419	69-0280 X	69-0356 X	69-0228 X
69-0524 F	69-0285 X	69-0358 X	69-C231 X
1424	69-03C4 X	69-0371 X	69-0233 X
69-0344 N	69-0319 X	69-C375 X	69-0234 X
69-08C6 N	69-0321 X	69-0379 X	69-0236 X
1434	69-0323 X	69-0411 X	65-C237 X
69-1080 F	69-0324 X	69-0439 X	69-0238 X
1437	69-0326 X	69-0445 X	69-0239 X
69-1080 G	69-0328 X	69-0446 X	69-0240 X
1448	69-0330 X	69-0450 X	69-0241 X
69-0524 G	69-0331 X	69-0451 X	69-0245 X
1467	69-0333 X	69-0452 X	69-0246 X
69-0908 N	69-0335 X	69-0453 X	69-0250 X
69-0909 N	69-0367 X	69-0454 X	69-0251 X
69-0910 N	69-0376 X	69-0455 X	69-0252 X
1536	69-C41C X	C9-C457 X	69-0259 X
69-15C8 M	69-0418 X	69-0458 X	69-0260 X
1541	69-042C X	69-0459 X	69-0261 X
69-0524 F	69-0424 X	69-C460 X	69-0268 X
1553	69-0427 X	69-C461 X	69-0284 X
69-1080 G	69-0430 X	69-0464 X	69-0287 X
1564	69-0432 X	69-0469 X	69-0292 X
69-2621 N	69-0433 X	69-0470 X	69-0293 X
69-0524 N	69-0435 X	69-C493 X	69-0363 X
		69-C489 X	69-0465 X

69-0035 Y
0040
69-0035 Y
0042
69-0035 Y
69-1080 F
0043
69-0035 Y
0044
69-0035 Y
0046
69-0035 Y
0047
69-0021 Y
0048
69-0035 Y
69-0098 Y
0050
69-0035 Y
0051
69-0035 Y
0053
69-0035 Y
0054
69-0007 Y
0055
69-0035 Y
0056
69-0007 Y
0057
69-0035 Y
69-0555 V
0058
69-0035 Y
0059
69-0035 Y
0060
69-0021 Y
0062
69-0035 Y
0063
69-0035 Y
0064
69-0035 Y

Figure 5.13 Continuity index: Information Science Abstracts. [Reprinted from Information Science Abstracts, Vol. 4, Dec. 1969, p. 374, by permission of Information Science Abstracts.]

6 | Publishing

6.1   PREPARING THE ABSTRACT PUBLICATION

After the abstracts have been checked, edited, and provided with cross-references, they are assembled and sent to the printer. The editorial process still continues, for there will be galleys and page proofs to correct. Even the design, or layout, of the entire publication periodically will need to be reviewed and possibly modified.

6.1.1   Assembling the Abstracts

Categorized abstracts are readied for publication by an editor or arranger who separates abstracts on which cross-references have been indicated and who has prepared the inter-sectional cross-references that guide users of the service from one section (category) to another. Patents and book reviews may be published separately from the abstracts of papers. If so, the arranger then separates the abstracts, book reviews, and patents into sections. Subcategorization, as was mentioned in Chapter 5, is ad hoc and is done by the arranger according to a plan that is reasonably flexible. Each section has a different set of subcategories, which are altered as the subject field grows and changes. Exceptions to procedures for subcategorization can be made for good reason, such as to bring series and like abstracts together. Users of abstract services pick up the pattern of subcategories rapidly and find it helpful in limiting their skimming and searching.

Once the abstracts have been arranged in sections, and in a systematic order within sections, they are prepared for shipment to the printer. Publishing and printing are two separate, although complementary, processes. Printing of abstract journals is seldom done in the establishment of the publisher. Thus, shipment of manuscript, galley proof, page proof, and instructions to the printer are important processes in the production cycle and must be controlled. It is essential to ensure against loss en route to and from the printer.

Manuscript and typescript are similar to archival materials; they are unique. Replacement is costly, and may not be possible. Protection against loss in mailing is worthwhile, and a number of techniques are commonly employed. The *detection* of loss can be handled by numbering all abstracts with a consecutive-numbering stamp. These stamped numbers give quantitative data useful in predicting expansion of the service and in calculating budgets, and the loss of an abstract is immediately visible as a missing number.

The prevention of loss is necessarily more expensive than numbering abstracts. Copies need to be made. This can be done by Xeroxing; however, microfilming is a less expensive way to protect against loss. Automatic cameras photograph rapidly and produce 16-mm microfilm that can be stored until the proof has been checked, read, and received by the printer. It is unnecessary to develop the microfilm after it has served its purpose of insurance against loss.

The printer is usually notified of a coming shipment of manuscripts by a separate letter, which informs him of the number of abstracts in the shipment. He is also sent a postcard to be returned when he has received the material shipped. All these checks and precautions may seem to be excessive until one wonders what to do about a block of index cards in, say, the Ms that turns out to be missing; or if a section of manuscripts of abstracts does not appear in a package opened by the printer. The effect would be close to catastrophic. Logging (making a list of receipts and shipments) manuscripts and index cards in and out of the premises of the publisher and printer is considered good practice. A record is invaluable in the event of a mishap.

Shipments are insured, but sent in the least expensive way possible.

Different carriers may vary considerably in rates, insurance, dispatch, and so on. Mail, Parcel Post, Railway Express, and local and air transport services should all be investigated and the best service selected.

Printing is a highly specialized craft, and there are many kinds of printing, including computer-controlled, photo-offset, and hot-lead processes. Discussing the merits of each is outside the scope of this text, but all kinds should be explored carefully before signing contracts and committing resources. Factors to be watched include cost, legibility, promptness of output, unionization, artistic quality, number of type fonts, paper quality, peak loads, equipment utilization and maintenance, and prior commitments.

6.1.2   Checking and Proofreading

The printer sets the manuscript in type justified according to the column and page size of the publication. Errors can and do occur in typesetting and so checking and proofreading the galleys and page proofs are always necessary to ensure that what was sent to the printer will appear correctly printed in the abstracts and their indexes.

A *galley proof* is a sheet approximately 30 inches long. It is the first impression made of the typeset manuscript before the type is divided into page-size units. These galleys are sent by the printer to the publisher for checking and proofreading.

Just as with the typed manuscript, there are two processes involved: checking and proofreading. The checker makes sure that numbers and proper names in proof are the same as in manuscript. Proofreaders have no way of finding errors in numbers and proper names except by checking them against manuscript. It is less expensive to have checkers do this.

Proofreading consists of examining each printed character for perfection, each word for spelling, each sentence for grammar and sense, each paragraph for organization, and the entire abstract for correctness of content and format. Type may become damaged—for example, the dot may be missing from an *i* and the letter will have to be marked for replacement. Misspellings may occur at any point in the process and may be carried through to galley proof. Nonsense and incorrect grammar may have escaped notice by the abstractor, editor, and printer. Proofreaders must be exceptionally alert to watch all these items simultaneously and to see to it that all errors are corrected.

Corrections are made in the margin of the galleys. Proofreaders' marks, which are the same for both the proofreader and the printer, are used. (See Figure 5.1 for a list of proofreaders' marks.) Obviously, the cost of making corrections on the typeset galleys is greater than the cost of making the same corrections on the typed manuscript. Corrections are even more expensive on the page proofs. The point is that corrections should be made early, and only absolutely necessary changes should be made after the manuscript has been typeset.

Galley proof is logged in and out, and records are kept of who is checking and reading, and the days and hours. A rubber stamp can put the appropriate record form at the top of each galley for signatures, dates, and days and hours by checkers and proofreaders. Checkers always use manuscripts. Proofreaders have the manuscript available, but use it only for further checking. Proofreaders usually specialize in subject areas indicated by sections of the abstract service. Specialization results in greatly increased efficiency. It is much less a strain for the proofreader to proofread subject matter with which (s)he is familiar than to read completely foreign material. Also, the quality of product is much higher for abstracts in the reader's subject field. Often abstract editors double as proofreaders, shifting back and forth during the publication cycle. Such change is welcome.

. Galleys, when checked and proofread, are shipped back to the printer in batches on an agreed-upon schedule. The printer acknowledges receipt of the returned galleys. He corrects the type and transfers the galleys into chases (metal frames) of page size, which are then locked. A *page proof* is made to show exactly what the printed page will look like. It also provides assurance that the galley errors have been corrected and that type has not been pied (accidentally mixed up) during transfer to the chases. (This applies principally for Monotype.) It is rarely necessary to make corrections on the page proofs, but this does not mean that proofreading should not be done. The page proof is the last chance to correct errors, and the final reading should be a careful one.

With the return of the corrected page proofs to the printer, the normal editorial processes end. The rest of the production cycle is handled by the printer. He produces the journal and mails it to the subscribers.

6.2   JOURNAL LAYOUT

This chapter would not be complete without some discussion about the appearance of the abstracting journal. Although the content, quantity, and quality of the abstracts are the main criteria for determining the value of a journal, the layout design—the covers, title page, type fonts, arrangement, and organization—contributes to the readability and the usefulness of the publication. Librarians, the major purchasers of abstracting services, need to be especially alert to these features.

6.2.1 Outside Covers

Covers can do more than encase the interior pages of the journal. A well-designed cover is durable, attractive, and informative on all three of its outside surfaces—the front, the back, and the spine.

A durable cover to each issue of the abstract journal is essential, for the abstracts and especially the indexes are heavily used. The printer should be consulted in selecting cover stock, for he will be working with this material for both printing and binding, and a wrong choice could add to production costs. The use of color should be considered. The cover should, in addition to being durable, have a pleasing texture and appearance; it should take ink well and not be too expensive.

The printed matter on the cover greatly affects the use and usefulness of the entire journal. The goal is to make the outside cover informative and attractive. In a good design, these two attributes can be complementary and not competitive.

The following items are needed to identify a particular abstract journal, and set it apart from the others in a collection:

Title
Volume number
Issue number
Date of publication
Abstract numbers
Publisher
Sponsoring organization

It is suggested that the first four or five of these items be printed on the front, back, and spine of each issue, so that no matter how the journal is placed on either a shelf or a reading table, these identifying items will be visible. The publisher and sponsor need appear only on the front cover.

The most important item on the cover is the title. This should be given prominence. The largest type and the most prominent position—the space between the upper edge and the center line—are reserved for the title. Large letters make rapid identification from a distance possible. A colophon, or emblem of the service, also helps to identify the journal. The title should be informative and distinctive. Catchy but obscure titles are inappropriate. Brevity without confusion is the goal. The wealth of available type fonts makes it possible to combine legibility and visibility in a pleasing format.

After the title, the items of next importance are the volume and issue numbers and date of publication. These can be printed close to the top edge of the cover, on the left side, since the eye, in reading, starts from the left. Large, easily readable type is desirable. Titles and numbers on covers of abstract journals should appear consistently in the same place; deviation in position from issue to issue is disconcerting and irritating. A different style of type from that chosen for the title may be appropriately used for the numbers on the cover. The year is important in determining the coverage when searching, so it should be given a prominent position, for instance the center top of the cover. The size and style of type for the year number can be the same as for volume and issue numbers, or the year can be set in lightface type for contrast and less emphasis. The identification numbers, or the accession numbers, of the abstracts included in the issue should be listed and may be printed in the same or slightly smaller type.

In addition to these four kinds of numbers (volume, issue, date, and abstract), the name of the organization publishing the abstract journal needs to be clearly indicated on the front cover. The publisher's name, and the name and address of the organizational parent to the publisher, if there is such an organization, can also appear in smaller type.

The spine should, if possible, bear an abbreviated title plus volume and issue numbers. These aid identification when the journals are arranged in an upright position on library shelves.

Only rarely does the identifying information completely fill the space on the front and back covers. The editor and publisher have room to exercise their artistic and creative talents. Some journals carry bright color designs or photographs. Others print the table of contents on either the front or back cover. Still others sell the back cover space for advertisements. Many arrangements are possible. The only general recommendation that can be made is that the cover design should be tasteful, informative, and attractive.

6.2.2   Inside Covers

For the two inside covers, there are also many treatments possible. Since abstract journals must conserve paper and space, the inside covers are rarely left blank. Tables of contents can be printed on the inside cover as can names of the editor, editorial board members, editorial staff, abstractors, section editors, and indexers. An introduction to the journal is appropriate on the inside front cover, as is a policy statement describing the major features of the journal, such as scope, coverage, and editorial rules. A publisher's statement and announcements of related products or services may appear on the inside cover, as may a copyright statement. The publisher's statement should include issue frequency, dates of issue, publisher's name and address, subscription price, where to send notices of change of address, invitations to abstractors, postal regulations, and so on. Again, there is much room for individuality.

6.2.3   Title Page

The title page is needed when binding the journal, for at that point the covers are removed. It should appear in at least the first and last issues. Several title pages may be needed if several volumes are to appear each year. The title page should contain complete identifying information: the name of the journal, colophon, publisher, volume, issue, year, abstract numbers, period covered, place of publication, and so on. A list of abstractors could be printed on the verso of the title page.

If all information about the abstracting journal has not been carried on the cover and title page, then one or more additional pages are devoted to this data, which could include the following: sponsoring organization; slogan; publication period; printer and address; editorial, business, and branch offices; relations to other organizations; objectives; caveats for errors; scope; coverage; copyright data, including permission or restriction on copying; mailing class and privileges, etc.; subscription information; other products or services; contents of the volume or issue; and sections of the abstract journal complete with names and page numbers in the issue. The staff of the journal, including section editors, may be listed. A brief introduction may include these: announcement and description of a list of periodicals abstracted; how to obtain articles, patents, or other literature; pricing policies; special services; and announcements of indexes supplied with the publication.

6.2.4   Abstract Section

Since the abstract journals operate at a loss or for only modest profits, economy of paper, space, words, and so forth is a necessity. White space on pages is held to a minimum. The layout is carefully organized for maximum legibility and usefulness with relatively small-size type. Eight-point type has been found to be satisfactory. Two columns per page make for easier reading than one column in which the lines of print are so long that the eye may return to the same line or skip a line.

On the first page of abstracts it is usual again to list the name of the journal, volume, issue, and date. If the journal is divided into sections, the section number and title follow the journal identification data; for example, "1—Apparatus, Plant Equipment, and Unit Operations." The name of the section editor can appear just below this title. He is responsible for contents of his section and deserves proper recognition. In fact, his only recognition may be that his name is at the head of the section in each issue and in the list of section editors. If the page is divided into columns, then column numbers are more convenient than are page numbers. Columns may even be subdivided into fractions so that the index can lead directly to the relevant abstract with a minimum of skimming. The fractions of the column may bear letters rather than numbers, since letters are more legible in the small type used in indexes than are superscript numbers, which are even smaller type. Margins may be a little larger than ordinary to provide for rebinding the volumes of abstracts several times; this prevents print from being trimmed off in rebinding.

The running heads on subsequent pages of abstracts consist of column numbers, the abbreviated name of the journal, volume number, year, section number, and section name. All these data are exceedingly useful to the reader in making notes during his search. Running heads inform the searcher exactly where he is and when he has arrived at the proper place. More journals should use these aids.

Each section of the abstract journal follows the first section, without wasted page space. Each section is headed in the manner of the first section and the title is used in the running heads. The sections are arranged in a logical order according to the subject field of the abstract journal. This order aids those users who need to consult several sections, for it places related sections adjacent to each other.

6.2.5   Indexes

At the end of each issue, after the abstracts, it is customary to place the indexes to the abstracts in that issue. Subject indexes should be placed first. Next may come author indexes, and then patent-number or other indexes. A fixed order for indexes is a convenience to users of the abstract journal as are fixed orders of other parts of the journal. Searchers are inconvenienced by irregular variations in format.

Special symbols used in the index, such as asterisks, should be explained at the beginning of the index, just following the title of the index.

Issue indexes may be printed in as many as five columns per page. Line length is important in ease of search and can be explored with the printer who can supply different formats for selection.

Annual indexes appear after the issues for the year or volume have been completed. The layout for cumulative indexes should include introductions and instructions. Indexes are never simple devices, although indexers try to make them as self-explanatory as possible. Introductions to indexes help guide the user and should contain definitions of special symbols used; data on nomenclature and terminology; instructions on search strategy; special features; exceptions; and the like. Such an introduction normally precedes the index for which it is intended.

6.2.6   Concluding Comments

There is more to publishing an abstract journal than collecting and printing abstracts. Journal layout is important, and it is a complex, technical task. A poor format detracts from the usefulness of the journal. A good layout design adds to its attractiveness.

III | MANAGEMENT, AUTOMATION, AND PERSONNEL

7 | Abstracting Services

Abstracting services have had continuous and rapid growth. In the years following World War II, the literature of science and technology was abstracted in most of the technically advanced countries of the world. Indeed, there were so many abstracting services that it was difficult to know them all. The first directory to A&I services in the United States was published in 1961 by the National Federation of Science Abstracting and Indexing Services (organized in 1958). This directory was later expanded into *A Guide to the World's Abstracting and Indexing Services in Science and Technology* (NFSAIS, 1963). This directory, too, soon became out of date. A two-volume international directory, *Abstracting Services: Science and Technology* (Volume I), and *Social Science and Humanities* (Volume II), was published by the International Federation for Documentation (FID—Fédération Internationale de Documentation) in 1965. A revised edition was published in 1969. Approximately 1500 abstracting services are listed (FID, 1969).

Growth is measured not only in terms of the number of existing abstracting organizations, but, more important, by the number of items abstracted.

The National Federation of Abstracting and Indexing Services (NFAIS), as the organization is now called, regularly surveys its members and collects data on the number of items covered by the member and affiliate services. Table 7.1 shows the publication growth of a few of these services. The table was copied with permission from the National Federation of Abstracting and Indexing Services Newsletter (NFAIS, 1975, Pp. inserted between 14 and 15). In interpreting these figures, it is important to recognize that over the years some changes were made in the way the data were collected and presented, and so the NFAIS appropriately cautions against comparisons with other published data. The table is presented only to show the increase in the number of services and in the size and importance of a few selected services.

Still another measure of growth is the increase in number of the newer types of alerting services that supplement abstracting and indexing publications. Many of these new services use the computer for control and publication of bibliographic information. For example, the Institute for Scientific Information of Philadelphia, Pennsylvania, publishes the *Science Citation Index*, which includes a *Permuterm Subject Index*, and provides other specialized, individualized, and group-oriented services designed to help the researcher keep abreast of the current literature and retrospectively search the older literature. Another example is the *Concise Clinical Neurology Review* of categorized titles and terse conclusions (Friedlander, 1974). Such services, provided for many disciplines, are as useful as are the abstracting publications.

7.1   ORGANIZATIONS PROVIDING ABSTRACTING SERVICES

Organizations that publish abstracts and indexes are generally characterized as *secondary services*. The *primary services* are those that publish original contributions, most commonly journal articles and reports. The abstracting and indexing (A&I) services provide condensed, organized, subject access to a specified set of primary publications by means of abstracts and indexes. They are found in both governmental and private-sector organizations. The latter can be subdivided into four categories: societal, industrial, commercial, and institutional. These groups differ as to type of organization (profit and nonprofit), distribution policies (public or restricted), and affiliation (nature of affiliated organization, which influences policy).

Figure 7.1, taken from the System Development Corporation (SDC) study of abstracting and indexing services, shows the relative production

Table 7.1
Growth of Abstracting and Indexing Services, 1957–1975*

FULL VOTING MEMBERS	1957	1962	1967	1970	1971	1972	1973	1974	Estimate 1975
American Dental Association	—	—	6,681	7,289	7,358	7,388	7,514	7,200	7,200
American Geographical Society[a]	6,500	6,500	6,500	6,500	6,500	7,000	8,200	9,000	7,000[b]
American Geological Institute	—	—	11,450	35,000	45,000	42,000	35,000	39,733	50,000
American Institute of Physics	—	—	—	20,000	27,000	30,000	30,000	33,369	20,000
American Mathematical Society[c]	9,200	13,382	17,141	18,211	18,784	16,558	20,410	—	—
American Meteorological Society	5,000	12,000	9,000	10,244	7,500	7,200	7,200	7,200	7,200
American Petroleum Institute	11,615[d]	21,977	29,151	41,851	26,018	32,983[e]	37,606	40,000	65,000
American Psychological Association	9,074	8,776	17,202	21,722	23,000	24,000	24,409	25,558	26,250
American Society for Information Science	—	—	—	655	1,333	1,337	1,355	—[f]	—[g]
American Society for Metals	8,219	11,542	23,800	24,255	28,100	24,400	29,219	26,325	28,000
Applied Mechanics Reviews	4,245	7,200	8,802	10,030	10,300	10,300	10,700	10,825	11,400
BioSciences Information Service	40,061	100,858	125,026	230,026	230,020	240,006	240,000	240,000	240,000
Chemical Abstracts Service	102,525	175,138	269,293	309,742	350,105	379,048	356,549	375,663	413,000
Center for Applied Linguistics	—	—	—	84	108	122	92	121	110
Documentation Abstracts, Inc.	—	—	1,327	3,129	3,309	3,618	3,722	3,750	4,100
Engineering Index, Inc.	26,797	38,120	51,670	67,600	85,243	83,653	73,376	89,393	95,000
Exxon Research & Engineering Company[h]									
Index to Religious Periodical Literature[i]	1,100	2,300	3,241	4,326	3,538	5,939	4,050	5,315	5,560
Medical Documentation Service[j]	1,500	1,500	1,692	3,425	4,000	2,500	2,500	2,500	2,500
National Association of Social Workers	—	—	896	1,034	1,066	1,068	1,109	1,069	1,100
Philosophy Documentation Center[k]	—	—	—	—	—	—	—	5,628	6,000
Primate Information Center (Seattle)[k]	—	—	—	—	—	—	—	4,102	4,300
University of Tulsa	—	10,816	15,519	16,247	16,924	15,502	16,775	17,958	18,000
Sub Total	225,836	410,109	598,391	831,370	895,206	934,622	909,786	944,799	1,011,720

(Continued on p. 134)

Table 7.1 (Continued)

	1957	1962	1967	1970	1971	1972	1973	1974	Estimate 1975
UNITED STATES GOVERNMENT AFFILIATES									
Defense Documentation Center	21,015	23,897	52,972	44,319	43,251	36,900	34,899	32,335	34,500
Energy Research & Development Administration	14,042	34,149	47,055	53,080	60,296	60,848	62,167	66,236	90,000
National Agricultural Library[l]	98,409	94,968	102,198	61,460	105,988	124,592	112,774	114,000[m]	115,000
National Library of Medicine	104,517	150,000	165,000	210,000	206,000	221,000	207,000	210,000	210,000
National Oceanic and Atmospheric Administration[a]	876	—	1,224	2,988	3,284	2,760	3,974	2,789	3,500
National Technical Information Service	—	—	29,500	43,650	48,670	54,980	55,597	59,001	66,400
Water Resources Scientific Information Center	—	—	—	10,500	14,000	15,000	15,300	13,500	13,000
Sub Total	238,859	303,014	397,949	425,997	481,489	516,080	491,711	497,861	532,400
FOREIGN AFFILIATES									
Commonwealth Scientific and Industrial Research Organization[o]									179,000
INSPEC	16,452	39,272	71,032	144,442	147,332	154,074	154,269	164,646	
International Labour Office[o]									
National Library of Australia[o]									
TOTAL	481,147	752,395	1,067,372	1,401,809	1,524,027	1,604,776	1,555,766	1,607,306	1,723,120

* From NFAIS, 1974, by permission of the National Federation of Abstracting and Indexing Services.

a Coverage varied between 6,000–7,000 from 1957–1971 inclusive.

b Reduction in content has been necessitated by the Society's serious financial difficulties and the subsequent retrenchment of library members who analyze and catalog literature received on geography and related environmental and social sciences.

c No longer Federation member as of 1974.

d Literature (world-wide) only.

e Augmented patent coverage in cooperative effort with Derwent Services.

f Clearinghouse ceased operation on December 31, 1973.

g ERIC/CLIS transferred to Stanford January, 1974. No documents processed.

h EREC believes that the statistics for its in-house abstract bulletins are not parallel to those for other member services. In recent years EREC has shifted extensively to equivalent bulletins published outside, chiefly by the American Petroleum Institute. Internal documents are still computer-based indexed, however.

i Does not include multiple entries or book reviews. Figures for the years 1960–1970 are estimates.

j Additional abstracts are prepared for client publications. Figures for the years 1957–1966 are estimates.

k New Federation member as of 1974.

l Figures represent indexing citations published in *Bibliography of Agriculture*. Since 1970, *B of A* produced by commercial publisher from data on CAIN (Cataloging and Indexing) tapes purchased from NAL.

m Estimate. Final issues for 1974 not yet published.

n 1958–1966 figures not available.

o New Federation Foreign Affiliate. Statistics not yet available.

volumes of abstracts published by organizations in 1962. Although the absolute figures have increased, the relative percentages are still useful indicators (SDC, 1966).

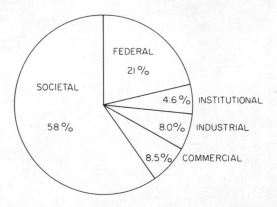

Figure 7.1 *Relative production volumes for abstracts in 1962. Total volume in 1962: 1,037,604. Estimated volume for 1966: 1,440,000. [Reproduced from SDC, 1966, p. 15, by permission of System Development Corporation.]*

7.1.1   Federal Organizations

Federal organizations are the government producers of A&I publications. These organizations are reasonably similar to one another. All but the Library of Congress belong to the executive branch of government, and they include the Departments of Agriculture; Commerce; Defense; Health, Education, and Welfare; and the Interior; as well as the Atomic Energy Commission and the National Aeronautics and Space Administration. These organizations produce abstracts and indexes for specific subject areas of governmental concern; the private-sector abstracts and indexes may or may not overlap. Obviously, these are nonprofit organizations, and the distribution of material (except for reports of a military or classified nature) is not restricted. Federal organizations publish approximately 21% of the total number of abstracting publications.

7.1.2   Societal Organizations

Professional societies are generally nonprofit organizations that exist to serve their members and to advance knowledge in their fields. In pursuance of these aims, they publish original reports (primary literature), and some of them provide A&I publications.

A few representative societies of the many that regularly produce abstracts and indexes are the following:

American Ceramic Society
American Chemical Society
American Dental Association
American Geological Institute
American Institute of Physics
American Mathematical Association
American Meteorological Society
American Psychological Association
Association for Computing Machinery

Professional societies account for about 58% of the total number of all abstracted and indexed items. Distribution is unrestricted but primarily for members.

7.1.3   Industrial Organizations

Industrial organizations include both individual companies and associations of companies. The Exxon Research and Engineering Company, for example, produces abstracts for its internal use. The American Petroleum Institute is an industrial or trade association to which many oil companies belong. It, too, produces abstracts, but it has a broader field of interest and serves the collective information needs of all its sponsors. The cost of publication is underwritten by all the members. Distribution is generally controlled; the abstracts are provided to the sponsoring organization and association members. They may, in addition, be sold to outside users.

A short list of industrial organizations producing abstracts follows.

American Can Company
American Petroleum Institute
American Potash Institute, Inc.
Bell Telephone Laboratories
Burroughs Corporation
Exxon Research and Engineering Company
Merck, Sharp and Dohme Research Laboratories
National Paint, Varnish & Lacquer Association

Industrially produced abstracts make up about 8% of the total abstract production.

7.1.4   Commercial Organizations

Industrial organizations manufacture a product. They produce abstracts for their research and development departments. A commercial abstracting organization, by way of contrast, is in the business of producing and selling abstracts and indexes. Knowledge transfer is not a sideline but the main activity.

Some of these commercial abstracting organizations are as follows:

American Bibliographic Service
Cambridge Communications Corporation
H. W. Wilson Company
Information for Industry, Inc.
Institute for Scientific Information
Pergamon Press
Williams and Wilkins Company

Commercial organizations are anxious to sell their products and the sale is unrestricted. It is estimated that commercial abstracts constitute about 8.5% of the total abstract production.

7.1.5   Institutional Organizations

By definition, institutional organizations are not part of the federal government and are nonprofit. They are dedicated to furthering the arts, sciences, and humanities. Many of them are universities that publish and distribute abstracts and indexes of specialized literature.

Examples of institutional organizations are

Arizona State University
Battelle Memorial Institute
California Institute of Technology
The John Crerar Library
Mellon Institute
New York Public Library
Rutgers Center of Alcoholic Studies

Institutional organizations produce approximately 4.6% of the total number of available abstracts.

7.2   PRODUCTION PROCESSES

As can be inferred from the volume figures presented, the need to provide access to the world's literature by abstracting and indexing has resulted in a multimillion-dollar service industry. The production cycle consists of the following six steps:

1. policy formulation and document acquisition;
2. article selection and assignment;
3. abstractor selection;
4. classification and cross-references;
5. editing, composition, and printing;
6. distribution and storage.

The management of these related steps is a significant administrative task. Previous chapters have discussed these steps from the point of view of the abstractor. This section seeks to provide an overview of the management aspects of the production cycle.

7.2.1   Policy Formulation and Document Acquisition

If one thinks of an abstracting service as a specialized information system analogous to a library, the necessity for a selection policy becomes obvious. The problem is one of determining what documents should be acquired for abstracting in order to serve a selected group of patrons when there is always a limited budget and a limited amount of page space. Abstracting services generally have policy statements specifying the completeness of subject coverage, the journals that are and are not abstracted, the types of information materials covered, and those that will not be abstracted.

In light of the phenomenal growth of the scientific and technical literature throughout the world, the ideal goal of achieving complete coverage of almost any discipline is difficult and expensive. Some restriction of coverage may be necessary. Let us suppose that we are dealing with a discipline-oriented service, such as *Psychological Abstracts*. (The reasoning holds true for a mission-oriented service.) The ideal would be to provide complete coverage of the literature of psychology. For the moment, let us ignore budget and space and concentrate on the decisions needed to attain complete coverage. Should all medical psychiatry be abstracted, for clearly this impinges upon clinical psychology? Should articles on psychopharmacology—the use of drugs for the study and treatment of mental illness—be abstracted? What articles are appropriate for abstracting in the area of educational psychology? How would one select articles germane to psychometrics without trying to cover some of the related field of applied statistics? Clearly, some policy guidance is needed. Does complete coverage imply all languages and all countries of publication? Should the service abstract German, Russian, Portuguese, Hebrew, Arabic, Japanese, and so on? Would the journal be providing a useful service by printing abstracts of documents that are written in languages that the average reader cannot understand and from journals that are difficult to obtain, or would this frustrate the user and clutter the pages with useless material? Again, a policy decision is needed.

What type of documents should be abstracted? Scholarly journals, of course. But how about popular periodicals? If the *Ladies Home Journal* carries an article by a well-known psychologist, should this be abstracted? Should patent literature be covered? Should conference proceedings, textbooks, and monographs be abstracted? All or some? Which? How does one decide? What is the policy?

An even more difficult decision that needs to be made is to provide guidance on the types of material that should *not* be abstracted. For example, should brief communications and letters to the editor be abstracted? How about editorials? What should be done about notices of meetings and reports of meetings? Should biographies and obituaries be noted? Clearly, it is not sufficient to state that one will abstract all communications of importance. That is begging the question; policy must help the editor determine what is important.

Another problem related to selection has to do with documents that are appropriate for more than one service, for example, for psychiatry and psychology, or biology and chemistry. The policy question that arises is whether one service should not abstract the document since the other service is certain to abstract it. The decision has generally been for both services to provide abstracts, because otherwise one group of users would be disadvantaged. Abstracting the same article more than once is costly, and all concerned would like to avoid unnecessary duplication. However, each service has its own standards of quality, style, and coverage, and each prepares abstracts appropriate to the needs of its own users. Because of differing requirements of users in different disciplines, abstracts written for one service may or may not be suitable for a related service.

The policy statement prepared by the abstracting service should be basic and modifiable, for the scope of the service must keep pace with changes in the field. The formulation of a selection policy is normally a function of the management board and the editors. The assigners, editors, and abstractors are responsible for implementing the policy. The subscribers provide feedback by indicating whether their needs are being served and, particularly, where scope needs to be expanded.

The scope of the journal is determined by a compromise between the users' desire for complete, conveniently arranged coverage and the economics of publication. A large abstract journal is costly; a small service may cause users to miss material, which is always awkward, and may force the user to consult other services, which may be even more costly. Publishers of abstracting services often seem to err on the side of inclusion of related material as the least of the evils.

7.2.2   Article Selection and Assignment

The primary journals and other materials are distributed to an assignment editor who is responsible for selecting articles within each journal that are appropriate for abstracting. Not everything published is within the scope of the abstracting journal's policy. Guidance for the assignment editor is provided by a number of policy statements or rules. Specific services will, of course, make their own rules; the rules that follow provide general guidance.

1. *Policy concerning articles to be abstracted.* An article should be abstracted if it is
   a. pertinent to the subject areas of the users of the abstracting service;
   b. an original contribution to the literature of the field;
   c. significant;
   d. a technical report of a research or development project; and
   e. published in a journal that the abstracting agency has agreed to abstract in full.
2. *Policy concerning articles not to be abstracted.* An article is not to be abstracted if it is
   a. unoriginal;
   b. only of marginal interest to users of the abstracting service;
   c. trivial or of no lasting importance;
   d. a preliminary progress report;
   e. published in an unknown source; and
   f. published in a source that the abstracting agency has agreed not to abstract.
3. *Policy concerning books.* As a general rule, books are not abstracted. However,
   a. Relevant books are simply cited, for it is assumed that the title,

      author name, and publisher will be as informative as a brief ab-
      stract would be.

  b. Abstracts may be published for books reporting new research
      results. Chapters may be abstracted separately.

  c. If the book is an anthology or a collection of papers, as for con-
      ference proceedings, the book is cited; in addition, separate ab-
      stracts may be prepared for each of the papers, reporting new
      material.

4. *Policy concerning review articles.* Since a review article is another
   type of surrogate, it is generally not desirable to abstract it. Consequently, reviews are usually cited, and the scope of the review
   and the number of references may be noted.

In addition to the selection policy, assignment editors are usually
provided with a list of all serial publications of possible interest to the
readers of the abstracting service and which, therefore, may be abstracted. These publications will most likely be divided into three
categories:

1. journals to be abstracted completely, including all articles, plus
   communications and notes of lasting interest;
2. journals to be skimmed regularly for articles of interest;
3. journals that are peripherally related to the field but that occasionally
   carry articles of interest.

When issues of journals are received by the abstracting service, they
are sorted into these three categories. Journals in the first category are
immediately assigned to abstractors, and those in the other two categories
are reviewed by a senior editor or abstractor who marks the articles to
be abstracted.

As a result of selection, all appropriate articles are marked for abstracting and are assigned for processing to the most qualified abstractor
available. This may be a full-time staff member or a part-time volunteer.
Most organizations use a combination of a small full-time staff supplemented by a large number of volunteers.

The physical process of assigning material for abstracting is comparatively straightforward, although many variables need to be considered.
In general, the assignments must be matched to the interests and capabilities of the abstractors in terms of language competence, subject
knowledge, special requests, and the amount of work previously assigned.
Few abstractors are willing to abstract a document written in a language
they cannot read fluently, nor should this be expected of them. More

abstractors are willing to abstract outside their specialty fields, but one should avoid making assignments that are too far removed from the abstractor's area of expertise. The assigner must also keep track of the amount of work that a given abstractor has ahead of him and how much he has requested, as well as special requests of the abstractor, such as, "No patents," "No microfilm," "No German," or "No steroid chemistry." Limitations on assignments may also be imposed by the assigner or by editors of the service as they discover limitations of abstractors. "Don't send Joe any more German; he's guessing." "Stop all assignments to Harry; he's out of the country on vacation." "Send Fred extra assignments; he's on vacation in the Maine woods, and he wants to read." "Al is slow in returning assignments." Assignment is often a compromise between what the assigner wants, who is available at the time, and how much delay can be tolerated.

It is, of course, impossible for the assigner to keep the requirements and status of all the abstractors in a group of several hundred in mind at all times. Records need to be kept. Records on 3-by-5-inch cards are most common. Changes (additions and deletions) are easy to make in such a card system—an important factor where changes must be made frequently. Three different files are maintained: the abstractor file, the language file, and the subject file.

In the *abstractor card file* each card contains the name of the abstractor; his/her title; address; subject areas; languages; amount of material requested for a given period of time; special limitations; and space for comments by assigner, editors, and indexers. This file is alphabetized by abstractor's name—last name first. Assignment slips (also 3 by 5 inches in size) are put into this file as a way of keeping track of how much work an abstractor has ahead of him. They also help keep track of special requirements. For example, if an abstractor is given the first part of a series of papers, it is considered courteous and tactful also to give him the second and following parts. As the abstractor completes his work and returns the abstracts, the corresponding slips are removed from his file. Some abstractors apparently enjoy being overloaded; others consider it an imposition. The assigner must pay attention to these individual differences.

Another file is arranged by *language*, with more than one card for the abstractors who ask for assignments in several languages. Assigners quickly learn who can handle what languages, but the file cards help them distribute the work more equitably. The third file is arranged by *subject*. The assigner matches the new document to be abstracted to the abstractor by language and by subject area. By carefully observing the special limitations noted in the file, and by going through these files regularly and systematically, the assigner can distribute the assignments fairly.

Besides individual assignments (of separate papers, patents, and so on) there are also "journal assignments" in which an entire journal is assigned to an abstractor, who selects the articles to be abstracted—through his knowledge of the scope of the service and selection rules. He has the option of asking that another abstractor handle any item that is out of his field of competence. Whole journal assignments are made mainly for homogeneous publications in a relatively specialized field of knowledge. For example, *Science, Nature,* and *Naturwissenschaften* are unsuitable for whole journal assignments. Journal assignments are recorded in the abstractor's file so that overloading can be avoided. Some abstractors handle individual as well as whole journal assignments. The abstractor given responsibility for selecting articles from a journal must also be given guidance rules and all updatings relating to the scope of the service. The content of both mission- and discipline-oriented services changes from time to time, and these changes are reflected in their publications. The abstracting service must be aware of these developments, and the materials selected for abstracting reflect the changes.

7.2.3   Abstractor Selection

The publisher of the secondary service views production in terms of the resources needed to prepare quality abstracts at a minimum cost. In selecting abstractors, he has a number of alternatives. Abstracts may be prepared by

1. the author of a work
2. in-house employees (professional abstractors)
3. outside contractors
4. subject-expert volunteers

The previously cited SDC report indicates that "the use of author abstracts and contractor-generated abstracts shows a small but probably significant increase relative to the use of abstracts prepared in-house" (SDC, 1966, p. 28).

Author abstracts cost nothing and, being already prepared, are promptly available. Many primary scientific and technical papers are now accompanied by an author abstract; the trend seems to be increasing. When policy permits the use of author abstracts, fewer subject specialists may be needed, and the professional abstractor will apply his talents to editing the author abstracts and to formatting it for publication. This process may prove to be more costly than is the cost of subject-expert produced abstracts. It has been found to be difficult to edit some author-written abstracts without careful study of the original work.

The use of volunteers is the next most cost-effective choice for the publisher. The vast majority of abstractors are volunteers. They are selected for their subject knowledge and language competence. They may consider the task to be a part of their professional responsibilities, or they may abstract in order to keep up with the literature, or to prevent hard-won language skills from being lost. Their only "pay" may be an occasional honorarium or a subscription to the abstract journal.

Outside contractors are often used to prepare abstracts of materials requiring skills that are not available in-house, such as articles in specialized fields, or foreign-language literature in the less common languages (e.g., Chinese, Japanese, and Arabic). (For years, however, *Chemical Abstracts* was able to cover the literature of chemistry and chemical engineering by subject-expert volunteers and without the help of contractors.) Although it is much more expensive to use contractors than volunteers, precisely because they are paid, contractors should be expected to complete their assignments on time.

In-house abstractors are, of course, the most expensive source of abstracts. They also are the most prompt source, except for the author abstracts already prepared.

7.2.4   Classification and Cross-References

The value of a collection of abstracts, such as a journal, depends on the ease with which the collection can be used either as a surrogate or as a means to identify and locate relevant documents. A classification scheme and various indexes provide the capability for browsing and searching. As each document is selected for entry into an A&I publication, it is classified by categories that have developed with the discipline and designed to satisfy the aims and objectives of the publisher. The classified arrangement of abstracts facilitates browsing by subject area and thus helps the reader to keep up, or at least become acquainted, with the newly published literature on a given topic.

Indexing uses more specific terminology than classification and is designed to guide the user to documents by author name, corporate source, and subject, for example. For policy guidance, a number of management decisions have to be made. As always, there is a trade-off between costs and benefits. Indexing by author names may appear to be simple, but as was discussed earlier (Chapter 4), one must decide whether to index by all the author names for an article, or by only the first author; whether to print full first and middle names or only initials, and so on. Corporate sources become complicated to list in an author index, particularly at the government-agency level, but also for corporations that have many branches and affiliates. Organizations' name changes cause difficulties.

By far the most complex form of indexing is subject indexing (see Chapter 5), and again there are a number of choices to be made, e.g., "free" vocabulary, specified vocabulary, permuted title, and special indexes. An increase of indexing density (number of the subject entries per abstract), sometimes called *depth of indexing*, adds to publication bulk and cost. Some indexes are printed in the same issue as are the abstracts. Issue indexes may or may not be cumulated while edited indexes are often produced at intervals, such as quarterly, semiannually, and annually.

In addition to the classification and indexing of abstracts selected for publication, some form of cross-referencing among abstracts is needed, because abstracts can often fit well into several categories. Indexes also need cross-references to handle synonymy, broader and narrower concepts, and the like. Policy guidance in classification is provided by the publisher; the categorization may be done by the abstractor or the editor. The cross-references that are not added by the abstractor are added by the editor who corrects the omissions that he detects.

7.2.5   Editing, Composition, and Printing

After the abstract has been prepared and checked by the abstractor, it is checked by the publisher and edited by an editor who corrects all errors of content and form according to the policy of the journal. This editor also improves grammar and ascertains for informative abstracts whether data have been omitted. If data have been omitted, the editor supplies them.

After the abstracts have been edited, they are forwarded to the printer for typesetting, proofreading, and printing. These processes have been described in Chapter 6. The task is complex, for it requires the skills of many specialized craftsmen, such as typographers, proofreaders, pressmen, and, if the journal is printed by offset, lithographers, layout artists, and photographers. Most A&I services employ a publication coordinator who is responsible for organizing all the input elements into a functional and attractive product within a given budget and hopefully within time limits.

7.2.6   Distribution and Storage

Distribution techniques vary with the type of service organization. The federal government and the private sectors use different techniques to put their publications into the hands of users. All A&I services, or their printers, maintain an address file of subscribers. The methods of updating and printing a mailing list from this file may vary from manually addressing envelopes or typing labels, through the use of Addressograph plates, to computer techniques. The method of choice depends upon costs, the size of the operation, and the availability of equipment. It is necessary to note that postal regulations require that bulk mailings be sorted and tied by zip code. Small inefficiencies in distribution may be costly.

Storage costs and facilities are other areas that require the attention of management. Back issues of the abstract publication are an important source of revenue. If the journal is popular, new library subscribers may request copies of earlier volumes. These requests can be met by authorizing overprinting or reprinting. Overprint copies need to be stored; management must strike a balance between costs and services.

There is still another aspect of storage, and that is the storage of primary journals in the library of the abstract publisher. A decision has to be made as to whether these journals should be stored after they have been abstracted, and if so for how long. Complaints may be received about the quality of an abstract, an abstract may be lost, and one may need to check the original article during indexing. Also, some subscribers may write the publisher to request a copy of the original journal article, which he may not be otherwise able to obtain. Either for courtesy or for profit, should the publisher of abstracts provide copies of the original article? There is, of course, a copyright problem that has been solved by the Institute of Scientific Information, for example, by encouraging readers of *Current Contents* and subscribers to *Automatic Subject Citation Alert (ASCA)* to order tear sheets through *Original Article Tear Sheet* (OATS) service. Each A&I service should examine the questions involved in the distribution and storage functions and base its decision on the costs and benefits of these services.

7.3   FUNCTIONS OF JOURNAL LITERATURE

Journal literature serves three essential functions (Herschman, 1970):

1. It disseminates information among members of a scientific community who have similar or overlapping interests and who need to main-

tain a *current awareness* by keeping up with developments in their fields of interest.

2. It links producers and users of information by a record of achievements that can be used for *retrospective searching*. The journal provides a public record, prepared with quality control through the editor-referee system, a means for establishing priority, and an orderly basis for transforming data into information and for relating new knowledge to prior knowledge so as to form a corpus. It packages results of research and development.

3. It performs an important *social function*, for it conveys prestige and recognition upon its authors.

The functions themselves have not changed over the years, but the relative importance accorded them has. It is this change in *emphasis* that has economic and social implications for both primary and secondary publications. Changes in emphasis have been brought about, in part, by the enormous numbers of journals published (35 to 70 thousand).

7.3.1   Primary Publications

Primary journals (those containing original contributions) and research reports were initially published to inform members of a discipline of the work of their colleagues. A century or so ago, travel was slow and uncomfortable. There were few national and international conventions to attend where one might listen to papers, or exchange information with colleagues. Scientists have always preferred vocal exchange of information.

Times have changed. Travel is now fast and convenient, and there are more conventions than one has time or money to attend. These meetings and symposia are even more important now than earlier, and it has been shown that scientists often make their first report of research activity at these meetings (Garvey, 1972). The journal article reaches the scientific community after a considerable delay, and thus the current-awareness function of the journal is lessened.

Another factor that has reduced the current-awareness role of the primary journal is the growth of the primary literature. One no longer has to document the fact that the literature of almost every discipline has now expanded to such an extent that every person is experiencing difficulty in keeping up with his own field of interest. An individual can read and assimilate only so much. The so-called information explosion is not due to greatly increased productivity of the individual scientist but is a natural outcome of the increase in the number of working scientists. The information problem is further compounded by the interdisciplinary nature of science and by the need for awareness of relevant literature in other languages. Furthermore, relevant articles may be published in such a variety of journals that even if one subscribes to and reads the core journals in his field, he must still miss a significant portion of the relevant material.

The conclusion that must be drawn from this analysis is that the role of the primary journal as a current awareness tool for the user is weakening. A similar conclusion was drawn by H. W. Koch from his examination of the effect of growth on the role of the primary journal in physics (Koch, 1970).

However, although the current-awareness function of the journal is decreasing in importance, its archival services maintain their importance. There are many reasons for this shift in the use of the literature, but perhaps the most obvious is this: since the reader is unable to keep up with the current advances in his field, he must search the accumulated record when faced with a problem in his field that he is seeking to solve. Users rely on the fact that articles published in learned journals have been properly referred and thus have quality control. They rely on the published record. Younger scientists, who are not members of the "invisible college" (groups of active researchers who keep in contact by meetings, mail, or phone) and who do not have access to preprints and to informal contacts and publications, are even more dependent upon the journal literature in keeping up. If one cannot keep current—and it is a fact that no one can—then one must become aware of the relevant literature by searches of the primary literature. The results of these searches may now often be more material than the searcher can read and digest.

One important consequence of this changing role of the primary journals is that fewer people subscribe to the journal. Koch, in the course of an analysis of the economics of primary publications in physics, stated that, although journals of the American Institute of Physics (AIP) are produced to serve individual subscribers, "Unfortunately, individual subscriptions to journals are not increasing as fast as the population of physicists is increasing" (Koch, 1969, p. 12). The basic reason is an economic one:

> Even though a member can subscribe at phenomenally low prices per page, the number of pages to which he should subscribe is going up so fast that the absolute subscription cost is becoming intolerably high for the individual member. The solution for a growing number of physicists is the photocopying of pages out of library journals. Even though the photocopying costs may be ten times the subscription cost per page, the

selectivity provided by the physicist makes his own customized "separates" journal attractive and relatively inexpensive. [Koch, 1969, p. 12]

Because of the growth in the amount of literature and the cost of publication, the role of the primary journal has changed in two basic ways:

1. The main function of the primary journal is archival; it preserves the validated record of scientific accomplishments. Current awareness is a secondary function.
2. The main support for the primary journal has shifted from the individual subscriber to the library or institutional subscriber.

7.3.2   Secondary Publications

Secondary publications provide necessarily delayed access to the primary literature. Even though this role remains the same today as it was in the past, there are some subtle differences in publication practice and function that are directly attributable to the previously discussed functional changes in primary publication. To keep up with these changes, some secondary services have increased coverage, changed form, and become more economical.

When current awareness was the main function of the primary journal, the A&I services provided guidance to some of the articles and offprints that the individual subscriber had in his personal collection. Coverage for some services was of a core collection of primary journals rather than of all the literature in the discipline. Now, however, the A&I services provide access to primary publications with the primary journals themselves as archival material. The emphasis for the A&I services has to be on completeness. With this need for completeness, the size and cost of these publications have increased even more than those of the primary journals. Because few individuals can afford to subscribe, abstracts and indexes are used mainly in the library. And so the library's role as a provider of access has grown in importance.

The quality of the A&I services has improved, but as a consequence their cost, already high, has become higher. Up to the point of subscription-income return, all the activities of A&I services have resulted in expenditure of capital. Money has been spent to acquire the primary publications not received as exchanges or as gifts, to select articles, to prepare and edit the abstract, to compose, to print, to bind, and to mail the abstract publication. Library budgets are limited and, in many instances, are not keeping pace with inflation. Subscriptions even to worthwhile journals have been stopped by some libraries because of a lack of funds. Our society values research more than its record and consequently allocates dollars for research and cents for the communication of its record. This puts a premium on the quality of the publication and on its use.

Quality can be improved by making the abstracts more informative, so that they can function as surrogates, especially where the original article is in another language. The user will, with increasing frequency, have to rely on the abstract to provide the information he needs and also to help decide whether, in some cases, it will be necessary to order a copy of the article. Copies can be obtained from the author, the publisher, and tear-sheet services, and through interlibrary loan.

Quality can also be improved by providing better indexing; greater variety of indexes; and secondary publications that lead promptly to conclusions of authors, and their data and findings.

Providing increased coverage and improved quality in the presence of inflation is costly, yet the third requirement is that price must be perceived to be reasonable. The problem is a difficult one, but there is some hope that change in perceptions and developments in publication procedures and services may provide part of the solution.

7.4   TRENDS IN PRODUCTION PROCEDURES AND SERVICES

Journal publishers are acutely conscious of increasing costs. Interest in the economics of information transfer can be gauged from the substantial growth in the quantity and the quality of literature on this topic. The Special Interest Group on Cost, Budgeting, and Economics of the American Society for Information Science has prepared a bibliography and commentary on the economics of information transfer (Olsen, 1972). Also, Volume 8 of the *Annual Review of Information Science and Technology* (Cuadra and Luke, 1973) has two chapters on this topic: Michael D. Cooper's "The Economics of Information" (Chapter I), and Elwood K. Gannett's "Primary Publication Systems and Services" (Chapter 8). These references provide a more comprehensive analysis than will be attempted in this section, for here we will limit our analysis to an examination of three developments that show promise of improving the cost-effectiveness of secondary reference publications and services. These developments are (1) changes in printing methods; (2) increased cooperation among journal publishers; and (3) the development of integrated information systems.

7.4.1   Printing Methods

Scientific publications have a limited audience and a small print order of between 2000 and 15,000 copies. With few exceptions (and all of them of an experimental nature), most scientific and technical journals were composed on Monotype machines and printed by letterpress until the late 1960s or early 1970s. About this time a number of important technical innovations took place and some procedures changed. The impetus was the need to find a less costly method of printing journals. A number of acceptable alternatives have become available. Perhaps the most significant change has been the replacement of letterpress by offset printing. "By the end of 1973, virtually all of the larger scientific and technical societies will have converted to offset printing" (Gannett, 1973, p. 250). Since even the large professional societies do not own their own printing plants, it can safely be assumed that they will turn to the least expensive form of printing that is acceptable. One of the cost-saving advantages of photocomposition is that the printing plates can be made directly from the typewritten copy, if one is willing to accept the typography and increased bulk of the product. This means that the journal can be composed on a typewriter. Typewriters have been improved over the past 50 years and can now be obtained with a variety of attractive type fonts and the capability for mixing fonts. Special characters are available as well as partially proportionally spaced letters. The net result is that through typewriters and photocomposition, one can achieve a serviceable product that costs less for setting than does the aesthetically superior Monotype composition.

The American Institute of Physics (AIP) and the Institute of Electrical and Electronics Engineers (IEEE) are producing some of their publications by typewriter composition and reducing typesetting costs by about 25%; although this reduction is offset somewhat by increased copy-editing costs and by the increased bulk of the publication. The bulk is increased because more characters can be placed in a line of Linotype or Monotype composition than in a line of typewriter type. Additional cost savings of as much as 50% of the production process can result from requiring the author to serve as his own editor and compositor (Gannett, 1973). The use of author-prepared copy is fairly common in the production of conference proceedings, but thus far it has not been widely used in journal publishing. Quality is an important factor.

The printing technique that may hold the most promise is computer composition. This method is no longer a novelty, but neither has it fulfilled its promise (Landau, 1971). Although the hardware is available, the capital investment is high and the existing software needs improvement. The great, but as yet latent, advantage of computer typesetting may not be in its cost advantage but in its extended capability to produce automatically the secondary abstracting and indexing journals from the material already keyboarded for the original article. The fulfillment of this promise requires extensive research and cooperation among the primary publishers and the secondary services.

7.4.2 Cooperation among Journal Publishers

Primary and secondary publications do not compete; their services are complementary. Secondary services provide access to the primary literature, and the primary journals need to be abstracted and indexed in order to fulfill their archival functions and to provide readers with a method of retrieving the original articles. The two types of publications need and support one another. Through the organized efforts of the International Council of Scientific Unions Abstracting Board (ICSU–AB) and NFAIS, the editors and publishers have increased contact and greater opportunities for exchanging information and exploring ways of improving services. Various avenues for cooperation are being investigated.

Many primary journals require that articles submitted for publication include an abstract prepared by the author. It has been suggested that when the article is accepted for publication, or when the page proof is printed, the complete citation and abstract, and possibly the entire article as well, be sent to the secondary service. This is already being done to a limited extent. Such a procedure allows the A&I service to prepare its copy earlier and reduces the publication time lag.

With the advent of computer typesetting, the interfacing between primary and secondary services can be further improved. Magnetic tapes can be exchanged, and the costs for keyboard composition and editing for both services can partially be shared.

The secondary services are also engaged in cooperative studies. One such effort began in April 1970 when the Biosciences Information Service of *Biological Abstracts* (BIOSIS), the Chemical Abstracts Service (CAS), and Engineering Index, Inc. (Ei) announced a joint five-part study with five objectives:

1. To measure overlap among the journals each of the services abstracts.
2. To determine why the same articles are abstracted by two or three services.

3. To compare editorial policies and procedures of the three services as they relate to the form, format, and content of references and abstracts.
4. To measure the compatibility or interconvertibility and reliability of the computer files of each service.
5. To compare indexing policies through index entries. [Wood *et al.*, 1972, p. 36]

The first two parts of this study have now been published, and the results provide data on the amount of overlap in the publications of these three major services.

The initial study (see objective 1) sought to identify the amount of overlap in the lists of primary source journals that each of the three services abstracts. A total of 14,592 journals was abstracted. Of these, the BIOSIS and CAS lists contain entries for 13,060 different currently published scientific and technical journals. Of the list, 23.6% (3112 journals) was scanned by both BIOSIS and CAS. CAS and Ei abstract from 10,815 different journals, of which 1078 (10%) are monitored by both. Between BIOSIS and Ei, 9470 different journals are covered, but only 171 are common to both (1.8% of the total). Finally, 140 journals are abstracted by all three services, and this is less than 1% of the more than 14,000 journals that are covered (Wood *et al.*, 1972, p. 36).

Whereas the 1972 study dealt with the *journals* that the three services abstracted, the second study investigated the extent to which the same *article* was abstracted by any two, or all three, of the services (Wood *et al.*, 1973, p. 25). The method used was this: a list was made of journals monitored in common, and then each service examined its selection records to determine the number, and the identity of, the articles selected for coverage from the journal issues with publication dates of July 1969 through June 1970, inclusive. Once the articles had been identified, it was possible to compare one service's selection against one or both of the others to determine whether the same article had been abstracted more than once.

In studying article overlap for all three services, BIOSIS, CAS, and Ei, the articles in the 140 overlapping journals were counted—a total of 29,182 authored articles. The BIOSIS records indicated that 6970 had been selected; CAS selected 16,766; and Ei selected 5627. Next, the number of selected articles were listed by journal issue.

For example, the issues of the journal *Acoustica* for the year studied contained 144 articles. Of these BIOSIS had selected 15, CAS 9, and Ei 39. Thus, if any three-way overlap had occurred, it could have only occurred on the 9 articles that CAS selected from this journal. When the maximum possible overlap was calculated for each journal and totaled, it was found that only 822 of the 29,182 might have been covered by all three services. [Wood *et al.*, 1973, p. 26]

By similar procedures, it was determined that for BIOSIS and Ei, the total number of articles published by the 171 common journals was 30,529 and that the maximum number of articles that could have been selected by both services was 1428.

The amount of overlap between CAS and BIOSIS and CAS and Ei was estimated using both a counting and a sampling procedure. The results are shown in Table 7.2.

These two overlap studies provide the most accurate data available on the extent to which the same articles are selected for abstracting by more than one service. The results indicate that although the amount of overlap among all three services is negligible, as is overlap between BIOSIS and Ei, some overlap does exist between CAS and BIOSIS and between CAS and Ei. As a result, the three services will continue this cooperative study to gather information for policy guidance and for planning improved and less costly publications and services.

7.4.3   Integrated Information Systems

The cost of information services can be reduced by adopting innovative printing methods and by cooperation among journal publishers. But are these efforts sufficient? Are we trying to cure by a Band-Aid when surgery is necessary? Such indeed may be the case, and plans for a more inte-

Table 7.2
Overlap Study of Journals Selected for Coverage by BIOSIS, CAS, and Ei[a]

	Overlap	
Services	Journals monitored	Articles abstracted
BIOSIS, CAS, & Ei	140	822
BIOSIS & Ei	171	1,428
BIOSIS & CAS	3,112	48,856
CAS & Ei	1,078	21,580

[a] Source: Data from Wood (1973).

grated system for gathering, processing, and disseminating information have been proposed. The System Development Corporation (SDC, 1967), in a study conducted for the Committee on Scientific and Technical Information (COSATI) of the Federal Council for Science and Technology, characterizes the present information-handling system in the United States as being one in which the many independent units in government, universities, professional societies, and industry go their separate ways with little or no awareness of the larger national scene. The report states that "there is no national long-range plan or planning body to bring about any cohesion in these separate efforts. There is a need for the development of national policy regarding S&T [Science and Technology] information and documentation problems" (SDC, 1967, p. 118). It goes on to recommend that a "capping agency" be established, preferably as a bureau within the Executive Office of the President and that this agency be responsible for formulating policy, establishing standards, collecting statistical data, and developing long-range plans in order to bring about a national document-handling system for science and technology. Note that in the proposed plan, the bureau will not gather or provide access to information. Operations will be decentralized but there will be centralized planning and coordination. This proposal was not implemented, but neither was it forgotten.

In 1969, the Committee on Scientific and Technical Communication (SATCOM) of the National Academy of Sciences (NAS) again studied the "pressing national problem" of scientific and technical communication (SATCOM, 1969). After an intensive effort, the Committee found that

> Today in the United States, scientific and technical communication exhibits the characteristic heterogeneity of a system that evolved by fits and starts through adaptations to locally perceived needs and opportunities. No master plan prepared by experts guided its evolution, nor are our information services staffed by an organized body of such experts. . . . Though the performance of this heterogeneous aggregate of activities has been criticized on many counts, there is no evidence of critically inefficient operation or catastrophic failure. Nevertheless with the necessary and continued expansion of information services, scientific and technical communication presents increasingly diverse problems, and our ability to maintain high-quality services under such unstructured coordination and leadership is frequently questioned. As long as it continues to function reasonably well, the present dispersed system of decision-making is a source of great strength. . . . Therefore, rather than urging immediate and radical change at the present time, we see the implementation of recommendations directed toward more effective coordination, planning, and decentralized management as the best means of coping with the growing and increasingly varied demands for scientific and technical information. [SATCOM, 1969, pp. 20–21. Reprinted by permission of the National Academy of Sciences.]

The Committee made 55 recommendations for improving the transfer and utilization of information. SATCOM's first recommendation was for the establishment of a Joint Commission on Scientific and Technical Communication, which would report to the Councils of NAS and the National Academy of Engineering (NAE). The Commission would be responsible for integrating the interests of all groups in the government and in the private sector, including both profit and nonprofit organizations, for the purposes of formulating national policies and programs throughout the community. In essence, the Commission would assume the task of creating a planned diversity of coordinating services out of the existing chaotic diversity. These recommendations also have not been implemented.

Other nations are engaged in planning integrated information systems. UNESCO has sponsored a number of missions to various developing countries for the purpose of advising on the organization and establishment of national scientific and technical information systems (Borko, 1972—Brazil; Lazar, 1972—India; Samarasinghe, 1969—Ceylon). The Organization of American States (OAS) has sponsored other missions to South American countries for planning national information systems (Gonod *et al.*, 1971—Colombia; Gonod *et al.*, 1971—Peru). All these plans differ in accordance with the political structure, goals, and state of development of the country in question. All are similar in that they recognize that information is an important resource that has contributed to the economic and cultural development of the nation. The purpose is to create a structure that will ensure the efficient and systematic gathering, processing, and dissemination of information. In almost all cases, the national plan calls for an integrated, although not necessarily a monolithic, infrastructure.

Just what is an integrated information system? Perhaps the most succinct description has been provided by A. I. Chernyi, the Assistant Director of VINITI (the All Union Institute for Scientific and Technical Information in the USSR).

By an integrated information system we mean a multifunction automated informative system which, once an information item has been fed into it, will repeatedly use that item in accomplishing all kinds of information tasks; it is intended for collecting, analytical-synthetic processing, storage, retrieval, and dissemination of scientific and technical information to satisfy fully [the] comprehensive meeting of the information needs of scientists and practical specialists. In other words, exhaustive data on the contents and form of every scientific document are entered into the automated information system only once to be stored in it; the complete (exhaustive) description of the document is used by such a system as a basis for producing all printed aids and conducting all types of information service that do not imply any additional creative processing of that input information on all kinds of requests. [Chernyi, 1972, p. 167]

VINITI is, or is developing into, such a system. It is a highly centralized organization performing the following functions:

a. Indexing, annotating and abstracting all world scientific and technical literature, and on that basis,

—production of current-awareness bulletins in the various fields of science and technology, subject and problem areas;

—production of the abstract journal, *Referativnyi Zhurnal,* with indexes in the various fields of science and technology, subject and problem areas;

—dissemination, on a subscription basis, of magnetic tapes with indexed retrieval files in the various fields of science and technology, subject and problem areas;

—selective dissemination of information on sci-tech literature of the world serving a certain group of patrons;

—retrospective search of documents and information on individual requests in the whole accumulated file.

b. Preparation of surveys of the type *Advances in Science and Technology;*

c. Production—on user's requests—of copies of any scientific documents reflected in current-awareness bulletins and the abstract journal.

d. Translation—on users' requests—of foreign scientific and technical publications into Russian. [Chernyi, 1972, p. 186]

The basic design principle for an integrated information system is that each document—journal article, progress report, patent, and so on—is to be processed one time only and the results put into the computer for subsequent repeated and multiple use. This is the system that VINITI is currently implementing.

On a still broader scale, UNESCO has completed a study on the feasibility of establishing UNISIST, a World Science Information System (UNESCO and ICSU, 1971). This is not to be a "world system" in the sense of being a preplanned, integrated organization under a single manager. On the contrary, "The ultimate goal is the establishment of a flexible and loosely connected network of information services based on voluntary cooperation" (UNESCO, 1973). UNISIST is an international effort that will attempt to integrate the diverse national philosophies, programs, and policies, and to encourage the free flow of scientific and technical information across national borders. The problems, as one can imagine, are immense. Not only are there problems in politics and policy, but also in different levels of development, education, and training, of language, document identification, classification, indexing, and so on. The encouraging aspect is that UNISIST is making progress. The need for improved information services is recognized everywhere and efforts are being made, nationally and internationally, individually and cooperatively, to provide fast, efficient, effective, and economical access to all the world's literature to all who may need it. Abstracting and indexing services will necessarily play an important role in these integrated information systems.

8 | Automatic Abstracting

Interest in automatic abstracting began in the early 1950s as a result of the natural confluence of two major development streams—computer technology and machine translation. Before the 1950s, the few computers that were available were used exclusively for computing. When it was realized that computers were actually symbol manipulators, and that they can process alphabetical as well as numerical symbols, new areas of application opened and became appropriate for investigation.

Machine translation (MT) was among the first of the language-processing applications. The computer was provided with a large bilingual dictionary, a set of grammar rules, and was programmed to translate from one language to another. The initial results were encouraging. It was reported that the programs were able to achieve 85–90% accurate translations. Improving these percentages was extremely difficult, and eventually the research emphasis switched from MT to more basic work in computational linguistics.

Although interest in MT was still high, the domain of computer language processing was expanded to include research in automatic abstracting, automatic indexing, and automatic document classification. The

161

question challenging the researcher was this: If the computer could be used to translate a document from one language to another, could it not be used to create a condensation of the document in the same language? H. P. Luhn was perhaps the first to respond to this challenge when, in 1952, he wrote that "there now exists the possibility of taking advantage of technological advances of recent years for solving this (information) problem to a degree which should mark a distinct advance over previous methods" (Luhn, 1952, p. 35). A few years later, Luhn published a paper describing a method for the automatic creation of literature abstracts (Luhn, 1958). This paper, along with Luhn's other work in information retrieval, provides the start from which other investigations proceed.

8.1   POSSIBLE BENEFITS OF AUTOMATIC ABSTRACTING

A number of practical reasons spurred the research efforts in automatic abstracting. The volume of journal literature was increasing; this, of course, led to an increase in the size and in the importance of the secondary publications. It became difficult to keep up with the literature, and the lag between the publication of the original article and the publication of the abstract increased in some instances. In order for the secondary publications to be complete and current, more abstractors were needed. It was postulated that not enough people had the required skills and interests to do this work. The professional abstractors who were available required high salaries, and this further increased the cost of the publication. If less-qualified abstractors were utilized, the quality of the publication dropped. Something had to be done, and so exploratory research was undertaken to produce abstracts by computer.

Obviously, these autoabstracts had to be of sufficient quality so that they would be useful and used. Thus, while an attempt was being made to automate the production of abstracts, simultaneous efforts were directed toward studying how humans write abstracts and toward formulating the criteria for evaluating the quality of the products of both humans and machines.

One of the initial benefits of the research in automatic abstracting was a better understanding of how humans prepare abstracts. The first attempt at automation involved having the computer select key sentences verbatim for inclusion in an "extract." The methods and the consistency of sentence selection by humans were investigated. At IBM, a series of studies on this topic was conducted by Rath, Resnick, and Savage (1961b).

To study sentence selection, Rath and co-workers gave six subjects 10

Scientific American articles and asked them to pick the 20 most representative sentences from each. Then the subjects were asked to rank these
sentences by how well each represented the article it was from. It was
found that 47% of the sentences selected by the subjects were topic
sentences; that is, they were either the first or last sentence of a paragraph. Five different autoabstracting programs also selected and ranked
sentences from the same 10 articles. All six subjects agreed on an average
of only 1.6 sentences of the 20 selected for each article. If the criterion of
agreement was five out of six subjects, then agreement was reached on
an average of 6.4 out of the 20 sentences. The five computer programs
were more consistent, but there was little agreement among the
sentences selected by the humans and those selected by computer.

A second study measured human consistency in sentence selection after
a lapse of eight weeks. Only 55% of the same sentences were selected the
second time, although the subjects were able to identify correctly their
previous selections 64% of the time. There was more intrasubject consistency than intersubject consistency.

One may conclude from these studies, although they are certainly not
definitive, that human extractors tend to choose topic sentences as being
representative, and that representative sentences can be selected with
only moderate consistency.

Once it became possible to prepare computer-produced extracts, researchers faced the problem of evaluating their acceptability, but it was
impossible to evaluate automatic extracts without at the same time
evaluating the quality of manual abstracts and extracts. What were
needed were criteria by which all abstracts could be judged. Borko and
Chatman (1963) began their search for such criteria by studying the
instructions to abstractors provided by editors of scientific and technical
journals. The results of this study were reported in Chapter 3. The study
is mentioned here as yet another example of the benefits—both direct and
indirect—that accrued from the efforts to automate the preparation of abstracts. It was not until it became necessary to evaluate the acceptability
of computer-produced extracts that the acceptability of any abstract was
studied empirically. Programming the computer to select "significant
representative sentences" required precise operational instructions, and
this in turn led to some understanding of how humans select sentences,
prepare abstracts, and evaluate the results.

8.2   METHODS OF AUTOMATIC ABSTRACTING

"The ultimate goal of research in automatic abstracting is to enable
a computer program to 'read' a document and 'write' an abstract of it

in conventional prose style, but the path to this goal is full of yet un-conquered obstacles" (Wyllys, 1967, p. 128). In the rest of this chapter, we will examine the progress made on the path to this goal and the obstacles that still remain to be overcome.

Altough the chapter title is "Automatic Abstracting," the name is neither descriptive nor accurate. For one thing, there is nothing auto-matic about using a computer, and we agree with Mathis (1972, p. 39n) that abstracting by computer should preferably be called *computer-based abstracting*. More important, the present-day process—by any name—does not now produce a true abstract. The output of the computer processing is an *extract;* that is, a number of significant, representative sentences are identified, extracted from the original article, and printed as a computer-produced extract of the article. Although the phrases *computer-based extracting* and *computer-produced extracts* are more accurate and more descriptive of both the process and the product, the terms are not com-monly used; *automatic abstracting* is more often found in the literature. All these terms will be used, but with appropriate nuances.

Computer-based extracting consists of the following steps:

1. putting the article to be extracted into machine-readable form, by keypunching or by other methods;
2. determining operational measures of "significance" and/or "rep-resentativeness" for individual words and for sentences;
3. analyzing the input text by computing representativeness scores for each word and sentence, and by selecting that set of sentences constituting the extract;
4. formatting and printing the extract.

Each step is briefly discussed in the following sections.

Keypunching. The task of converting technical documents into machine-readable form is much more complex than one would anticipate. Most technical articles are printed in a variety of type fonts and with many more symbols than uppercase and lowercase letters and numbers. Many contain tables, graphs, and other illustrations. How are these features to be keypunched? A simple solution, and the one most often adopted, is to pre-edit the text and to eliminate those portions of the document that cannot be directly processed on the input device, which is generally a card punch. This solution is not the best one, for discarded information such as boldface, italic, and special characters; captions and tables, graphs, and pictures; and other special text features might contribute significantly to the design of abstracting algorithms. Decisions made at this stage will affect all the succeeding work; thus, keypunching decisions should be made with care and forethought.

Determining measures of sentence significance. The most important features of extracting programs are the measures used for calculating the "significance" and/or "representativeness" of the words and the sentences in the text. Researchers have devised different measures for determining sentence selectability. Their measures, rationale, and results will be discussed under Survey of Research Studies.

Analyzing text and selecting sentences. Once the selectability criteria have been defined, programs can be written to analyze the input text, to assign weights to all words, to calculate the significance scores for each sentence, and to select those sentences that will constitute the computer-based extract.

Formatting and printing. Extracts are usually printed on an off-line printer with the sentences arranged in the order of their appearance in the original article. Generally the printing is done all in uppercase characters. The format is unattractive and the print hard to read. Little, if any, effort is spent on improving the appearance of the printed extract.

8.3   SURVEY OF RESEARCH STUDIES

This section reviews significant studies that have contributed new methods for producing extracts and abstracts by computer. These reports are necessarily neither complete nor evenly balanced. Readers needing more detailed information should refer to the original reports. Readers content with state-of-the-art summaries, but wanting more data than are presented here, are referred to Wyllys (1967), and to Mathis (1972). The sections that follow draw heavily on both these sources.

8.3.1   The Luhn Study

Luhn's (1968) paper on autoabstracting (actually autoextracting) was the prototype study. It described many of the procedures that other researchers then went on to modify and improve.

The text of an article was first keypunched into machine-readable form for computer processing. As each word in the input text was read by the computer, it was designated as either a common word or a content word. *Common words,* sometimes called *function words* or *nonsubstantive words,* consist of conjunctions, pronouns, prepositions, articles, auxiliary verbs, and certain adjectives and adverbs. These words were listed in a previously prepared dictionary for table lookup (search of a list by a computer). Common words were arbitrarily assigned a zero significance value. *Content words* are words that by definition are not common words; that is, words that are not listed in the table of common words. These words were alphabetized, consolidated (words with the same root form, such as *program* and *programs* were combined), and counted. Content word types whose frequency exceeded a predetermined value *V* were considered *representative* of the content of the article; all word types that did not exceed this value were labeled *nonrepresentative*.

Thus, Luhn's procedures for measuring the representativeness of individual words in a document were rather simple and made use of a two-valued scale. All common words were by definition nonrepresentative. Content words that exceeded a predetermined frequency value were considered representative; all others were not.

To measure the representativeness of sentences, two criteria—frequency and proximity—were combined. Luhn wrote that "whenever the greatest number of frequently occurring words are found in greatest physical proximity to each other, the probability is very high that the information being conveyed is representative of the article. . ." (1958, pp. 160–161). Sentences were divided into substrings, each of which was bounded by significant words separated by no more than four nonsignificant words. If a significant word was separated from other significant words by more than four words, it was labeled an *isolate* and dropped from consideration. A representative value (r_i) for each nonisolate substring was calculated by squaring the number of representative word tokens (p_i) in the cluster and dividing by the total number of word tokens in the cluster (q_i):

$$r_i = \frac{p_i{}^2}{q_i}$$

To select sentences for inclusion in the extract, one of two criteria were used: (1) r_i had to be higher than some prescribed value, or (2) a predetermined number of sentences with the highest r_i values were to be selected for the extract.

Because of its historical importance, and in order to demonstrate the effectiveness of these procedures, a number of exhibits from Luhn's paper are reproduced. (See Figures 8.1, 8.2, and 8.3.)

8.3.2   The Baxendale Study

Phyllis Baxendale was more interested in automatic indexing than in automatic abstracting. However, the two tasks are related, for they both involve the identification of the representative words in a document. She

Significant words in descending order of frequency (common words omitted).

46	nerve	12	body	6	disturbance	4	accumulate
40	chemical	12	effects	6	related	4	balance
28	system	12	electrical	5	control	4	block
22	communication	12	mental	5	diagram	4	disorders
19	adrenalin	12	messengers	5	fibers	4	end
18	cell	10	signals	5	gland	4	excitation
18	synapse	10	stimulation	5	mechanisms	4	health
16	impulses	8	action	5	mediators	4	human
16	inhibition	8	ganglion	5	organism	4	outgoing
15	brain	7	animal	5	produce	4	reaching
15	transmission	7	blood	5	regulate	4	recording
13	acetylcholine	7	drugs	5	serotonin	4	release
13	experiment	7	normal			4	supply
13	substances					4	tranquilizing

Figure 8.1 *List of representative words and their frequencies. [Reprinted from Luhn, 1958, by permission of IBM Corp. Copyright 1958 by International Business Machines Corporation.]*

was the first to consider the possibility of using topic sentences for selecting highly representative words, and the studies of Rath *et al.* (1961a,b) were based, in part, on her work.

Baxendale experimented with three methods for selecting words and groups of words from an article: (1) deleting function words; (2) selecting content words found in topic sentences; and (3) selecting words found in the prepositional phrases in the text.

Method 1: Deleting function words. By using a list of 150 function words (noncontent words), Baxendale was able to eliminate over half the running text from further consideration. The remaining content words were given a score based upon their absolute and relative frequency in the text. The words with the highest scores were considered to be the most representative.

Method 2: Topic sentences. Baxendale argued that the topic sentence is "the fulcrum on which the paragraph rests." Furthermore, she stated

Total word occurrences in the document:	2326
Different words in document:	
Total of different words	741
Less different common words	170
Different non-common words	571
Ratio of all word occurrences to different non-common words . . .	~4:1
Non-common words having a frequency of occurrence of 5 and over:	
Total occurrences	478
Different words	39

Figure 8.2 *Word counts. [Reprinted from Luhn, 1958, by permission of IBM Corp. Copyright 1958 by International Business Machines Corporation.]*

Exhibit 1

Source: The Scientific American, Vol. 196, No. 2, 86-94, February, 1957

Title: Messengers of the Nervous System

Author: Amodeo S. Marrazzi

Editor's Sub-heading: The internal communication of the body is mediated by chemicals as well as by nerve impulses. Study of their interaction has developed important leads to the understanding and therapy of mental illness.

Auto-Abstract*

It seems reasonable to credit the single-celled organisms also with a system of chemical communication by diffusion of stimulating substances through the cell, and these correspond to the chemical messengers (e.g., hormones) that carry stimuli from cell to cell in the more complex organisms. (7.0)†

Finally, in the vertebrate animals there are special glands (e.g., the adrenals) for producing chemical messengers, and the nervous and chemical communication systems are intertwined: for instance, release of adrenalin by the adrenal gland is subject to control both by nerve impulses and by chemicals brought to the gland by the blood. (6.4)

The experiments clearly demonstrated that acetylcholine (and related substances) and adrenalin (and its relatives) exert opposing actions which maintain a balanced regulation of the transmission of nerve impulses. (6.3)

It is reasonable to suppose that the tranquilizing drugs counteract the inhibitory effect of excessive adrenalin or serotonin or some related inhibitor in the human nervous system. (7.3)

*Sentences selected by means of statistical analysis as having a degree of significance of 6 and over.
†Significance factor is given at the end of each sentence.

Figure 8.3 Automatic abstract. [*Reprinted from Luhn, 1958, by permission of IBM Corp. Copyright 1958 by International Business Machines Corporation.*]

that "an investigation of a sample of 200 paragraphs [revealed that] in 85 percent of the paragraphs the topic sentence was the initial sentence and in 7 percent the final" (Baxendale, 1958, p. 355). Her procedure was to select representative words from only the first and last sentences of each paragraph and to weigh these for significance.

Method 3: Prepositional phrases. The third method was to select as representative the words in prepositional phrases, for "the phrase is likely to reflect the content of an article more closely than any other simple construction" (Baxendale, 1958, p. 357). This method had the additional advantage of selecting word groups rather than individual words, as for example "discrete energy levels" and "forbidden energy region." Furthermore, this could be done by means of a relatively simple computer program.

Since these methods were not actually used for selecting representative sentences for automatic extracting, their effectiveness can be evaluated only indirectly. However, Baxendale's experimental work is influential and important and has stimulated other researchers.

8.3.3   The Oswald Study

Oswald was also more interested in automatic indexing than in abstracting. His study (Edmundson, Oswald, and Wyllys, 1959) involved a technique for automatically generating indexes that included multiword terms as well as single words. He stated that when selecting sentences for automatic extracting, scores should be computed by the number of representative groups of words in the sentence.

The basic procedures included, first, ascertaining the frequency of content-word tokens in the document. After the highest-frequency words were identified, it was necessary to determine whether or not another significant word, with a frequency greater than 1, was located adjacent to the first word; if so, these constituted a multiword term. For automatic extracting those sentences with the greatest number of multiword terms were selected.

Oswald did not have a computer, and so he hand-simulated these procedures. In evaluating his results, Oswald candidly admits that the automatic extracts produced by these methods exhibited a "range in quality from fairly good to disappointing. The longer articles were extracted more satisfactorily than the shorter ones" (Edmundson *et al.*, 1959, p. 17).

8.3.4   The ACSI-Matic Study

The ACSI-matic study was conducted by IBM for the Department of the Army, Assistant Chief of Staff for Intelligence (ACSI) (IBM, 1960, 1961). The automatic extracting procedures developed in this study have been implemented as part of an operational computer-based extracting system. The procedures work; they produce extracts, and for this reason, if for none other, they deserve special recognition.

The extracting techniques used in the ACSI-matic study were those developed by Luhn, with some very significant modifications and extensions.

Word Selection Techniques

As an initial step in processing, documents to be extracted were divided into three groups, called *normal, blah,* and *detailed.* A slightly different technique for selecting representative words was applied to the documents in each group.

For *normal* documents, it was determined that the average document in this group contained between 48% and 56% function words. Also, the average sentence ranged in length from 18 to 26 words. For these normal documents, words with frequencies equal to or greater than the average word frequency in that text were designated as representative words.

For *blah* documents, the percentage of function words was higher than 56%, and the content words with the highest frequencies were so general as to be useless and nonrepresentative of the document. Content words with a frequency exceeding 1% of the total words were simply eliminated and the remainder designated as representative.

Detailed documents usually had less than 48% function words and a larger number (greater than 35% of the different words in the text) of content words that appeared only once. For detailed documents, the procedure selected as representative those words whose frequency was *less than* or equal to the average word frequency.

Sentence Scoring

Once the representative words in a document were identified, representative sentences could be scored. Luhn's original procedure was to count those clusters of representative words that were separated by not more than four nonrepresentative words. In the ACSI-matic study, sentences were scored by adding the total number of representative words in a sentence to the sum of a set of fractions calculated from the pattern of the nonrepresentative words in the sentence. An example will make the procedure clear. Suppose we have a sentence with the following pattern of nonrepresentative words (N) and representative words (R):

$$N \; R \; N \; N \; R \; N \; N \; N \; R \; N \; N$$

R-words are given a value of 1, terminal N-words have a value of zero, and nonterminal N-words are given a value of $(\frac{1}{2})^n$, where n is the number of N-words between successive R-words. So, the sentence pattern will be scored as follows:

$$0 + 1 + (\tfrac{1}{2})^2 + 1 + (\tfrac{1}{2})^3 + 1 + 0 + 0$$
$$1 + \tfrac{1}{4} + 1 + \tfrac{1}{8} + 1 = 3\tfrac{3}{8}$$

Number of Sentences

To determine the number of sentences to be included in the extract, the following formulas were used: (a) if the document had fewer than 200 sentences, the extract was to contain 10% of the total number of sentences; (b) if the document had more than 200 sentences, the number of sentences was divided by 10; 20 was subtracted from the quotient; and the remainder was divided by 32. The number of sentences in the extract was this quotient plus 20.

For example, if the document contained 1000 sentences, then,

$$1000/10 = 100$$
$$100 - 20 = 80$$
$$80/32 = 2.5$$
$$2.5 + 20 = 22.5$$

Thus the extract would contain 23 sentences.

Sentence Selection and Elimination of Redundancy

After the number of sentences to be included in the extract was determined, the n sentences with the highest scores were selected and called *abstract sentences*. A second group of sentences numbering $n/4$ were selected from those having the next highest scores. These were called *reserve sentences*. Here another variation from the Luhn procedure was introduced. The set of candidate sentences was examined for possible redundancy. Highly redundant sentences, that is, those containing a number of matching words greater than one-fourth of the total number of the words compared, were eliminated and a new sentence added from the set of reserve sentences.

The ACSI-matic system of automatic extracting has a number of sophisticated features. Although no recent reports have appeared in the unclassified literature, it is reported that the system is operational, and so one can assume that the users are satisfied with the results.

8.3.5   The Edmundson and Wyllys Studies

These studies on automatic extracting, directed by H. P. Edmundson, spanned the 1960s and took place in a number of different organizations although the bulk of the work was done while the principal investigators were employed by Thompson Ramo Wooldridge, Inc., of Canoga Park in Los Angeles, California. The studies were comprehensive and covered four main lines of investigation: (1) consistency of human extracting; (2) the mathematical and logical foundations of automatic extracting formulated in terms of the inductive probability of selecting a given sentence for inclusion in the extract; (3) the semantic structure of individual sentences as a means of determining representativeness; and (4) the development of computer programs for sentence extraction. Each of the separate studies is important and has contributed to our knowledge of abstracting; however, for this summary, we are primarily concerned with the new procedures used in sentence selection for automatic extracting. In describing the research method, Edmundson stated, "The goal was to replace the subjective notion of 'significant' by an operational procedure. A methodology was sought whereby a computer could produce extracts as useful as conventionally created abstracts. The approach was to look for selection criteria among manually selected and rejected sentences" (Edmundson, 1969, p. 267). Four basic methods of sentence selection were identified and called the *Cue, Key, Title,* and *Location* methods.

1. *Cue Method.* "The Cue method is based on the hypothesis that the probable relevance of a sentence is affected by the presence of pragmatic words such as 'significant,' 'impossible,' and 'hardly' " (Edmundson, 1969, p. 271). Selected words were pre-stored in a Cue dictionary with three subdivisions: Bonus words that had a positive value or weight, Stigma words that had a negative weight, and Null words that were irrelevant. In this method, the significance value of a sentence was the sum of the Cue weights of its constituent words.

2. *Key Method.* The principle involved was similar to the one suggested by Luhn, and was based on the hypothesis that high-frequency content words could be used to select sentences relevant to the content of the document. The Key weight of a sentence was the sum of the Key weights of its constituent words.

3. *Title Method.* This method was based on the hypothesis that the title and the subtitles that partition the body of a document summarize its contents. A Title glossary was created consisting of all nonnull words in the title, subtitle, and other headings for that document. In determining the significance value of a sentence, title words were assigned a higher weight than subtitle words, and the sentence value was the sum of the Title weights of its constituent words.

4. *Location Method.* The Location method assigned weights to sentences according to their occurrence under certain headings (such as "Introduction," "Purpose," "Conclusions") and their position in the text (i.e., first or last paragraphs, and first or last sentences of paragraphs). The Location weight for each sentence was the sum of its Heading weight and its Ordinal weight.

Edmundson explained the rationale of these four methods by stating that sentence representativeness may be based on structural and/or linguistic cues. His concepts are summarized in Figure 8.4, which is reprinted from his article (Edmundson, 1969, p. 274).

A number of experiments were performed to determine the best combination, and weighting, of these four extracting methods. The final system used a simple linear function:

$$a_1 C + a_2 K + a_3 T + a_4 L$$

where a_1, a_2, a_3, and a_4 are parameters (positive integers) for the Cue,

		Structural Sources of Clues:	
		Body of Document (Text)	Skeleton of Document (Title, Headings, Format)
Linguistic Sources of Clues:	General Characteristics of Corpus	CUE METHOD: Cue Dictionary (995 words) (Includes Bonus, Stigma, and Null subdictionaries)	LOCATION METHOD: Heading Dictionary (90 words) (Location method also uses ordinal weights)
	Specific Characteristics of Document	KEY METHOD: Key Glossary	TITLE METHOD: Title Glossary

Figure 8.4 Rationale of the four basic sentence selection methods employed by Edmundson. [Reproduced from Journal of the Association for Computing Machinery, *Vol. 16, No. 2, 1969, p. 274. Copyright 1969, Association for Computing Machinery, Inc., reprinted by permission.]*

Key, Title, and Location weights respectively. The length of the extract was also parameterized so that it could be adjusted, but in the experiments, it was left at 25% of the number of sentences.

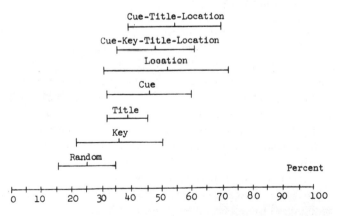

Figure 8.5 Mean coselection scores showing the percentage of the number of sentences coselected in automation and target extracts, for the sentence selection methods—Cue, Key, Title, and Location—employed by Edmundson. [Reproduced from Journal of the Association for Computing Machinery, *Vol. 16, No. 2, 1969. Copyright 1969, Association for Computing Machinery, Inc., reprinted by permission.]*

Figure 8.5 (Edmundson, 1969, p. 274) shows the percentage of the number of sentences coselected in both the automatic and the target extracts for each of the extracting methods, separately and in combination. The figure shows the intervals encompassed by the sample mean plus and minus one standard deviation. The Cue–Title–Location method has the highest mean coselection score, whereas the Key method, when used in isolation, has the lowest score. Based upon these data, the Key method was discontinued.

A sample of an automatic extract, prepared by Edmundson, is reproduced in Figure 8.6 (Edmundson, 1969, pp. 282–3).

Two methods were used to evaluate the automatic extracts (1) similarity rating of the automatic extracts versus the corresponding human-prepared target abstracts and random extracts of the same length; and (2) a "statistical error analysis" based upon the number of coselected sentences containing the same information as other sentences in the target extract, and upon sentences that should have been selected for the automatic extract. Neither the utility of the target extract nor of the automatic extract was studied.

Although his report was in a sense an interim report, Edmundson concluded that "it is now beyond question that future automatic abstracting methods must take into account syntactic and semantic characteristics of the language and the text; they cannot rely simply upon gross statistical evidence" (Edmundson, 1969, p. 284).

8.3.6   The Earl Studies

For a period of nine years, beginning in 1964, Lois Earl and her associates at the Lockheed Missiles and Space Company, Sunnyvale, California, conducted a series of research projects directed toward the development of automatic indexing, abstracting, and extracting systems. These studies, supported by the U.S. Office of Naval Research, included basic investigations in English morphology, phonetics, syntax, semantics, and representations of pictorial data. A series of reports describing this project has been written. (See Earl, 1973, for a complete bibliography. See also Earl, 1970.)

The approach taken by the Lockheed researchers has been to develop linguistic criteria by which a subset of text—words, phrases, or sentences —can be recognized by a computable algorithm. During the initial period, a *word data base* was established, together with an algorithm for determining the existence of linguistic similarities between sentences, for producing abstracts.

These morphological studies led to the development of a *sentence dictionary* of syntactic types. It was hypothesized that there might be a relationship between the syntactic structure of a sentence and its "significance" for deriving index and extract terms. Experiments were designed to test the hypothesis that the part-of-speech structure could make a binary distinction between representative and nonrepresentative sentences—sentences that contained an indexable term and those that did not. Unfortunately, the results of these experiments showed that although the text corpus contained over 3000 unique part-of-speech patterns, only 34 of these occurred more than once. Clearly, these strings made too fine a distinction among sentences. New experiments were designed and executed to test the applicability of phrase structures for automatic abstracting, but this too proved to be too fine a distinction, and the results were again negative. It was concluded that indexable and nonindexable sentences cannot be distinguished by structure alone.

The next approach was to experiment with the use of a combined frequency–syntax method for identifying significant words and sentences for extracting. This approach made use of a phrase-identifying syntactic analyzer, which identified all noun phrases and excluded function words within the noun phrase. The nonfunction words were then alphabetized, counted, and rearranged in descending order of frequency. All frequencies lower than a cutoff frequency were discarded, and the words making up the remaining frequency counts were extracted from the original list and arranged in ascending order according to their associated page and sentence number. A sentence was considered representative and was selected for the extract if it contained three or more high-frequency words from these noun phrases, or two high-frequency words if that pair had not occurred together in a previously selected sentence.

The procedure just outlined is similar to Luhn's frequency method of identifying significant sentences for automatic extracting with the important modification that only nonfunction words in noun phrases are used in determining frequency.

Earl characterized the results of these experiments as mildly encouraging. She suggested that the computer-produced extracts could be used to decide whether the original article contains material of interest to the reader. She stated that "all four extracts cover the territory rather well and convey the subject matter and tone of the text. For screening purposes, it is felt that the extracts produced by this algorithm are quite acceptable" (Earl, 1970, p. 327).

8.3.7   The Ohio State University Studies: The ADAM System

Professor James A. Rush at the Ohio State University and his students, particularly R. Salvador, A. Zamora, and B. A. Mathis, conducted a series of studies on automatic abstracting (Rush, Salvador, and Zamora, 1971;

PAR   SENT   DOCUMENT NUMBER   6   1

ABSTRACT BASED ON HUMAN SELECTION

EVALUATION OF THE EFFECT OF DIMETHYLAMINE BORINE AND SEVERAL OTHER ADDITIVES ON
COMBUSTION STABILITY CHARACTERISTICS OF VARIOUS HYDROCARBON TYPE FUELS IN PHILLIPS
MICROBURNER (AD87730)
R. L. BRACE

1   0   SUMMARY

2   1   AT THE REQUEST OF THE NAVY BUREAU OF AERONAUTICS, PHILLIPS PETROLEUM
COMPANY UNDERTOOK THE EVALUATION OF DIMETHYLAMINE BORINE AS AN ADDITIVE
FOR IMPROVING THE COMBUSTION CHARACTERISTICS OF AVIATION GAS TURBINE TYPE
FUELS.

2   2   BECAUSE OF THE SAMLL AMOUNT (100 GRAMS) OF DIMETHYLAMINE BORINE RECEIVED
FROM CALLERY CHEMICAL COMPANY. THIS EVALUATION HAS BEEN LIMITED TO THE
MEASUREMENT OF ITS EFFECT ON THE FLASH-BACK CHARACTERISTICS OF THREE
PURE HYDROCARBONS (TOLUENE, NORMAL HEPTANE AND BENZENE) IN THE PHILLIPS
MICROBURNER.

2   3   DIMETHYLAMINE BORINE CONCENTRATIONS OF FROM 0.1 to 1.0 PER CENT BY WEIGHT
WERE EVALUATED.

3   1   FOR COMPARATIVE PURPOSES TWO COMMON IGNITION ADDITIVES (AMYL NITRATE
AND CUMENE HYDROPEROXIDE) WERE ALSO EVALUATED DURING THIS STUDY, AS
WELL AS CONCENTRATIONS UP TO 20 PER CENT BY WEIGHT OF PROPYLENE OXIDE -
A RELATIVELY HIGH FLAME VELOCITY FUEL.

3   2   PREVIOUS STUDIES IN PHILLIPS 2 INCH TURBOJET ENGINE TYPE COMBUSTOR HAD
INDICATED THAT SUCH MATERIALS COULD SUBSTANTIALLY INCREASE THE MAXIMUM
RATE OF HEAT RELEASE ATTAINABLE, ESPECIALLY WITH LOW PERFORMANCE
FUELS SUCH AS THE ISO PARAFFIN TYPE HYDROCARBONS - PARTICULARLY WHEN
OPERATING UNDER SEVERE CONDITIONS FOR COMBUSTION (I.E., HIGH AIR FLOW
VELOCITY OR LOW COMBUSTION PRESSURE).

4   4   WITH RESPECT TO THE DIMETHYLAMINE BORINE, ITS EFFECT AS A FUEL ADDITIVE
WAS NOTEWORTHY, 0.1 WEIGHT PER CENT IN TOLUENE BEING EQUIVALENT TO 20
PER CENT BY WEIGHT OF ADDED PROPYLENE OXIDE.

4   5   IN GENERAL, ADDITIVE CONCENTRATIONS OF ONE PER CENT BY WEIGHT IN THE
SEVERAL PURE HYDROCARBONS WHICH NORMALLY DIFFERED QUITE WIDELY IN PER-
FORMANCE, PRODUCED UNIFORMLY SUPERIOR COMBUSTION STABILITY CHARACTERIS-
TICS AS MEASURED USING THE PHILLIPS MICROBURNER.

5   0   I. INTRODUCTION

8   0   II. DESCRIPTION OF PHILLIPS MICROBURNER (MODEL 1A)

10   0   III. DESCRIPTION OF TEST APPARATUS

14   0   IV. DESCRIPTION OF TEST FUELS

15   2   THESE FUELS REPRESENT VARIATIONS IN CHEMICAL STRUCTURE WHICH WILL IN
TURN PROVIDE INDICES OF BOTH GOOD AND POOR COMBUSTION STABILITY PER-
FORMANCE.

17	0	V. TEST PROCEDURE
21	0	VI. RESULTS
24	1	THE REGION OF STABLE OPERATION IS DEFINED AS THE STATE OF FLASH BACK— THE CONDITIONS OF COMBUSTION WHERE THE FLAME WOULD BECOME ANCHORED TO A FLAME HOLDER - AS IN STABLE GAS TURBINE OR RAM JET COMBUSTOR OPERATION - IF THE FLAME HOLDER WERE PROVIDED IN THE BURNER TUBE.
25	0	VII. DISCUSSION
26	2	THE ASSUMPTION IS MADE THAT THE GREATER THE ALLOWABLE HEAT INPUT RATE AT A GIVEN VELOCITY, THE GREATER THE DEGREE OF STABILITY.
31	3	ALL FOUR ADDITIVES INDICATED THEIR ADDITION TO BE SUBJECT TO THE EFFECT OF DEMINISHING RESULTS UPON FURTHER ADDITION - THAT IS, THEIR EFFECT WAS NOT ESSENTIALLY A BLENDING EFFECT.
32	1	MENTION SHOULD BE MADE OF THE FACT THAT DURING THE COMBUSTION OF THE DIMETHYLAMINE BORINE-HYDROCARBON FUEL BLENDS NO NOTICEABLE ODORS OR SMOKE WERE OBSERVED.
33	0	VIII. CONCLUSIONS
36	1	3. THE ADDITION OF ADDITIVE CONCENTRATIONS (UP TO 1 PER CENT) OF AMYL NITRATE, CUMENE HYDROPERIOXIDE, AND DIMETHYLAMINE BORINE ALL RESULTED IN IMPROVED STABILITY PERFORMANCE; THE GREATEST INCREASES WERE SHOWN WHEN B_ENDED WITH A FUEL OF POOR PERFORMANCE CHARACTERISTICS - SUCH AS TOLUENE.
36	2	BENEFICIAL EFFECTS WERE APPRECIABLY LESS WHEN BLENDED WITH A FUEL OF GOOD PERFORMANCE CHARACTERISTICS - SUCH AS N-HEPTANE.
37	0	IX. RECOMMENDATIONS
38	1	BASED ON THE EVALUATION OF THE EFFECTS OF ADDITIVES ON THE FLASHBACK LIMITS OF THE ADDITIVE-FUEL BLENDS TESTED IN THE MICROBURNER (MODEL IA) IT IS RECOMMENDED THAT DIMETHYLAMINE BORINE SHOULD BE FURTHER INVESTIGATED.
38	2	THIS FUTURE WORK SHOULD INCLUDE STUDY OF COMBUSTION STABILITY AND COMBUSTION EFFICIENCY EFFECTS IN THE PHILLIPS 2 INCH COMBUSTOR AND AN INVESTIGATION OF ITS INFLUENCE ON COMBUSTION CLEANLINESS.

81c

Figure 8.6 Example of an extract produced by Edmundson's system. [Reproduced from Journal of the Association for Computing Machinery, Vol. 16, No. 2, 1969, p. 269. Copyright 1969, Association for Computing Machinery, Inc., reprinted by permission.]

Mathis, Rush, and Young, 1973). Their system was named ADAM (automatic document abstracting method). It is briefly described by Mathis (1972). The two basic components were a dictionary, called the Word Control List (WCL), and a set of rules for implementing the functions specified for each WCL entry. The goal was to produce a true abstract and not just an extract.

One of the most significant aspects of the ADAM system was the development of rules and procedures for identifying and *rejecting* those sentences in the original document that should not be included in the abstract. ADAM emphasized rejection criteria rather than selection rules Sentences to be excluded were those that contained historical data, results of previous work, explanations, speculative material, and the like. Use was made of modified location and cue criteria, plus word-frequency and coherence considerations for assigning both positive and negative weights to each sentence.

The *location criterion* considered the position of the sentence in the document (e.g., the first sentence of the concluding paragraph), but it also took into account the location of words and phrases within a sentence as determined by punctuation marks. These sentence elements were given syntactic values indicating whether the sentence should be considered for retention or rejection.

Cue words, contained in the WCL dictionary, had two components: a syntactic value and a semantic weight. Such phrases as *our work, this paper,* and *present research* provided semantic cues identifying sentences that gave the purpose of an article and were important enough to be considered for inclusion in the abstract. The cue method also matched the words in a sentence against those in the WCL and invoked decision rules to determine whether the weighting should be positive or negative. It was found that although numerous cue words could be used by authors to indicate important notions in sentences, only a relative few were indicative of sentences that could be rejected. Thus, by emphasizing the rejection approach to abstract production, Rush and associates were able to keep the WCL to fewer than 700 cue-word entries.

Frequency criteria, as used in ADAM, stated that if any cue-word expression exceeded a given frequency threshold, its value was to be reduced so that if the expression in question had a positive weight, it would be made less positive, and if it had a negative weight, it would be made less negative. High-frequency words or phrases reduced the likelihood that the sentence would be accepted and also reduced the likelihood that the sentence would be rejected. Word-frequency considerations were used to modify the weight of the cue words when the information content value of a sentence was calculated. Consideration was also given to the words in the *title;* that is, the words of each sentence were matched against the words in the title, and if any content words matched, the sentence was a candidate for selection. If the title words appeared with high frequency, the weight given to those words was reduced.

Coherence criteria took into consideration semantic interrelationships among the sentences selected for possible inclusion in the abstract. If a candidate sentence required an antecedent, that is, if it contained cue words such as *these cases,* or *this method,* then the previous sentence was also included in the abstract even though the calculated value of that sentence was low. In this way the ADAM system attempted to produce abstracts in which the progression of ideas flowed smoothly and coherently from sentence to sentence. Later work (Mathis *et al.*, 1973) resulted in other procedures for modifying sentences initially selected by the abstracting system, and in some instances creating new sentences. Sentence modification has further improved the coherence and readability of the automatic abstracts. The results more closely resemble manually prepared abstracts than those of any other computer-based extracting system (see Figure 8.7).

Improvement of Automatic Abstracts by the Use of Structural Analysis

We have undertaken to extend the capabilities of the abstracting system described by Rush, Salvador and Zamora by adding to the system a modification procedure that could be employed to make the abstracts produced by the system more acceptable to the reader. Results of this study are reported in this paper. Our purpose is to present a rationale for the modification phase of an abstracting system and to describe several modification rules whose implementation is an initial step toward the automated production of abstracts that contain sentences written especially for the abstract. We have described several methods for improving the readability of abstracts produced by computer program. The research described in this paper was performed as a part of a larger project whose aim is the development of an operational automatic abstracting system. 18 references are given.*

BETTY A. MATHIS, JAMES E. RUSH and
CAROL E. YOUNG

Department of Computer and Information Science
The Ohio State University

* This abstract was produced by the Rush, Salvador, and Zamora automatic abstracting system and the procedures described in this paper.

Journal of the American Society for Information Science—March–April 1973

Figure 8.7 Automatic abstract: The Ohio University Studies, ADAM system. [*Reproduced from Mathis* et al., *"Improvement of automatic abstracts by the use of structural analysis,"* Journal of the American Society for Information Science, *Vol. 24, No. 2, 1973, pp. 101–109.*]

8.4   EVALUATING THE QUALITY OF ABSTRACTS

Measuring the quality of an abstract is complex. Yet it is necessary that we do so, for unless we can evaluate the product, we cannot improve it.

A number of criteria can be devised for evaluating the quality of an abstract. These include

1. a global rating or judgment of quality;
2. adherence to a standard for writing abstracts such as that proposed by the American National Standards Institute (ANSI), or by the International Standards Organization (ISO), or by some other authoritative body, such as the Chemical Abstracts Service;
3. inclusion of significant information and exclusion of unimportant information;
4. lack of errors;
5. consistency of style and readability.

To these criteria of quality can be added criteria on the "effectiveness" of the abstract, that is, the benefits derived from using the abstracts. Such effectiveness criteria could include the following:

6. for indicative abstracts—ability to alert the reader to the existence of a relevant document;
7. for informative abstracts—ability to provide the reader with significant specific information contained in the document and thus to serve as a surrogate for the original;
8. for any abstract—adequacy as a source of indexing terms.

If this list of eight criteria is accepted in principle, and one can delete some criteria and add others, then one can develop various evaluation techniques for measuring the quality and the effectiveness of abstracts— manual abstracts as well as computer-produced abstracts.

For example, it is possible to design a rating scale and have users evaluate the overall quality of abstracts. This would be a very general measure and perhaps not a very useful one for pointing out specific deficiencies. Using the second criterion, adherence to standards, one can develop a specific checklist, with or without rating scales, asking such questions as: Are the primary objectives of the study stated and Is the size of the sample population given? Additionally, one could check and determine whether the abstract includes all mentioned chemical compounds, reactions, types of equipment, specific results, and so forth. Errors in the abstract, such as misspelled names or wrong·

dates, are obvious items for inclusion in the checklist, as are inconsistencies in the use of abbreviations, in transliteration, and so forth. Readability may have to be a global rating, but it can also be evaluated using such criteria as the length of time it takes to read the abstract, the number of polysyllabic words, and the number of punctuation marks. Once the quality of an abstract is operationally defined, and the variables that determine quality are agreed upon, it is a relatively simple task to design tools and techniques for measuring these variables.

Editors of abstracting publications containing manually produced abstracts use a procedure similar to the one suggested above, but theirs is an informal procedure. Formal checklists and rating scales are unnecessary, for the editor has internalized the criterion concepts and measures to be used as evaluation standards. (S)he no longer needs to be conscious of them. There is, however, one evaluation aspect of which the editor is very conscious and that is the user response. The ultimate test of user acceptance is the marketplace; although the number of paid subscriptions reflects much more than just the quality of the abstracts, it is both an important factor in the success of the publication and a measure of its quality. If the publication is needed, it may succeed although of low quality.

Effectiveness, as well as overall quality, of the abstract can also be measured. Several researchers have conducted experiments designed to measure the effectiveness of both indicative and informative abstracts. Rath *et al.* compared the effectiveness of abstracts, titles, and complete text in relation to (1) determining whether a document is relevant for a specific purpose, and (2) obtaining relevant information in order to answer examination questions. They concluded that "there is no major difference between the Text and Abstract groups in their ability to pick appropriate documents, but the Text group obtained a significantly higher score on the examination" (Rath *et al.*, 1961a, p. 130).

Edmundson (1961) studied the effectiveness of computer-produced extracts by measuring the degree of similarity between an automatic extract and a manual extract prepared from the same text. Similarity was defined as the number of sentences selected in common and was measured by means of a correlation coefficient—the higher the coefficient, the better the extract.

Payne and his associates at the American Institute for Research (Payne, 1964; Payne, Altman, and Munger, 1962) conducted a series of experiments on the effectiveness of informative abstracts. They tested the ability of a group of subjects to answer questions on data contained in informative abstracts and compared the results with those obtained when the subjects used the complete, original documents. The effectiveness of the abstract was measured by the ratio of correct answers obtained using the abstract to those obtained using the original document. It was concluded that abstracts are effective purveyors of information.

Mathis (1972, p. 113) proposed a two-step procedure for the evaluation of abstracts: (1) Determine if the abstract conformed with the criteria for an acceptable abstract, such as the ANSI standards; (2) determine the data coefficient for the abstract.

For step 1, Mathis suggested the following criteria, which might be used as a checklist:

a. maximum length;
b. minimum length;
c. bibliographic citation format;
d. subject orientation;
e. error level;
f. style;
g. sentence completeness;
h. form (block verses paragraphed);
i. type (indicative, informative, etc.);
j. timeliness. (1972, p. 116);

For step 2, it was necessary first to define a data coefficient that would reflect the desired property of abstracts. The following formula was proposed:

$$DC = C/L$$

where

DC = data coefficient
C = data retention factor
$\quad = \dfrac{\text{the amount of data in the abstract}}{\text{the amount of data in the document}}$
L = length retention factor
$\quad = \dfrac{\text{the length of the abstract}}{\text{the length of the document}}$

This formula required the identification and measurement of the number of *data elements* in both abstracts and documents. A data element was defined as the equivalent of one concept. It was represented by Name–Relation–Name patterns, which were language strings composed of words representing names and relations. In a simple sentence, the first name corresponded to the subject, the relation to the predicate, and the second name to the object. The number of data elements, expressed as N–R–N patterns, would always be greater than or equal to the number of sentences in the text being examined. The rules for identifying data elements were precise, but a certain amount of subjectivity remained. Length was the simple sum of the number of words in the text. Thus, all the variables in the formula could be calculated. Once this was done, the results could be interpreted as follows:

a. If $DC < 1$, the abstract was unacceptable.
b. If $DC = 1$, the abstract was at a minimum level of acceptability.
c. If $DC > 1$, the abstract was acceptable.
d. The higher the DC value, the better the abstract.

The method proposed by Mathis is probably the most precise procedure now available for measuring the value of abstracts and extracts. It has particular significance for measuring the effectiveness of automatic abstracts. She applied her formula to the evaluation of the ADAM system and concluded that "the average data coefficient produced by the abstracting system was 1.063. This indicates that the system produces abstracts that are acceptable, but not outstanding" (Mathis, 1972, p. 166). This is probably a fair summary of the present state of the art for all existing automatic abstracting systems.

8.5   PROBLEM AREAS AND FIELDS FOR FUTURE RESEARCH

Having reviewed the various automatic abstracting and extracting procedures and the methods for evaluating abstracts, let us now turn our attention to some of the existing problem areas that may also serve to identify principal fields for future research. Earlier in this chapter we discussed the processes involved in computer-based abstracting. These consisted of three broadly inclusive tasks:

1. input processing;
2. specifying measures of representativeness for words and sentences;
3. formatting the abstract.

How adequate are our present procedures for implementing these steps?

8.5.1   Input Processing

For the most part, it is still necessary to edit and keypunch the text of an article in order to convert the printed version into a machine-readable form for computer processing. This procedure may change as a result of improvements in computer typesetting. Some technical journals are already being typeset by computer, which means that a machine-readable record exists, and thus one can avoid rekeyboarding. A certain amount of editing to remove errors and to specify which special features should, or should not, be included would still be necessary. It is safe to predict that more and more machine-readable texts will be available for computer processing, abstracting, and indexing. The input problem is being solved.

8.5.2   Measures of Representativeness

The survey of automatic abstracting experiments mentioned a number of different criteria—statistical, textual–syntactical, and semantic—that have been used to identify representative words in a text.

It was H. P. Luhn who first proposed a *statistical criterion*, based upon the absolute frequency of content words in a document, as a measure of a word's representativeness to the topic discussed. Although this criterion seems reasonable, and is reasonably useful, it has a number of deficiencies. Some content words appear with high frequency, but they are of a general nature and are unrelated to the specific theme of the article. Some highly specialized words might be used only once but are important indicators of content. To correct for such errors, *textual cues* need to be added to the list of criteria for determining representativeness. These textual cues are of both a positional and an editorial nature. The positional cues are dependent upon the position of the sentence with respect to the document as a whole. The editorial cues include such features as paragraph subheadings, specialized type fonts, capitalization, and punctuation marks. Although these criteria are helpful, they are dependent upon the author's style of writing and the journal's style of presentation, and these differences result in a great deal of inconsistency. *Semantic criteria* consist of cue words that authors frequently use in sentences having more than average importance (e.g., conclude, demonstrate, prove, summary). These words may be considered to be *positive semantic cues*. Semantic criteria may also have negative weights and these words can be used to identify nonrepresentative sentences.

The above measures are sometimes useful in selecting representative sentences for automatic abstracting. They cannot be relied upon to work consistently. Language is ambiguous; the same word may mean different things, and different words may mean the same thing. Sentences can obscure meaning as well as clarify it. The truth of the matter is that we have no really satisfactory automatic means of determining the representativeness of text units. One may, perhaps, also question whether we know enough to select representative text units by human intelligence. The problem is an extremely difficult one and is related to the more general question of measuring the importance of information.

8.5.3   Formatting the Abstract

In the early work on automatic extracting, sentences in the original document were assigned representativeness values based upon a formula that made use of one or more of the criteria discussed previously. The sentences were then ranked according to these values, and only the top few were selected for inclusion in the extract. The length of the extract, or the number of sentences to be selected, was determind by limiting the size of the extract to a certain number of words or sentences, or to a percentage of document length. Once the number of sentences was determined, those with the highest representativeness scores were selected and printed in the order in which they appeared in the article. Generally, that is all that was done to format the abstract.

This formatting procedure, although simple, is not very satisfactory. The sentences may be unrelated and repetitious, and they may refer to items described earlier but not included in the extract. It is difficult to fill in the gaps between the sentences, and so the extracts are difficult to read and to use. A number of things can be tried to alleviate these difficulties. Sentences can be checked for redundancy, and if two of the high-scoring candidate sentences contain some of the same content words, one sentence can be rejected. The Ohio State University programs achieved greater coherence and clarity by identifying sentences that required antecedent information and selecting these sentences as well. Some success has also been achieved in combining phrases and clauses from a number of sentences into one sentence, thus forming a *new* sentence for the abstract; this is almost genuine autoabstracting.

The task of creating an abstract involves more than simply extracting a few representative sentences from a document and listing these in order of occurrence. Completeness and coherence are needed, and those qualities have thus far not been achieved by computer processing.

8.6   COMMENTS

Both automatic extracting and abstracting may be within the current state of the art. A number of approaches and programs have been experimentally demonstrated and shown to work to a limited extent. But automatic abstracting consists of more than the design of computer programs that process a document and produce an abstract. Now, research in automatic abstracting must have as its goal the production of reasonably high quality, useful abstracts that are also cost effective. Computer-based abstracting systems need to operate on a high cost–performance–benefit ratio as compared with manual systems for extracting and abstracting.

The goal is difficult to achieve, much more difficult than simply producing computer-generated extracts. However, it may be, we believe, within the current state of the art if all that we know could be assembled and applied. Indeed, much progress has already been made. Programs are available that can produce different extracts from the same document. The quality (performance) of these results can be measured, and so can their effectiveness. Cost, until now, has not been a matter of concern, and extracting systems (except possibly for ACSI) have not been tested on a sufficiently large scale to determine operational costs. However, this can and should be done.

The initial research efforts in automatic extracting have concentrated on demonstrating that it is possible to program a computer to take machine-readable input and prepare an extract. This has now been demonstrated. In a second stage, research emphasized improving the quality of the extracts, and much effort was expended in measuring the quality, representativeness, and effectiveness of the results. These efforts did lead to improved quality; although clearly, research in this area will need to continue. For one thing, we need to learn how to program for selection of novel information. Perhaps now, we are almost ready to enter into the third stage of research, that stage immediately preceding development, when the research efforts need to be directed toward improving the quality, utility, and the cost effectiveness of the product.

Much has been accomplished; much remains to be accomplished.

9 | Career Opportunities

Since abstracts are an important product of the information industry, it follows that there are opportunities for those who wish to make abstracting a career, or a sideline for an organization or for themselves. Some abstractors create for themselves "external memories" (collections of indexed abstracts) of works important to their own personal interests. The producers of abstracts are publishers employing editors and proofreaders as well as abstractors and indexers. Most of the abstracting services provide some on-the-job training for their personnel, but of course, prior formal training will help one to get the position initially. One can seek full-time employment as an abstractor or, more often, one may look upon abstracting as a part-time job, even as an avocation. Many opportunities are available.

Abstracting services compete in their search for qualified personnel. Salaries for professional abstractors are commensurate with the educational background and professional experience of the individual and are comparable for analogous positions in the same location. Starting salaries for abstractors are generally the same as for beginning librarians. Part-time subject-expert abstractors may donate their services; some receive an honorarium.

In addition to salary, one can expect to receive the usual fringe benefits of vacation, insurance, hospitalization, and retirement programs. Above and beyond these normal accoutrements of employment, the working conditions in an A&I service are generally pleasant and stimulating. Intellectual attainment is prized and many of the services encourage employees to get advanced degrees. The Chemical Abstracts Service, for example, has a continuing-education program for all employees that pays 75% of tuition for satisfactorily completed courses in recognized academic, technical, and business curricula.

Abstractors can also obtain paid part-time work. Part-time abstractors usually work at home during evenings and weekends. This work can be a means of supplementing their main income. Some graduate students abstract to help pay their way through school. Since they are working in their own fields of specialization, abstracting provides income and opportunity for keeping up with the literature as well as having their names brought to the attention of their peers.

Part-time abstractors are paid either by the hour or by the abstract. The rate of pay or honorarium varies widely and, in a few cases, may be dependent upon the technical difficulty of the subject matter, the language in which the article is written, the expertise of the abstractor, the policy of the journal, and so on. No meaningful average price can be given. Some abstracting services have held that, for an abstractor who knows a subject area or a language, abstracting is no more difficult than for another abstractor who knows a different subject area and language. Consequently, these services pay the same for all languages and subjects.

The vast majority of abstractors are subject-expert volunteers who contribute their efforts and skills abstracting as a professional responsibility and an opportunity. They derive no financial benefits, although they may receive a free subscription to a journal or two. The benefits received by the volunteers are in their feeling of satisfaction that they are keeping up with the literature on a regular basis, making a contribution to their profession, and receiving recognition from their colleagues and peers. Theirs is a labor of love and not a labor for money. Without volunteers, many, if not most, abstract journals would be unable to continue publication or their circulation would be so reduced by high price as to affect their usefulness.

Abstractors, whether they are paid or volunteer, need subject knowledge. They need to be able to understand and appreciate the significance of what the author has written. Lack of this ability is one of the reasons programmers have difficulty in getting computers to abstract. How much subject knowledge is needed for the writing of abstracts is still a matter of debate. One does not have to be a recognized expert, but one needs more than a casual acquaintance with the field of study. The value of subject knowledge in abstracting can be easily demonstrated. It is merely necessary for the skeptic to select an article in a subject field with which he is unacquainted and attempt to abstract it. Difficulties immediately arise from not knowing what is discussed, not knowing the significance of what is presented, not knowing the new contributions that are made, not knowing the precise meaning of significant words, and not knowing what, in the article, is worth abstracting. Experience has shown that an abstractor who does not know the field makes more errors than one who does, and the errors are more serious. Thus, if one wishes to be an abstractor, either as a full-time career, as a part-time employee, or as a volunteer, one must—as an absolute requirement—have knowledge of the literature in the field in which one will be abstracting. If an applicant does not have such subject knowledge, the publisher or manager of the abstracting journal would not consider employing him or her on any basis. To enhance one's employment possibilities, it would be a decided advantage to have, in addition to this subject knowledge, formal training in abstracting; although, as was pointed out, on-the-job training may be provided.

9.1   PERSONNEL

The large A&I services are diversified publishing organizations that produce many products and provide career opportunities for people with different backgrounds and interests. The discussion in this section is limited to job opportunities for abstractors, indexers, proofreaders, and editors. Nevertheless, the career-oriented reader should keep in mind that there are many challenging assignments available as qualified managers, system analysts, computer programmers, librarians, and other specialists.

9.1.1   Abstractors and Indexers

The tasks of abstractors and indexers of scientific and technical journal literature have been described in great detail throughout this book. While preparing the abstract, one may also select keywords. It may be less expensive for the publisher to have both these tasks done by the same person. In some cases, indexing may not be separated from abstracting as a job category. Indexing is often done without abstracting. Nothing new can be said about the abstracting and indexing tasks at this place in the book, but a short statement about job qualifications and working conditions is appropriate here.

Generally an abstractor is a college graduate with a major in the subject of the abstract journal. He should know the technical literature. If he does research, he will find abstracting highly interesting. He must have a fairly large vocabulary and should be able to write in clear, simply constructed sentences that convey the exact meaning of the original article. This ability requires training; it does not come naturally, but some people have a greater aptitude for this kind of writing than do others.

Subject-expert abstractors who volunteer their services are often outstanding people in their subject fields. Their abilities and names lend authority and prestige to their abstracts and to the abstracting services. They enjoy working for an A&I service because the job provides an opportunity to be with colleagues and peers who have similar technical interests.

Full-time abstractors in large organizations are paid commensurate with their educations and experience. There is opportunity for advancement into editing, indexing, index editing, and for moving into management. It is also true that experience as an abstractor has been an advantage in seeking other industrial employment. Abstractors, whether full- or part-time, whether paid or volunteer, are known for their cooperative spirit, subject interest, keeping up with the literature, and ability to think and write clearly. These are all abilities that employers value.

9.1.2   Editors

Although editors are usually hired for editorial positions, some of the most knowledgeable and successful abstractors and other staff members may be promoted to become editors. Good editors, in addition to having the ability to write well, must also have the ability to find and correct errors. Some administrative ability is required for editors who make assignments and who direct activities of personnel. The latter are administrators in responsible positions; they have commensurate salary and prestige.

Editors apply the policy of the service. In some journals, they specialize in subject areas. They edit the abstracts that have been prepared by the staff and by outside contributors. They must be skilled writers as well as subject specialists with an ability to recognize errors of commission and omission. Editors for some services also check the initially selected index-heading terms and edit these so as to reduce subject scattering. They may also provide appropriate cross-references. They may help to plan the journal layout, and they do edit galley proofs and page proofs of each issue.

Editors are usually active members in their professional societies and they often get together with fellow editors and abstractors at national meetings where they talk shop and share experiences. They have a responsible position. They generally enjoy their work, mainly because they get to see so much of the literature of the subject field in which they are interested.

9.1.3   Proofreaders and Proofcheckers

The proofreader is responsible for quality of proofs (galley proofs and page proofs) before the final printing. He checks for all kinds of error, including factual, omission, grammatical, typographical, and composition errors. He does this after the checker compares the original copy with the proof. He corrects the errors, inconsistencies, and omissions that he finds. Marked proofs are returned to the printer for correction.

As described in the *Encyclopedia of Career and Vocational Guidance* (Doubleday & Company), the proofreader must have good eyes, a lively mind, and the ability to read with understanding the enormously wide range of material that may come before him. He must see to it that printing follows copy and that the copy itself makes sense. To correct mathematical composition, he should be a mathematician, to correct foreign languages he should be a polyglot, to correct chemical formulas he should be a chemist, and so on. He must have a passion for correctness, an orderly and meticulous mind, and a desire to learn endlessly. A skilled and knowledgeable proofreader is a thoroughly respected and relatively well-paid professional person. The quality of the service is in his hands.

In many organizations, there is a division of labor between proof-reading and proofchecking. Proofcheckers need not have subject knowledge; their sole task is to compare the original manuscript with the proof. They normally check for those items that proofreaders cannot be expected to find, such as numbers, dates, correct spelling of names of people and places, and the like. Division of labor between proofreading and proof-checking usually is economical.

9.2   TRAINING

There are essentially four means for training abstractors: formal course work in educational institutions; short courses or training institutes; on-the-job training; and self-teaching through use of manuals and other instructions.

9.2.1   College Preparation

Few students enter college with the clear objective of becoming an abstractor. This is a choice generally made later in life and as a result of opportunities and maturing interests. A college education provides the knowledge and enrichment needed for reading and understanding scientific and technical literature in a given subject field. An undergraduate degree in science, social science, or the humanities helps the potential abstractor to become familiar with the technical literature in his field of specialization. Such knowledge is a necessary prerequisite for the more-specialized training that will follow.

Abstractors must know how to write well. University courses on abstracting, technical writing, and editing are appropriate. Such courses may be taught in the Department of English in the School of Journalism, and in the School of Information and Library Studies of the university. Practice in writing, such as is provided by working on the school newspaper (particularly editing and writing headlines) provides valuable experience.

Training in librarianship is an extremely useful preparation for abstractors, particularly if coupled with indexing and with an undergraduate major in the sciences. Abstracting and indexing services are often of major importance in reference services. Researchers seeking access to the journal literature may ask the librarian for help in the use of A&I publications. The alert reference librarian quickly learns to identify which publications have complete coverage, and which have incomplete; which services provide informative abstracts, and which provide indicative, and so on. The reference librarian comes to know which abstract publications are useful and used. This knowledge makes a librarian a valuable member of the staff of an A&I service, provided that he or she also has subject competence. This last point cannot be over-emphasized.

The most relevant university courses for those people who are interested in learning to abstract are formal courses in abstracting and indexing. Such courses are generally taught in schools of librarianship and information science. However, the student should look elsewhere in the college catalog for similar courses that may be part of the curriculum in English, journalism, or chemical documentation.

University courses are more than workshops; they provide a broad perspective and show the relationship of abstracts to the rest of the discipline being studied. In addition, university courses help the student to look beyond the present state of the art to understand its development. University courses discuss theory and techniques, concepts and methods, current developments, and new research, all of which are related to the subject matter. A university course in abstracting helps the student to understand the why as well as the how of abstracting. It is for these reasons that university training in abstracting is the most desirable preparation for anyone wishing to work as an abstractor or editor in one of the secondary publication services.

9.2.2   Short Courses and Conferences

Short courses may last for a few hours or a few days. They are designed to meet the needs of those who have completed their formal education. The courses may be of a tutorial or a refresher nature.

Short courses relating to information services and to indexing and abstracting are offered by university continuing-education programs, by organizations such as the American Management Association, the National Federation of Abstracting and Indexing Services, and by professional societies such as the American Chemical Society, the American Society for Information Science, and the American Society of Indexers. Workshops usually accompany these courses and the sessions are designed to put a maximum amount of instruction and practical experience into a brief period of time. The instructors are generally men and women who work as abstractors, editors, and indexers and who wish to share their practical knowledge and experience.

Still another way of gaining information, keeping abreast of developments, and meeting people who are working in A&I services is to attend the meetings of professional societies. Papers of interest to abstractors are presented at meetings of the American Chemical Society, Chemical Documentation Division; the American Society for Information Science; the American Society of Indexers; and the Special Libraries Association. Frequently the societies present tutorial sessions either immediately before or after the convention proper. These are especially useful for the novice and for those who feel a need for a refresher course. Conferences are among the best settings for sharing professional information.

9.2.3   Self-Teaching

Most abstractors are self-taught through the use of instruction manuals, such as those that are discussed in the next section. Subject authorities cannot take the time to come to the abstracting organization to learn how to abstract; they learn at home or where they work around the world. The abstracting organization provides them with instructions, usually in the form of published manuals, sends them material to abstract usually at the same time, and edits their first abstracts with special care as part of the teaching process. Copies of their first few batches of abstracts are returned to them so that they can see how to improve their efforts. Later, they are instructed to keep carbon copies of their abstracts and compare them with the printed abstract to study the editorial changes made. This method of teaching has worked well for many decades.

9.2.4   On-the-Job Training

Although the concepts of abstracting are of general application, each service has unique, specific requirements for preparing abstracts for its particular publication. To teach the abstractor these special procedures, the organization provides some form of on-the-job training. The three most common procedures used for training newly hired and volunteer abstractors are (1) published instruction manuals, (2) tutorial training (coaching), and (3) continuing feedback and review. These methods are not independent of each other; all or some of them may be used as elements of an integrated training program.

Published Instruction Manuals

Large abstracting services with a worldwide staff of subject-specialist, volunteer abstractors rely heavily upon a published set of instructions. These instructions are made as specific as possible—the objective being to anticipate all the problems that an abstractor would encounter. The success of this method of instruction is attested by the number of services that publish abstracting manuals. Two manuals, which in the opinion of the authors are particularly good, are *Directions for Abstractors*, 1971, published by the Chemical Abstracts Service of the American Chemical Society, and the *API Abstracts of Refining Literature; Abstracter's*

Manual, 1969, published by the Central Abstracting and Indexing Service of the American Petroleum Institute.

The instruction manuals vary in style and in amount of detail. Typically, they include the following topics:

1. journals covered and journal abbreviations;
2. general instructions;
   a. how to prepare and submit the manuscript of the abstract;
   b. nature and length of the abstract;
   c. nature of significant content;
3. style:
   a. author and author's affiliation;
   b. journal references;
   c. title;
   d. chemical-compound nomenclature;
   e. transliteration table;
   f. punctuation;
   g. standard abbreviations and symbols;
4. special instructions with examples.

Abstracting manuals must strike a balance between being too general for effective standardization and being so detailed that they unnecessarily restrict flexibility and prove too costly to use.

Tutorial Training

In most A&I service organizations, both large and small, the newly recruited abstractor undergoes a period of apprenticeship training that may be more or less formal. He begins his training by studying the manual or other instructions, and then he is invited to start abstracting. Frequently he is asked to keep carbon copies of his efforts for training and then reference. Editors correct these first efforts more legibly and possibly more intensively than usual and return copies of the original manuscripts along with instructive comments. Abstracting is more effectively learned by working on material that will be published rather than by working on practice material. The new abstractor, by studying the original and the edited versions, improves his ability to abstract; he learns to adopt the style and procedures of the service. After a few corrected abstracts have been returned, the abstractor may be requested to follow changes in his work by comparing his carbon copies with published abstracts. The amount of training in abstracting may gradually be decreased. Almost without being aware of the transition point, the trainee becomes a full-fledged abstractor. This system of training, which

combines the use of published instructions with some tutorial help, works
very well and is the one most commonly used.

Training is a continuing process. Abstractors who do not maintain the
quality of their abstracts may be spent copies of their changed manuscripts and a reminder; changed manuscripts are also returned to the
abstractor if retraining is necessary and in order to introduce new rules.
Professional abstractors who are having difficulty in maintaining quality
work may be assigned material in a different subject field or language or
they may be given added coaching.

Coaching differs from tutorial training in that coaching uses individualized (one-to-one) instruction in a close and prompt working relationship.
By way of contrast, tutorial training can be characterized as intensive
editing. The coach is an experienced abstractor and a teacher. He meets
with the new abstractor to show the changes that he has made in the
submitted abstract manuscripts. There is room for disagreement. Also,
there is immediate vocal feedback with explanations and discussions.
Questions are asked and answered; learning proceeds rapidly.

Training in abstracting can also take place by means of specially prepared instructional material, such as that found in the appendix of this
book. Exercises are provided in subject selection, elimination of redun-
dancies and ambiguities, paraphrasing, and so on. Obviously, there is
more to abstracting than sentence selection and editing. However, these
formal exercises provide training on specific relevant topics and also help
the abstractor to apply the general instructions for writing concisely.
Their use has the further advantage of allowing the novice to progress at
his own rate and in privacy.

Continuing Feedback and Review

Training programs are not complete without feedback. The trainee
must know what has been accomplished and how well it has been done.
Feedback is also provided by the occasional return of corrected manuscript and by the users of the abstracting service. User comments or
complaints are effective in maintaining and improving quality of the
publication. Editors welcome all comments, complaints, and suggestions.
These indicate interest, needs, and opportunity for specific improvement.
Types of user feedback that are most helpful are the disclosure of errors
in abstracts; suggestions for grouping or regrouping abstracts; and detection of omissions and other errors in the indexes. If appropriate, the
editor may provide abstractors with anonymous feedback from users.

Training is an ongoing process. Various training programs are used for
new abstractors and for maintaining quality. All feedback includes

informing the abstractor of the editorial changes made in his manuscript and encouraging him continually to strive for improved quality. Good training and quality control are *essential* for a good product.

9.3   PLACES OF EMPLOYMENT

Who hires abstractors? Fortunately there are many organizations that require the services of abstractors on either a full-time or a part-time basis. The most obvious employers of abstractors are the many A&I services that publish abstract journals as their main product. In addition, there are a number of other organizations, generally special libraries, that prepare abstracts only for use in their own organization or for a special clientele.

9.3.1   Abstracting Services

Most full-time professional abstractors work for an A&I service whose main function is to prepare and publish categorized, indexed abstracts of current literature in a given discipline or subject field. These organizations may be commercial, profit-making organizations, such as the H. W. Wilson Company; they may be abstracting-publication units of scientific societies such as the American Psychological Association, publisher of *Psychological Abstracts;* or they may be governmental agencies with an assigned mission to prepare abstracts for dissemination, such as the National Technical Information Service or the Defense Documentation Center. They may be very large services employing hundreds of paid abstractors and many more volunteers, or they may be very small organizations staffed entirely by one or two part-time abstractors. If one wishes to make a living as an abstractor, one would probably seek employment with a commercial organization, a professional society, or a governmental A&I service agency. As was pointed out at the beginning of this chapter, positions do exist and salaries are competitive.

9.3.2   Special Library Services

Librarians, particularly those working in special libraries, may be required to abstract as a regular part of their positions. For example, the Technical Library Services of the Hughes Aircraft Company regularly prepare and compile abstracts on specialized topics for the sole purpose of keeping company personnel informed on the current literature. *Radar*

Abstracts is such an in-house publication; it is for company internal use only.

Another example of a special library publication is the *Abstracts of Computer Literature* prepared by the Business Machines Group Library of the Burroughs Corporation. This is an attractive publication that covers a number of computer-related subjects, including English-language abstracts of foreign literature. Corporate employees can order reprints of abstracted articles.

Public libraries also produce abstract publications for special-interest groups among their clients. Librarians often make abstracts of newly acquired books and make the loose-leaf notebook containing these abstracts available for browsing by patrons. Occasionally more special services are provided. These include abstract journals and other serial literature for selected groups of library users. A particularly impressive example of this type of publication is *Business Briefs*, prepared by the Pasadena Public Library. Each issue may contain abstracts of articles from *The Harvard Business Review, Fortune, Construction Reports, The Cleveland Trust Company Business Bulletin, Federal Reserve Bulletin, Wall Street Journal*, and the like. This publication is mailed to subscribers who may also order copies of the original articles.

Not only may abstractors seek employment; they also may become entrepreneurs and start their own abstracting services. This is not so unusual as it may sound except that abstractors are not usually entrepreneurs; it is the entrepreneur who becomes the abstractor and publisher. One such private enterprise publication is *The Communicator*. As its subtitle states, this is a "computer-news abstracting service." It is published 50 times a year since the editor–owner needs 2 weeks off for a vacation. This newsletter-like service provides brief reports of financial and technical events about the computer industry. The reports are abstracted from a number of computer-oriented news publications and prepared to save the reading time of managers and executives in the computer industry.

Again—there are many opportunities for people with an interest in, and a knowledge of, abstracting. Both salaried and volunteer positions are available. Employment opportunities may be sought in abstracting services, in special libraries of corporations, in public and academic libraries, in government library and information services, and in other publication and information service ventures.

APPENDIX:
EXERCISES

These exercises are designed to provide practice in abstracting techniques. Each set of exercises is preceded by instructions and followed by answers to the odd-numbered items. Although the answers were prepared by an experienced abstractor–editor, other responses may also be correct. The exercises are not, in any sense, a "test"; they are examples to be used in gaining experience in handling problems encountered when preparing abstracts. Five sections are provided, as follows:

I. Elimination of Redundancy, Ambiguity, and Obsolete Expressions (100 items)
II. Title Modification (10 items)
III. Common Editorial Changes (28 items)
IV. Subject Paraphrases (35 items)
V. Editing Abstracts (20 items)

I. ELIMINATION OF REDUNDANCY, AMBIGUITY, AND OBSOLETE EXPRESSIONS

The English language is full of redundancy. Abstracts are shortened by removal of redundancy. In belles lettres, scientific reports, and the like, redundancy serves the useful purposes of reinforcement, cogency, error reduction, and aesthetics. In abstracts, most redundancy has been found to be wasteful of the readers' time. It takes costly space. The kind of redundancy eliminated in this exercise involves superfluous terms and expressions. The first example is *the hoi polloi. Hoi* in Greek means "the." Thus, *the* is redundant and the expression should read simply *hoi polloi.* All of us are so accustomed to redundancy in common speech and writing that it takes a conscious effort to detect and remove it. The following exercise should help participants to become conscious of one kind of redundancy as well as to become sensitive to ambiguity and obsolete expressions.

Replace each expression in the following list by a shorter, clearer, unambiguous, and/or current expression:

1. the hoi polloi _____
2. putting up a new building _____
3. stated verbally _____
4. depreciates in value _____
5. noninflammable _____
6. wireless telephony _____
7. the sum of 100 dollars _____
8. the year, 1974 _____
9. lost Atlantis _____
10. at a later date _____
11. past history _____
12. two weeks' time _____
13. campanile bell tower _____
14. basic fundamentals _____
15. repeated over and over again _____
16. in close proximity _____
17. at the hour of noon _____
18. selective SDI system _____
19. typewritten manuscript _____
20. both of them _____
21. unselfish altruism _____

22. in the city of Buffalo _____

23. e.g., sugar, salt, and pepper, etc. _____

24. made out of _____

25. unexplained idiopathic etiology _____

26. during the course of _____

27. A Contribution to the
    Study of Sepia Synthesis _____

28. perhaps it may be that _____

29. will, in the future _____

30. somebody or other _____

31. Jack is too loquacious and
    besides that he talks too much. _____

32. by means of this device _____

33. dust particles _____

34. invited guest _____

35. meaningful experience
    of an educational nature _____

36. necessary requirement _____

37. self-confessed _____

38. present incumbent _____

39. irregardless _____

40. true facts _____

41. Roentgen rays _____

42. successful achievements _____

43. widow lady _____

44. undergraduate student _____

45. connective word _____

46. anthracite coal _____

47. attached together _____

48. continue on _____

49. fuse together _____

50. recoil back _____

51. to come by ⸺
52. standard norms ⸺
53. assembled together ⸺
54. more preferable ⸺
55. or, alternatively ⸺
56. new discovery ⸺
57. now pending ⸺
58. pair of twins ⸺
59. entirely completed ⸺
60. all of ⸺
61. later on ⸺
62. for the most part ⸺
63. over with ⸺
64. and moreover ⸺
65. bisect into two parts ⸺
66. audible to the ear ⸺
67. automobile accumulator ⸺
68. universally by all ⸺
69. every now and then ⸺
70. biography of his life ⸺
71. surrounding circumstances ⸺
72. 2 PM in the afternoon ⸺
73. sugar diabetes ⸺
74. immediately at once ⸺
75. blue in color ⸺
76. totally annihilated ⸺
77. few in number ⸺
78. after a period of 3 days ⸺
79. alphabetical order ⸺
80. final outcome ⸺
81. make a copy of ⸺

82. different facets _____

83. false illusion _____

84. undergoes change with time _____

85. square in shape _____

86. chronologically arranged _____

87. absolute perfection _____

88. after 5–7 days have elapsed _____

89. complete master _____

90. as a general rule _____

91. raised up _____

92. on a weekly basis _____

93. put into final completion _____

94. mechanical friction _____

95. in order to _____

96. another one _____

97. yellow jaundice _____

98. periodic intervals _____

99. invisible to the eye _____

100. added supplements _____

Possible Answers

1. hoi polloi	27. Sepia Synthesis
3. stated	29. will
5. nonflammable	31. Jack is loquacious.
7. $100	33. dust
9. Atlantis	35. educational experience
11. history	37. confessed
13. campanile or bell tower	39. regardless
15. repeated	41. x rays
17. at noon	43. widow
19. typescript	45. connective
21. altruism	47. attached
23. sugar, salt, pepper, etc.	49. fuse
25. idiopathic	51. to get

53. assembled	77. few
55. or	79. alphabetically
57. pending	81. copy
59. completed	83. illusion
61. later	85. square
63. over	87. perfection
65. bisect	89. master
67. storage battery	91. raised
69. sometimes	93. completed
71. circumstances	95. to
73. diabetes	97. jaundice
75. blue	99. invisible

II.   TITLE MODIFICATION

Titles of articles can sometimes be improved. Useless words can be deleted; ambiguity can be resolved by insertion of bracketed words, terms, or phrases.

Edit the following titles to shorten them and remove ambiguity. Insert bracketed material to remove ambiguity. Indicate, by a question mark, problems for which you do not have enuough information to solve. Delete unnecessary definitions and explanations.

1. A Study of Library Use by Teenagers

2. On Audiovisual Aids for Exceptional Children

3. Oil Prices in 1974

4. NASA vs. DoD vs. NIH in the Federal Budget

5. An Introduction to the Study of Programmed Instruction for a Modern Language

6. Fractured Economics

7. Documentation of COBOL (Common Business Oriented Language) Programs

8. Concerning Indexing of Filmstrips

9. Selective SDI for One Science

10. Terse Literatures: Part I. Terse Conclusions

Possible Answers

1. Library Use by Teenagers
3. [Cottonseed?] Oil Prices in 1974

5. Programmed Instruction for [French?]
7. Documentation of COBOL Programs
9. Selective Dissemination of Information for [chemistry?]

III.   COMMON EDITORIAL CHANGES

Through the years, editors of abstracts have found that certain errors and editorial changes are made frequently. The following 28 items include the errors found most commonly—except for errors of abbreviation. Find the errors and correct them:

1. Paper attempts identification—major qualities—subject indexes—suggests preliminary standards.
2. The authors mention that the techniques, well-known and accepted, for measurement and calculation of losses from omissions of subject-index entries are beyond the scope of this paper but they show that standards for completeness of subject indexes can be obtained from experience.
3. Library holdings averaged: 62% books, 4% government reports, 24% journals, and 10% patent specifications.
4. 2400 information centers and special libraries were studied.
5. Student use of carrels is frequent. Carrels were used for assignments and recreational reading. Restrict to school use.
6. Objectives of librarians are mixed and the mixture analyzed.
7. Much data has accumulated on journal selection for special libraries.
8. The technique of logging in acquisitions, which gave the best results, was too costly.
9. Local processing that had not been used previously proved to be inefficient.
10. Circulation for the local public library was measured using call slips.
11. Due to inaccurate shelf-reading, the book was "lost" for two years; this failure was owing to inadequate training of shelf readers.
12. The range of shelves of the "Z" collection in the Linda Hall Library was 10 times longer than in our library but 5 times shorter than in the Library of Congress.
13. Books were counted by students in the media center with an accuracy of 5%.
14. Similar experiments with information retrieval, which showed that document form, such as patent specifications, monograph, journal article, government report, etc., is irrelevant, are reported.

15. To accurately measure need for an information service, users were consulted.
16. When you are ready to report on your project, contact me for details.
17. React people in groups to determine their congeniality coefficient.
18. Grade-school students from 7–13 years old and high-school students between 15–20 were interviewed about media centers. 1–2% were opposed.
19. Electrical outlet containing carrels are termed *wet*.
20. More industrious students attend the universities with higher ratings.
21. Food-containing fat should especially be avoided by sedentary personnel.
22. Much higher intensity lighting is required in stacks when printing on books is gold.
23. Vitamin C deficient patients should be aware of effects of excessive vitamin A.
24. An important by product of catalog use is increased efficiency.
25. Twenty one students were chosen to participate in the experiment.
26. A. B. Jones, C. D. Smith and E. F. White collaborated on research project number 1234.
27. The work and personnel of the Technion in Haifa Israel are described.
28. On August 9 1970 the library was closed for inventory.

Possible Answers

1. This paper identifies the major qualities of subject indexes and suggests preliminary standards.
3. Average percent of library holdings: books 62, government reports 4, journals 24, and patent specifications 10. [Where is 2%?]
5. Student use of carrels is frequent. Carrels are used for assignments and recreational reading. Use should be restricted to school-work.
7. Many data have accumulated on journal selection for special libraries.
9. Local processing, which had not been used previously, proved to be inefficient.
11. Owing to inaccurate shelf reading, the book was "lost" for two years; this failure was due to inadequate training of shelf readers.

13. Books were counted by students in the media center with an accuracy of ±5%.
15. User consultation accurately measures need for an information service.
17. Cause people in groups to react to determine their congeniality coefficient.
19. Electrical-outlet-containing carrels are termed *wet*.
21. Food containing fat should especially be avoided by sedentary personnel.
23. Vitamin-C-deficient patients should be aware of effects of excessive vitamin A.
25. Twenty-one students were chosen to participate in the experiment.
27. The work and personnel are described of the Technion in Haifa, Israel.

IV. SUBJECT PARAPHRASES

Abstractors and indexers select subjects and paraphrase them. That is, they embody the subjects in words; they verbalize the subjects that they have selected. Often their first expressions (paraphrases) are verbose. Criteria that have been found useful in judging whether or not to remove material are:

1. Will removal of this expression, phrase, term, or word alter my decision to look up or not look up the original document from which the paraphrase was derived? If removal of the material will not alter this decision, then the material can probably be removed. Material essential for making this decision cannot be removed.
2. Will removal of this material substantially change the meaning of the paraphrase? If the meaning will remain substantially unchanged, then the material can safely be removed.
3. Will removal of this material substantially add to, or increase, the ambiguity? If removal has no substantial effect on ambiguity, then the material should be deleted.

Sometimes equivalent paraphrases, words, and terms can be substituted for material in the following exercises to result in substantial shortening.

Paraphrases in the following exercises are not sentences. They are of the type used in subject indexing.

Remove unnecessary words and add necessary words in editing the following subject paraphrases. Indicate by question marks all problems that you are unable to solve because of inadequate information.

Indexing can also be practiced on all the following exercises.

Group A

1. Electronic digital computer use in printing indexes matching selective-dissemination profiles of scientists in chemical research.
2. Promotional advertising effectiveness in media such as newspapers, magazines, TV, and radio.
3. Solutions to problems of too much to read in the limited reading time available; too many exotic languages unread by most readers and in which papers are written; and lack of access to documents to be read.
4. Study of the use of public-relation techniques in increasing use of public libraries.
5. Machine translation by computer in solving the problem of seventy languages in which technical material is now published.
6. Inadequacy of computerized control of waterworks.
7. Machine translation by electronic digital computers viewed as an unsolved problem in semantics (meaning).
8. Nitrogen trichloride as the factor that causes eyes to smart in swimming pools.
9. Distance from books in relation to use of said books for reading and reference vs decentralization policies of libraries.
10. Watch irregularity from oil on balance-wheel spring through faulty lubrication.

Possible Answers

1. Computer printing of indexes for SDI for chemists.
3. Solutions to problems of: too much to read, too many languages, and lack of access to documents.
5. Computer translation of 70 languages for published technical material.
7. Computer translation as unsolved problem in semantics.
9. Distance–use relation for books vs decentralization policies for libraries.

Group B

1. An introduction to the study of public library use by patrons of the library.

2. Results of an experiment designed to measure how a card catalog in a school library is used by pupils.
3. Acquisition, organization, and use of media other than books and magazines by school libraries—now commonly known as *school media centers.*
4. The following factors have been shown to influence library use: distance from user, application of policies regarding fines, and unpleasant personality of the librarian.
5. Promotion of librarians through consideration of: job performance as judged by time and motion studies; intelligence as measured by IQ vs observed intraoffice politics and vs managerial ability of the Director.
6. Specialized information-analysis-center design to repackage data important to engineers.
7. Relative costs of replacing stolen books and of hiring guards for exits of libraries.
8. Curriculum revision in library schools by cooperation of faculty and students to increase flexibility and coverage.
9. Fond reminiscences of a librarian for 20 years.
10. Paranoia as a symptom of malfunction of the cause–effect center of the brain.

Possible Answers

1. Public library use.
3. Acquisition, organization, and use of nonprint media by school media centers.
5. Promotion of librarians.
7. Costs of replacing stolen books vs hiring guards.
9. Reminiscences of librarian.

Group C

1. Secrecy is topic discussed. It is necessary to protect interests of individuals and organizations. Interests are security and competitive advantage.
2. Continuing education, the current name for adult education, is a proper function of such organizations. Libraries continue to serve after the diploma.
3. He does more than the reference librarian so he should be paid more. Information specialists not only extract data; they also organize and use it.

4. Its value to our civilization can be estimated from the Gross National Products of countries that use technical information and those that do not.
5. Loss may cost in well-known terms such as those expressed repeatedly.

Possible Answers

1. Secrecy in protection of competitive advantage and security of individuals and organizations.
3. Pay of information specialists and reference librarians.
5. Loss? cost? terms? expressed repeatedly.

Group D

1. Bedtime stories for adults.
2. This book has a section entitled, "Subject-Paraphrase Writing in Three Easy Lessons."
3. School librarians hold key to orienting children to a better balance between gaining information from the record (books, etc.) and gaining it from experience (experiment, observation, etc.).
4. Stimulus competition by television, radio, movies, magazines through subscription, etc. limits use of public libraries.
5. The image of librarians as "little old ladies of both sexes" is fading through the efforts of contemporary library schools.
6. Those who drive like lightning may crash like thunder.
7. Inadvertent duplication of research comes from ignorance of the record.
8. Measurement of value of libraries through use of Human Relations Area Files at Ridge Lea to determine relation between number of libraries and industry or Gross National Products of various countries.
9. De facto censorship from inability to read all, de jure censorship from a legal structure, ad hoc censorship, and censorship from social pressure in relation to censorship and the freedom not to read.
10. Omit verbs, articles, pronouns, expected information, data, definitions, what one is expected to know, repetition, redundancy, and unnecessary detail in writing subject paraphrases.

Possible Answers

1. Are the stories to make people sleepy or is this an allusion to pornography? This point must be settled before the paraphrase can be edited.
3. School librarians in orientation of children to information from the record vs from experience.
5. Library-school education and image of librarians.
7. Inadvertent duplication of research.
9. de facto, de jure, ad hoc, and social pressure censorship.

V.   EDITING ABSTRACTS

The following exercises provide practice in both subject paraphrasing and editing.

Group A

1. Abstract qualities. — Abstract qualities discussed: completeness, correctness, conciseness, cogency, currency, etc. Recommends checking. Loss intolerable. Errors of typography, fact, grammar. Verbosity, circumlocutions, redundancy, repetition avoided. Promptness and currency life- and dollar-saving. Sign for authority, reward, and responsibility. Guidance to related abstracts important. Typography important as guide to subtle qualities. Measurement difficult. Worthwhile maintaining.

2. The place of standards in the new technology of information science. — I feel that the paper purports to describe, "in plain language," the system by which American Standards are formulated, reviewed, and approved. The author attempts to show this for "information science." After talking down to his readers about the need for standards, the author potentially offends some by writing about "nuts" and "bolts" (people) in information science. He tries to analyze standardization of data elements, exhorts to action, and briefly gives the history of the Z39 subcommittees on machine-input records, filing, essential bibliographic elements, and abstract form. This article, in the opinion of the abstractor, is not worth reading.

3. Cast-iron alloys for corrosion-resistant uses. — 6 hard, corrosion-resistant, gray, cast Fe is made by heating to 1800°F an alloy containing 2.25% carbon, 10.5% nickel, 4% copper, .9% chromium, 1.5% silicon, 0.3% manganese, and 73% iron, rapidly cooling in liquid N and reheating to

500° with slow cooling. 25 uses of this ally include: engine blocks, radiators, pistons, cylinder heads, housings for differentials and transmissions, etc. Making the alloy, chromium is reacted with cast Fe between 7–13%. The alloying elements are mixed and the mixture heated to 1800°C. Heat treat the alloy to make it tough and resistant to shock fracture. Chromium containing alloy has corrosion-resistant properties. Corrosion of the iron alloy is 5 times smaller than unalloyed cast iron. Manganese was determined with an accuracy of 5% in the alloy using oxidation to permanganate and oxalate filtration. Due to cost, the alloy will be restricted to expensive automobiles.

4. Automatic indexing. — Automatic indexing depends upon syntax (structure) rather than semantics (meaning). Words are selected on the basis of being proper nouns (proper names); frequently used in the document; infrequently used in the field; in proximity in the phrase, clause, sentence, paragraph, chapter, or document; indicated by clue words (e.g., *new, especially,* and *important*); not on an exclusion list (e.g., prepositions and articles); and on an inclusion list (e.g., names of drugs); subjects, objects, or other parts of sentences. The relationship between words selected this way and those selected by indexers on the basis of meaning, novelty, emphasis, and extensive review is tenuous. Control of synonymy, guidance, etc., in the index produced automatically is not evident in the results; 99% of the words in technical documents are not suitable guides to subjects. Automatic selection of only the 1% seems improbable. Automatic indexing can be tested by embedding different paraphrases of the same subject in unindexable text and seeing if all are indexed identically.

5. Indexed abstracts have, for the past century, greatly helped scientists and engineers to keep up in their specialties, to avoid having to translate from many languages, and have functioned as surrogates for inaccessible documents. The 300,000 abstracts each year in chemistry have been prepared from documents in 70 languages. Each abstract generates an average of 6.1 subject-index entries. The 80 categories into which abstracts are placed enable their use for current awarness. The indexes are used for retrospective search.

Possible Answers

1. Abstract qualities. — Qualities of abstracts discussed include: completeness, correctness, conciseness, cogency, and currency. Checking of abstracts is recommended. Loss of information is intolerable. There may be found errors of typography, fact, and grammar. Verbosity,

circumlocutions, and other forms of redundancy and repetition are avoided. Promptness and currency of abstracts may be life- and dollar-saving. Abstracts are signed to indicate authority, provide reward, and place responsibility. Guidance to related abstracts is important. Quality of typography is a clue to the more subtle qualities of abstracts. Measurement of quality is difficult and worthwhile maintaining.

3. Cast-iron alloys for corrosion-resistant uses. — A gray cast-iron alloy that is hard and corrosion-resistant is made by heating to 1800°F an alloy of carbon 2.25, nickel 10.5, copper 4, chromium 0.9, silicon 1.5, manganese 0.3% and the rest iron. The part is rapidly cooled in liquid nitrogen and then reheated to 500°F with slow cooling. This alloy is used for engine blocks, radiators, pistons, cylinder heads, housing for differentials and transmissions, etc. In manufacture of this alloy, from 7 to 13% of chromium is treated with cast iron. Alloying elements are mixed and the mixture is heated to 1800°F. The alloy is heat-treated to make it resistant to shock fracture. This chromium-containing alloy is corrosion resistant. Corrosion is one-fifth that of unalloyed cast iron. Manganese was determined in the alloy to ±5.0% by solution, oxidation of the manganese(II) to permanganate and its titration with oxalate. Owing to its cost, use of the alloy will be restricted to expensive automobiles.

5. The 300,000 abstracts/year in chemistry are from documents in 70 languages and are arranged in 80 categories to enable current awareness. Indexing density is 6.1 subject entries per abstract.

Group B

1. The librarian has a responsibility beyond the collection of the many unusual items to go in a local-history collection. Her/his responsibility is to make them available as quickly as possible and to coordinate them with the general library. Many additional steps, such as the preparation of a clipping file and indexes should be taken. Yet, with all of these aids and especially without them, one must agree with Hobbs, "The tendency is to rely upon the knowledge gained by the local librarian. . . ." The librarian's knowledge of, and acquaintance with, local-history materials is indispensable for best service to the public.

2. This is not an apologia for the old guard book style name catalog, but forgetting rules for streamlined efficiency, let us admit that there is some character, some romance about it that a card catalog cannot rival. Cards just haven't personality or color, being unitary and strictly functional, an unconnected jumble without a common link to make them

homogeneous. The guard book catalog, for all its problems of maintenance and often cumbersome inefficiency, does make life more interesting for the cataloger—and the imaginative user.

3. Hungary, a place of fine food and hard-working people, is often overlooked by American librarians and bookdealers as a source of fine books. While doing research in Hungarian libraries and archives recently, I was pleasantly surprised to find that the bookstores and also the antiquarian book shops contain volumes that would add to any library shelf. Hungarian bookdealers are even anxious to sell books to American libraries and dealers.

4. Most bibliographies are reference books—that is, they are designed to be consulted, not read right through. What this definition means is clear—but what it doesn't mean is often not quite so clear to librarians. A reference book is not, ipso facto, a noncirculating book. Users should be able to borrow a bibliography. Probably there should be an extra copy for circulation or even, for goodness' sake, the one marked, "Reference," should circulate. Scott's stamp catalogs, for example—which are also bibliographies, should circulate. Things not designed to be read may be read. People may enjoy browsing through them.

5. With regard to legibility; not only the printed word, but also the paper may interfere with legibility. Here as a first example: A dingy or gray paper may not contrast with the color of the type enough. "Art" or lead-coated paper—a disagreeable term for an inferior thing—may have so high a "shine," and be so dazzling as to make the paper outshine the ink. Or, a paper with a watermark of parallel lines may have a pattern that competes with the printing.

Possible Answers

1. Librarians should collect many unusual items for a local-history collection, make them available quickly, and catalog them. They should also prepare a clipping file and indexes. Their knowledge of these materials is indispensable for best service.

3. Hungarian antiquarian book shops and bookstores are a source of fine books. The dealers are happy and even anxious to sell to American dealers and libraries.

5. Legibility depends also on paper. Dirty-colored or grayish paper may not contrast enough with the type. Reflection of art or lead-coated paper may hide printing. A watermark of parallel lines may interfere with reading.

Group C

1. Biological dictionary preparation, control and maintenance. – Preparation, control, and maintenance of a biological dictionary or thesaurus is described and use of the dictionary by the abstractor–indexer is illustrated by sample coding sheets and examples from the dictionary of cross-references, instructions, and scope notes (glosses). The use of specific authority lists, such as the World Health Organization Classification of Diseases is cited. One person, trained in biological science, has firm control, especially in the matter of synonyms and of family or generic entries. Without control, pertinent references can be lost in searches. Nonthesaurus, uncontrolled indexing is wasteful and unreliable.

2. Classification systems and their subjects. A general analysis of different kinds of classification systems characterized by different types of subjects. – Types of classification systems characterized by different types of subjects are analyzed. The most important types of subjects in documentation are documents and terms. Other systems for subjects are discussed. Systems of science are dealt with as an introduction to document systems. Systems should have structures that will fit the subjects. The hierarchies for documents and terms are not the same. Classification of a category of subjects into a system made for another category of subjects (for example, classifying terms of technical products according to a document system) causes difficulties. We should not be bound to existing systems. Each type of subject requires the best possible system or variant. A system of systems is wanted, where every individual system as far as possible—without distortion of its primary function—has common features with other systems. Principles for a universal document system based on concepts, current technology, and a universal term system are advanced.

3. Library catalog production on small computers. – The Columbia–Harvard–Yale (CHY) Medical Libraries Computerization Project is described, including: bibliographic data input, computer processing, output, error controls, human editing, and the complexity and variety of bibliographic organization for computer manipulation.

4. The optimum number of frames per microfiche. – In microfiche preparation for a collection of documents, the number of frames per microfiche has an optimum value that depends on the range of number of pages in documents of the collection. For example, the number of pages in documents of the NASA and DoD collections leads to 63 frames per microfiche. The ratio of pages to frames is then 0.57, and the ratio of documents to microfiche, 0.72. The existence of such an optimum

suggests that further significant filming reduction ratio should be accompanied by a corresponding reduction of mircofiche size.

5. Automatic indexing. — This encouraging experiment is based on the assumption that a subset of the words in a document can be an effective index to that document, and that a subject can be approximated by selecting those words from the document whose frequencies of use are unexpectedly high for the field of knowledge indexed. The results are not definitive because any index set chosen must be tested with a larger collection.

Possible Answers

1. Biological dictionary preparation, control, and maintenance. — Use by the abstractor–indexer is illustrated by sample coding sheets and by examples taken from the dictionary of cross-references, instructions, and glosses. The use of authority lists, such as the World Health Organization Classification of Diseases, is cited. One biological scientist has firm control of synonyms, generic entries, etc. Nonthesaurus, uncontrolled indexing is wasteful and unreliable because it causes loss on search.

3. Library catalog production on small computers. — Description of the Columbia–Harvard–Yale Medical Libraries Computerization Project includes bibliographic data input, computer processing, output, error controls, human editing, and the complexity and variety of bibliographic organization for computer manipulation.

5. Automatic indexing. — A subset of words whose frequencies are unexpectedly high for the field of knowledge indexed is assumed to be an effective index to that document. Results of the experiment on this kind of automatic indexing are not definitive because the index set chosen has yet to be tested upon a larger collection.

Group D

1. Computer-based composition at Chemical Abstracts Service. — The Chemical Abstracts Service has gone through the process of converting its abstracts and index-handling procedures from a strictly manual operation with hot and cold typesetting processes to a fully integrated computer-based process. All abstract issue and index services are now available in traditional printed form and in a machine-processable store useful for alerting, retrospective searching, and reorganization. The basic conversion was to be completed by 1970.

2. Designing an Author-Based Correspondence Information System. —

The problems associated with a centralized correspondence information system in a research and development environment are examined. These problems relate to receipt and control, retention periods, circulation, filing, and retrieval. Various mechanisms for solving these problems are considered and a correspondence information system based on filing alphabetically by author is described.

3. Citation of Articles from Volume 58 of the *Journal of Physical Chemistry*. — The self-citation intensity in references per 100 pages was found to decrease with a half life of 3.5 years, only partially counterbalanced by a doubling rate of journal size every 6 years. SCI data, on the other hand, suggest that the chance for citation of a given paper may be fairly constant. About 80% of the articles written in Volume 58 of the *Journal of Physical Chemistry* were cited in the sources surveyed. A superficial study of these uncited papers showed no noticeable difference from other papers in the journal except for a few, such as an introduction to a symposium, that might not be expected to be cited.

4. Procedures for Assessing Errors. — User confidence in the validity of chemical literature is directly related to the accuracy with which it is presented. The nature, types, and sources of errors that find their way into the primary and secondary journal literature are analyzed. A description of the various methods by which the effects of such errors can be minimized through abstracting and indexing techniques is presented.

5. Some Information Indexing Techniques in a Real-Time Hospital Computer System. — A phonetic indexing technique has proven useful for computer retrieval of filed information, especially in those cases where misspellings in the retrieval requests can readily occur. Further, the creation of special indexes to filed information can facilitate rapid selection on very large files.

Possible Answers

1. Computer-based composition at Chemical Abstracts Service. — The Service converted the handling of abstracts and indexes from manual typesetting to an integrated, computer-based process. All abstract issues and indexes are available in their usual printed form and also as a computer store useful for alerting, searching, and reorganization.

3. Citation of articles in volume 58 of the *Journal of Physical Chemistry*. — The citation of articles in the *Journal* by other articles in it decreased to half in 3.5 years. This decrease was only partly counterbalanced by the *Journal* doubling in size every 6 years. Data from the *Science Citation Index*, on the other hand, suggest that the probability

for citation of a given paper may be fairly constant. About 80% of the articles in volume 58 were cited in the sources surveyed. Uncited papers seemed like the cited papers except for a few papers that might not be expected to be cited, such as introductions to symposia.

5. Indexing techniques in a real-time hospital computer system. — Phonetic indexing of filed data for computer retrieval is especially useful if misspellings in retrieval requests easily occur. Special indexes to filed information can facilitate rapid selection from very large files.

References

American Bibliographical Center–Clio Press. *Policies and Procedures*, ABC, Santa Barbara, California (no date).

Applied Mechanics Reviews. *Guidelines for Reviewers*, Southwest San Antonio, Texas (no date).

Armed Services Technical Information Agency. *ASTIA Guidelines for Cataloging and Abstracting*, ASTIA, Arlington, Virginia, June 1962.

Ashworth, W. "Abstracting as a fine art," *The Information Scientist*, Vol. 7, No. 2, June 1973, pp. 43–53.

Bar-Hillel, Y. "A logician's reaction to recent theorizing on information search systems," *American Documentation*, Vol. 8, No. 2, 1957, pp. 103–113.

Baxendale, P. E. "Machine-made index for technical literature–an experiment," *IBM Journal of Research and Development*, Vol. 2, No. 4, 1958, pp. 354–361.

Bernier, C. L. "The indexing problem," *Journal of Chemical Documentation*, Vol. 1, No. 3, 1961, pp. 25–27.

Bernier, C. L. "Condensed technical literatures," *Journal of Chemical Documentation*, Vol. 8, No. 4, 1968, pp. 195–197.

Bernier, C. L. "Terse literatures: I. Terse conclusions," *Journal of the American Society for Information Science*, Vol. 21, No. 5, 1970, pp. 316–319.

Bernier, C. L. *Newsletter of Biomedical Terse Conclusions* (unpublished), 1971.

Bernier, C. L. "Correlative indexes," *Encyclopedia of Library and Information Science*, Vol. 6, 1971, pp. 189–205.

Bernier, C. L. "Multipackaging of data at source," *Journal of Chemical Documentation,* Vol. 12, No. 3, 1972, pp. 152–157.

Bernier, C. L. "International Council of Scientific Unions (ICSU)," *Encyclopedia of Library and Information Science,* Vol. 12 (A. Kent, H. Lancour, and J. E. Daily, executive editors), Marcel Dekker, Inc., N.Y., 1974, pp. 372–376.

Borko, H., and Chatman, S. "Criteria for acceptable abstracts: A survey of abstractors' instructions," *American Documentation,* Vol. 14, No. 2, April 1963, pp. 149–160.

Borko, H. *Brazil: Organization and Structure of a National System of Scientific and Technical Information (SNICT).* August 1972, Serial No. 2824/RMO.RD/DBA, UNESCO, Paris, Dec. 1972.

Bush, V. "As we may think," *Atlantic Monthly,* Vol. 176, No. 1, July 1945, pp. 101–108.

Chemical Abstracts. "Directions for Abstractors and Section Editors of Chemical Abstracts," 1960.

Chemical Abstracts Service of the American Chemical Society. *Directions for Abstractors,* The Ohio State University, Columbus, Ohio, 1971.

Chernyi, A. I. "Integrated information systems," in *Problems of Information Science* (A. I. Chernyi, editor), FID 478, VINITI, Moscow, 1972.

Collison, R. *The annals of abstracting, 1665–1970.* The School of Library Service and the University Library, University of California, Los Angeles, 1971.

Cooper, M. D. "The economics of information," in *Annual Review of Information Science and Technology,* Vol. 8 (Cuadra and Luke, editors), American Society for Information Science, Washington, D.C., 1973.

Crane, E. J. *CA Today, the Production of Chemical Abstracts,* American Chemical Society, Washington, D.C., 1958, p. 23.

Cuadra, C. A., and Luke, A. W. (editors). *Annual Review of Information Science and Technology,* Vol. 8, American Society for Information Science, Washington, D.C., 1973.

Defense Documentation Center. *Abstracting Scientific and Technical Reports of Defense-Sponsored RDT/E,* AD 667 000, Defense Documentation Center, Alexandria, Virginia, March 1968.

Department of Defense. "Military standard format requirements for scientific and technical reports prepared by or for the Department of Defense," MIL-STD-B47A, 31 January 1973.

Earl, L. L. "Experiments in automatic extracting and indexing," *Information Storage & Retrieval,* Vol. 6, No. 4, 1970, pp. 313–314.

Earl, L. L. *Automatic Informative Abstracting and Indexing. Part I.* Lockheed Missiles and Space Company, Inc., Palo Alto, California, LMSC-350104, May 1973, AD 762 456.

Edmundson, H. P., Oswald, V. A., and Wyllys, R. E. *Automatic Indexing and Abstracting of the Contents of Documents,* Planning Research Corporation, Los Angeles, California. Prepared for Rome Air Development Center, Griffis Air Force Base, New York, 1959, AD 231 606.

Edmundson, H. P. *Final Report on the Study for Automatic Abstracting,* Thompson Ramo Wooldridge, Inc., Canoga Park, California, 1961, PB 166 532.

Edmundson, H. P. "New methods in automatic extracting," *Journal of the Association for Computing Machinery,* Vol. 16, No. 2, April 1969, pp. 264–285.

FID (Fédération Internationale de Documentation [International Federation for Documentation]). *Abstracting Services: Science and Technology,* Vol. I; *Abstracting*

Services: Social Science and Humanities, Vol. II. FID, The Hague, Netherlands, 1969.

FID (Fédération Internationale de Documentation [International Federation for Documentation]). "Abstracting and indexing services." *FID News Bulletin,* Vol. 24, No. 1, 1974, pp. 3–4.

Freeman, M. E. "The Science Information Exchange as a source of information," *Special Libraries,* Vol. 59, No. 2, 1968, pp. 86–90.

Friedlander, W. J. (editor). *Concise Clinical Neurology Review,* Clinical Neurology Information Center, University of Nebraska Medical Center, Omaha, Nebraska 68105, 1974.

Gannett, E. K. "Primary Publication Systems and Services," in *Annual Review of Information Science and Technology,* Vol. 8 (Cuadra and Luke, editors), American Society for Information Science, Washington, D.C., 1973.

Garvey, W. D., Lin, N., Nelson, C. E., and Tomita, K. "Research patterns in scientific communication," *Information Storage & Retrieval,* Vol. 8, Nos. 3–6, 1972.

Gonod, P., *et al. OAS Mission to Colombia to Plan a National Information System,* OAS, Washington, D.C., Nov. 1971. (a)

Gonod, P., *et al. OAS Mission to Peru to Study Plans for a National System for Scientific and Technical Information,* OAS, Washington, D.C., November 1971. (b)

Gray, D. E., and Rosenborg, S. "Do technical reports become published papers?" *Physics Today,* Vol. 10, No. 6, June 1957, pp. 18–21.

Herschman, A. "The primary journal: past, present, and future," *Journal of Chemical Documentation,* Vol. 10, No. 1, Feb. 1970, pp. 37–42.

IBM Corp., Advanced Systems Development Division. *ACSI-Matic Auto-Abstracting Project, Final Report,* Vol. I, Yorktown Heights, New York, 1960.

IBM Corp., Advanced Systems Development Division. *ACSI-Matic Auto-Abstracting Project, Final Report,* Vol. III, Yorktown Heights, New York, 1961.

International Standards Organization (ISO). *Abstracts and Synopses,* ISO/R 214, Geneva, Switzerland, Nov. 1961.

Keenan, S., and Elliott, M. "World inventory of abstracting and indexing services," *Special Libraries,* Vol. 64, No. 3, March 1973, pp. 145–150.

Koch, H. W. *Economics of Primary Journals in Physics,* American Institute of Physics, New York, N.Y., ID 69–5, Dec. 1969.

Koch, H. W. *The Role of the Primary Journal in Physics,* American Institute of Physics, New York, N.Y., ID 70–1, Jan. 1970.

Lancaster, F. W., and Herner, S. "Modular content analysis," *Proceedings of the American Documentation Institute,* Vol. 1, 1964, pp. 403–405.

Landau, R. M. (editor). *Proceedings of the ASIS Workshop on Computer Composition* (Arlington, Virginia, 8–9, Dec. 1970), American Society for Information Science, Washington, D.C., 1971, 258 pp.

Lazar, P. *India: A National System for Science and Technology,* March–April 1972, Serial No. 2717/RMD.RD/DBA, UNESCO, Paris, July 1972.

Luhn, H. P. "The IBM Electronic Information Searching System," IBM Research Center, Yorktown Heights, New York, May 1952, p. 18. Also in H. P. Luhn, *Pioneer of Information Science* (Claire K. Schultz, editor), Spartan Books, New York, 1968.

Luhn, H. P. "The automatic creation of literature abstracts (auto-abstracts)," *IBM Journal of Research and Development,* Vol. 2, No. 2, 1958, pp. 159–165; also in *IRE National Convention Record, 1958,* Vol. 6, No. 10, Institute of Radio Engineers, New York, 1958, pp. 20–24; also in H. P. Luhn, *Pioneer of Information Science* (Claire K. Schultz, editor), Spartan Books, New York, 1968.

McCandless, R. F. J., Skweir, E. A., and Gordon, M. "Secondary journals in chemical and biological fields," *Journal of Chemical Documentation,* Vol. 4, No. 2, 1964, pp. 147–153.

Maloney, R. K., "Title versus title/abstract text searching in SDI systems," *Journal of the American Society for Information Science,* Vol. 25, No. 6, 1974, pp. 370–373.

Mathis, B. A. *Techniques for the Evaluation and Improvement of Computer-Produced Abstracts,* The Computer and Information Science Research Center, The Ohio State University, Columbus, Ohio, Dec. 1972, OSU-CISRC-TR-72-15.

Mathis, B. A., Rush, J. A., and Young, C. A. "Improvement of automatic abstracts by the use of structural analysis," *Journal of the American Society for Information Science,* Vol. 24, No. 2, 1973, pp. 101–109.

Murray, G. *Aeschylus. Septemquae supersunt tragoediae recensuit.* 2nd ed., Oxford Classical Texts, Oxford, 1957, p. 205.

Myatt, D. O., and Upham, T. E. "A quantitative technique for designing the technical information center," *Journal of Chemical Documentation,* Vol. 1, No. 3, 1961, pp. 18–24.

NFAIS (National Federation of Abstracting and Indexing Services). *History and Issues 1958–73,* Report No. 5, NFAIS, Philadelphia, Pennsylvania, 1973.

NFAIS Newsletter, Vol. 17, No. 1, February 1975, pp. 1–27.

NFAIS (National Federation of Science Abstracting and Indexing Services). *A Guide to the World's Abstracting and Indexing Services in Science and Technology,* NFSAIS, Washington, D.C., 1963.

Olsen, H. H. *The Economics of Information: Bibliography and Commentary on the Literature,* 2nd ed., *Information, Part 2; Reports—Bibliographies,* Vol. 1, No. 2, March–April 1972, pp. 1–40.

Payne, D. *Automatic Abstracting Evaluation Support,* American Institute for Research, Pittsburgh, Pennsylvania, 1964, AD 431 910.

Payne, D., Altman, J., and Munger, S. J. *A Textual Abstracting Technique, Preliminary Development and Evaluation for Automatic Abstracting Evaluation,* American Institute for Research, Pittsburgh, Pennsylvania, 1962, AD 285 032.

Rath, G. J., Resnick, A., and Savage, T. R. "Comparisons of four types of lexical indications of content," *American Documentation,* Vol. 12, No. 2, 1961, pp. 126–130. (a)

Rath, G. J., Resnick, A., and Savage, T. R. "The formation of abstracts by the selection of sentences: Part I, Sentence selection by men and machines; Part II, The reliability of people in selecting sentences," *American Documentation,* Vol. 12, No. 2, 1961, pp. 139–141, 142–143. (b)

Research Grants Index. U.S. Department of Health, Education, and Welfare, Public Health Service, National Institutes of Health, Division of Research Grants, Bethesda, Maryland, 1969.

Rush, J. E., Salvador, R., and Zamora, A. "Automatic abstracting and indexing. II: Production of indicative abstracts by application of contextul inference and syntactic coherence criteria," *Journal of the American Society for Information Science,* Vol. 22, No. 4, 1971, pp. 260–274.

Samarasinghe, L. E. *Ceylon: National Scientific and Technical Documentation Center,* Dec. 1968, Serial No. 1156/BMS.RD/DBA, UNESCO, March 1969.

SATCOM (Committee on Scientific and Technical Communication). *Scientific and Technical Communication; A Pressing National Problem and Recommendations for Its Solution. Publication 1707.* National Academy of Sciences, National Research Council, Washington, D.C., 1969.

System Development Corporation. *A System Study of Abstracting and Indexing in the United States,* SDC, Santa Monica, California, Dec. 1966, TW-WD-394: PB 174 249.

System Development Corporation. *National Document-Handling System for Science and Technology* (Launor P. Carter *et al.,* editors), John Wiley & Sons, New York, N.Y., 1967.

Taube, M., Gull, C. D., and Wachtel, I. S. "Unit terms in coordinate indexing," *American Documentation,* Vol. 3, No. 4, 1952, pp. 213–218.

UNESCO. "Guide for the Preparation of Author's Abstracts for Publication," pp. 5–7, in *Guide for the Preparation of Scientific Papers for Publication,* Paris, France, Aug. 1968 (SC/MD/5).

UNESCO. *UNISIST Newsletter,* No. 1, UNESCO, Paris, France, 1973.

UNESCO and ICSU. *UNISIST, Study Report on the Feasibility of a World Science Information System,* UNESCO and ICSU, Paris, 1971.

Weil, B. H. "Standards for writing abstracts," *Journal of the American Society for Information Science,* Vol. 21, No. 5, 1970, pp. 351–357.

Witty, F. J. "The beginnings of indexing and abstracting: Some notes toward a history of indexing in antiquity and the middle ages," *The Indexer,* Vol. 8, No. 4, Oct. 1973, pp. 193–198.

Wood, J. L., Flanagan, C., and Kennedy, H. E. "Overlap in the lists of journals maintained by BIOSIS, CAS, and Ei.," *Journal of the American Society for Information Science,* Vol. 23, No. 1, 1972, pp. 36–38.

Wood, J. L., Flanagan, C., and Kennedy, H. E. "Overlap among the journal articles selected for coverage by BIOSIS, CAS, and Ei.," *Journal of the American Society for Information Science,* Vol. 24, No. 1, 1973, pp. 25–28.

Wyllys, R. E. "Extracting and abstracting by computer," in *Automated Language Processing* (H. Borko, editor), John Wiley & Sons, New York, 1967.

Glossary

A&I. Abstracting and Indexing. (The making of abstracts and indexes.)

Abridgment. A shortened form of a work, made by omitting detail and retaining the sense and unity of the original. The process of making this form.

Abstract. An abbreviated, accurate representation of a document without added interpretation or criticism. It is usually in the author's words and the abstractor's phraseology. Also the process of producing the representation.

Abstractor. One who prepares abstracts.

Accession number. A serial number associated with an item acquired by, e.g., a library.

Acronym. A pronounceable abbreviation often formed from the initial letter or letters of a word or expression, e.g., ADAM.

ADAM System. Automatic Document Abstracting Method. An automatic abstracting system developed at The Ohio State University that depends, in part, on *rejecting* sentences.

Ad hoc. For this case alone. Done once and for the purpose at hand.

Affiliate. To band together. A band so formed.

Algorithm. A defined process or set

of rules that leads to a desired output from a given input through a series of steps, especially on a computer.

Alphabetize. To arrange in alphabetical and (or) numerical order.

Ambiguous. Having two or more meanings. Understood in two or more possible senses.

Annotation. A note of comment, criticism, or explanation. A note with an entry in a catalog, reading list, bibliography, etc., to evaluate or describe the subject and content of the entry.

ANSI. American National Standards Institute. The U.S. organization for issuing recommendations on production, distribution, and consumption of goods and services.

Aphorism. A terse conclusion. A concise definition or statement of a principle as in a science.

ASCI-matic. Assistant Chief of Staff for Intelligence Automatic extracting system.

ASTIA. The Armed Services Technical Information Agency, renamed Defense Documentation Center, DDC.

Attribute. A characteristic or quality.

Author index. An index to the names of authors of works. The process of producing such an index.

Automatic abstracting. Making extracts by computer. Ideally, making abstracts with little or no human intervention.

Automatic indexing. Indexing by computer or other than by human. Simulation by a human of machine indexing.

Automation. Functioning without human intervention or converting to such functioning.

Axiom. A self-evident principle or proposition usually expressed tersely. A proposition to which people in general agree.

Bibliography. A collection of related references. A list of references to maps, books, etc. on one subject, written by one author, printed by one printer, in one place, or during one period.

Boldface. Type that is blacker than other type and used for emphasis and distinction. Type with broader lines than normal.

Brief. A terse article, item, or statement.

Catalog. To prepare an entry guiding to a document. A collection of such entries.

Category. A group of like items that can be distinguished from other groups of things.

Caveat. An admonition, a caution, or a warning.

Check. The process of comparing manuscript, galley proof, page proof, index entries, etc., against the original work to eliminate error.

Chemical compound. A union of chemical elements. The unit of a compound is the molecule.

Chemical element. One of about 100 entities that make up all of the molecules, mixtures, and substances known.

Circumlocution. An unnecessary number of words to express an idea. A kind of redundancy.

Citation. Reference to earlier works or to earlier parts of the same work.

Citation index. A guide to works that refer to earlier works. Used for legal records and the scientific and social science literature.

Classified. Items related in some way. Also, material kept secret or restricted by the military or other governmental agency.

Classify. To bring like things together. Also, to label material as secret or restricted.

Code. A system of symbols for representing data and/or instructions in a computer. Also, symbols identifying a chemical compound, etc.

Collective index. A set of indexes bound together without merging the alphabets.

Command. A cogent order, directive, or mandate.

Common word. Function word, or nonsubstantive word, e.g., article, auxiliary verb, conjunction, preposition, and pronoun.

Communication system. Any organization, network, etc., for conveying information, especially from records.

Compendium. A collection of brief items of a subject field or system. A work that treats a large subject field briefly or in outline.

Computerization. Conversion to use of computers and related equipment.

Conclusion. The wisdom resulting from an effort, e.g., research. Inference drawing.

Concordance. A word index in which the words are placed in context or in partial context. An index to words, often in titles.

Condensation. Preparation of a surrogate with a reduced number of words in the original. The product of such an effort.

Content word. Any word that is not a common or function word, and thus a word that contains substantive subject information.

Corporate author. The place in which the work was done. An entry under the name of a society, institution, government department, etc.

Correlation. Relating two or more subject headings, uniterms, or descriptors.

Coselection. Choice of two words from the same sentence, etc.

Criterion. A measure or unit for judgment. A standard for decision or judgment.

Cross-reference. A guide in an index to another place in the index. Reference or direction from one heading to another.

Cue. A word or expression that supposedly guides computers and humans in selection of sentences, words, phrases, and passages.

Cumulative index. An index from several indexes alphabetically merged, and usually edited after merging.

Current awareness. Keeping up to date via the record.

Data. Any or all facts, numbers, letters, and symbols that refer to or describe an object, idea, condition, situation, or other factors. Basic elements of information that can be processed or produced by a computer.

Data base. A searchable collection of data, references, and abstracts, usually related to a single subject field.

Databook. A handbook or factbook having data organized conveniently.

Data element. One concept in a document.

Datum signature. A number plus its label. E.g., the boiling point of normal water at 760 mm of mercury pressure is 100° C.

DDC. Defense Documentation Center. The successor to ASTIA.

Descriptor. A subject heading, originally a very general one.

Discipline. A field of knowledge, e.g., chemistry.

Document. A verbal or coded record. A record or object that may serve as evidence of a transaction.

DoD. Department of Defense.

Epitome. Abridgment, abstract, or summary. A concise statement of the salient points of a work. A concise survey of a subject.

ERIC. Educational Resources Information Center.

Excerpt. An extract of a passage from a book, document, or report. An extract or selection. A verbatim extract from a book or piece of music.

Extract. A condensed surrogate made up of sentences selected verbatim from the original work. The process of producing an extract.

Feedback. A term originally from electronics to indicate return of part of the output voltage to the input in proper phase. Now used in many fields to mean the process of continual comparisons of output with input to make the system self-correcting.

FID. Fédération Internationale de Documentation (International Federation for Documentation). The Hague, Netherlands.

Font. Style of type. A complete assortment of type of one style and size, including uppercase and lowercase letters, small capitals, punctuation marks, numbers, and special characters.

Format. The arrangement of print on pages and of material in a work. The appearance and make-up of a book.

Formula index. An index of molecular formulas. usually of organic chemical compounds. E.g., $C_4H_{10}O$ is the molecular formula of ethyl ether. It is alphabetized under C_4.

Forte. A strongpoint.

Function word. Common word, morpheme, or nonsubstantive word. Examples are articles, auxiliary verbs, conjunctions, prepositions, and pronouns.

Galley. A printer's holder for type before making pages.

Galley proof. The printed material as long sheets for correction before pages of the material are made.

Generalization. That which is derived from specifics.

Genre. A class of literature.

Grant. A gift from an individual or organization, often for research projects.

Honorarium. A token payment for a service.

Identifier. A subject heading much more specific than other headings selected from a thesaurus or list of subject headings. E.g., a trade name or brand name.

Index. A guide to the record. The process of producing such a guide.

Information. Communicated or received knowledge or intelligence. A signal.

Information dissemination. Knowledge transfer, often by publication, meetings, etc.

In-house. Within an organization; a product produced within an organization, as a publication. Contrasted with publications produced outside of the organization.

Initialism. A label of first letters of words of an expression. If the label is pronounceable, it is called an acronym rather than an initialism.

Integration. Mental absorption into an organized assembly for effective use. Gathering conventionally the details that comprise a catalog entry.

Intelligibility. Conveying intelligence.

Interdisciplinary. Related to two or more fields of thought. Multidisciplinary.

Inversion. Words in inverted order. E.g., *Library, public,* which is an inverted subject heading.

ISO. International Standards Organization.

Isolate. A content word separated by two or more nonsignificant words.

Issue. Of a series publication. Part of a volume of a serial, e.g., a journal.

Issue index. An index to an issue of a publication.

Italic. Slanting type used for emphasis and distinction. A variety of type based originally on the handwriting of Italian official documents.

Keyboard. To use the keyboard of a typewriter, typesetting machine, etc.

Keystroke. The result of operating a key or space bar on a typewriter or typesetting machine; a space or character.

Keypunch. A machine for punching cards for computers and for automatic data-processing equipment. The process of punching cards with this equipment.

Keyword. A word or expression of an author that is used or suggests another word or expression that is alphabetized in an index to guide the user to material. It may or may not be a subject heading.

Keyword index. An index in which keywords are used in place of subject headings or in place of entire index entries.

Knowledge industry. All effort in transfer of information.

KWIC. Keyword in Context. A concordance, usually to titles, with the words in context.

KWOC. Keyword out of Context. A concordance, usually to words of titles. The alphabetized word is removed from its context and displayed at the left margin of the column.

Lag. Delay, as in the appearance of an abstract after the publication of the original work.

Layout. Structure of the page of printed work. A plan for or by a printer showing arrangement of type, illustrations, etc., with indication of type styles and sizes. Process of laying out.

Log. To record acquisition or release of a document. A registry of items.

Lookup. To consult a reference, document, word, etc.

Machine-process. To control or alter by machines—usually computers.

Machine-readable. In a form that can be used as actual input for a computer or other data-processing equipment.

Machine translation. Conversion of documents in one language into another language by computer. The product of such a conversion.

Manual. Accomplished by hand or mind—as opposed to accomplished by machine, e.g., computer.

Margin. The edge around printed matter on a page. The gutter margin is in the fold of a book.

Maxim. A saying of a rule or truth, especially of a proverbial nature.

Mission. A project with a stated objective, e.g., landing on the moon.

Modification. The part of the index entry between the heading and the reference (locator). The modification modifies the heading much as an adjective modifies a noun. Modifications are coined, subheadings are standard.

Molecular formula. A linear arrangement of the symbols for the elements and the number of each element in a molecule. E.g., $C_2H_4O_2$ is the molecular formula of acetic acid.

Monograph. A work, usually a book, on one subject. May be published as part of a series. A complete, systematic treatise on a specific subject.

Monotype. The trademark of a typesetting apparatus that perforates a roll of paper to code characters. The perforated paper then operates a caster to cast individual type and assemble them into justified lines.

Multidisciplinary. Related to two or more fields of thought. Also called *interdisciplinary*—less precisely.

Network. A series of interconnected points. The interconnection of a number of points (which may be geographically dispersed) by communication facilities.

NFAIS. National Federation of Abstracting and Indexing Services.

NFSAIS. National Federation of Science Abstracting and Indexing Services. The predecessor of NFAIS.

Nomenclature. A system for naming things, usually systematically. The names themselves. A system of names for a system of classes, or classification; its terms.

Numerical patent index—or simply patent index. An index to patent numbers arranged by country and serial number or classification.

Offprint. Separate. Printed after the regular run. Extracted article. Also called *overprint,* or *reprint.*

Omission. Index entries or words that should have been present.

Output. That which comes out of a process. Product.

Page proof. Printer's proof in the form of pages for making corrections.

Paradigm. An example, model, or pattern.

Patent concordance. A concordance that relates like patents of different countries.

Pica. Twelve points.

Point. Unit of type measurement. Pica type is 12 points. One point is equal to 0.01384 in., or nearly 1/72 in.

Post. To place a reference number under a subject heading, keyword, etc. E.g., to type the proper catalog entry and number at the top of a group of catalog cards.

Precept. A command, instruction, or order for a rule of action or conduct.

Précis. An abstract or epitome.

Prescriptive. Giving rules or directions.

Primary service. Derived from author(s) rather than from their writings. Abstracts, extracts, and their indexes are secondary services.

Procedure. A precise method for effecting a solution to a problem or for producing a product or service.

Processed data. The product of raw data subjected to calculation and computation.

Proofreader. One who reads galley or page proof. He discovers errors in type, punctuation, statement, etc.

Proprietary. Items owned and usually kept secret by individuals and organizations.

R&D. Research & Development. Discovery and putting the results to use.

Raw data. The record of observation with or without a minimum of processing.

Readability. How easy the material is to read.

Redundancy. Superfluous repetition or verbosity. Synonyms and related terms are redundant. Superfluity, tautology, pleonasm, verbosity, prolixity, diffuseness, circumlocution, periphrasis.

Reference. A bibliographic item referring to the same or other work. An indication referring to a document or passage.

Reference number. The number that guides from an index to the work indexed. *Locator* is a neologism.

Rekeyboard. To use a keyboard of a typewriter, typesetting machine, etc. for material already keyboarded once.

Relevant. Judged to be useful.

Report. A written or vocal presentation, often in response to a request.

Report number. The unique label assigned to a report. Often consists of letters and digits.

Representativeness. How well the word or sentence conveys the sense of the sentence or document.

Reprint. Printed again, usually by photo-offset. A more common term for *offprint* and *overprint*.

Research. Application and discovery of truth usually through hypothesis and experiment. Studious inquiry or examination. Critical and exhaustive investigation or experimentation to discover facts and theories or laws. Prac-

tical applications of new or revised conclusions.

Result. Output of research or other effort.

Résumé. An abridgment or summary.

Review. An organized collection of results and conclusions from other works. A periodical containing critical articles of new books, etc. Evaluation of literary work published in a periodical.

Ring compound. A chemical compound, usually containing carbon and consisting of one or more rings of atoms.

Ring index. An index guiding to names of rings of chemical compounds.

Ruly. Strictly following explicit rules—especially said of a language.

Running head. Words, expressions, and numbers at the top of a page that indicate the contents of the page.

Salient. Outstanding, as of data.

Scattering. Dispersion of related entries in an index.

Scope. Subject area of the work. Intent, import of a writing or discourse. Subject matter or theme.

SDI. Selective Dissemination of Information, usually in the form of references. An automated or manual system for identifying references in current literature matching the interests (profiles) of patrons.

Search. To look for data or documents. The process of looking.

Secondary service. An information product or service derived from an original source, e.g., paper or report.

Section editor. One in charge of a section (specific subject area) of an abstract journal or other publication.

Security. Protection of documents against disclosure.

Selectability. The quality of a word or sentence that determines its usefulness in indexing or extracting.

Selection. Choice of documents or their parts.

Serendipity. Fortunate discovery. The gift of finding valuable or agreeable things not sought.

Series. A continuation of a publication periodically or aperiodically. Series number indicates an independent set of volumes. Successive volumes of a serial numbered separately to distinguish them from other sequences of the same serial.

Significance. The value of a word, sentence, etc., in representing the content of a document from which it was selected.

Skim. To read rapidly and perhaps incompletely. To read, study, or examine superficially and rapidly. To glance through for the chief ideas.

Specialization. Concentration in a narrow field.

Specificity. The inverse of the degree of generality of a subject heading, modification, or statement.

Spine. The back edge of a book.

Sponsor. An individual or organization supporting, at least in part, research, etc.

Standard. A norm agreed upon and used.

String of characters. A line of symbols and spaces between them, e.g., syllable, word, phrase, sentence, expression, paragraph, etc.

Structural analysis. Determination of the grammatical structure of an expression or sentence.

Structural formula. A diagram of a chemical compound that shows which atoms are connected to which other atoms. E.g., $CH_3\text{-}CH_2OH$ is the stylized structural formula of ethyl alcohol.

Subcategory. Category under another category. A more specific category.

Subheading. A heading in an index that is under or beneath the subject heading, keyword, etc. Subheadings are usually standard; modifications or modifying phrases are coined for the index entry.

Subject. That about which the author writes, speaks, performs, etc. The theme or themes of a book.

Subject heading. The word or expression in an index that principally controls the alphabetical position of the entry and guides the user to the subject of the work. Scattering among synonymous subject headings is eliminated so far as possible.

Subject index. An index to subjects

reported by authors. The process of making such an index.

Summary. A brief statement of salient points already covered.

Summation. A summing up.

Supplant. To take the place of or substitute for.

Supplement. To add to the value of. Something that adds value.

Surrogate. A document that can be used in place of another.

Synopsis. A condensed statement of a work altering a general overview. An abstract, abridgment, epitome, conspectus, summary, or syllabus.

Terminology. Special terms or words in a special field. Jargon of the field. Technical or special terms or words used in a business, art, science, etc., also, nomenclature as a field of study.

Terse admonition. A warning expressed concisely and cogently. E.g., "The Surgeon General has determined that smoking cigarettes is dangerous to your health."

Terse advocacy. A recommendation expressed concisely and cogently. E.g., "Stop smoking cigarettes."

Terse conclusion. A conclusion, usually of an author, expressed in concise elegance. E.g., "That which is used, develops; that which is not used, wastes away."

Terse explanation. How things function, expressed concisely. E.g., "Sucrose depletes body chromium that prevents insulin from causing deposition of lipids

in arterial walls and causing arteriosclerosis."

Terse intention. A plan expressed concisely. E.g., "I will stop smoking cigarettes."

Terse literature. Condensation to about one-hundredth the number of words in the original document; expressed with elegance.

Terse organizations of data. Datum signatures categorized.

Topic sentence. A statement of the subject of the work, often at the start of the work or of a paragraph in it.

Transfer of information. Knowledge communication immediate or delayed.

Transliteration. Character-by-character representation of words in one alphabet by characters in another. E.g., transliteration from the Russian, Arabic, Cyrillic, Irish, or Greek alphabets into the Roman alphabet.

Ultraterse literature. Condensation of a set of original works to one-thousandth the number of words or less.

UNESCO. United Nations Scientific and Cultural Organization.

UNISIST. World Science Information System.

Verbatim. Repeated without change. Word-for-word reproduction of some original. Following the original exactly. E.g., a verbatim translation.

Virgule. The punctuation mark, /.

Wraparound. A feature of KWIC indexes in which the remainder of the title is placed ahead of the keyword that has been alphabetized.

Z-39. A committee of the American National Standards Institute on information and library science.

Subject Index